foundatio

BUSINESS OPTIONS

JON SUTHERLAND & DIANE CANWELL

CW01502255

Hodder & Stoughton

A MEMBER OF THE HODDER HEADLINE GROUP

Dedicated to the memory of Nan –
E M Sutherland 1898–1994

A catalogue record for this title is available from the British Library.

ISBN 0 340 63155 4

First published 1996
Impression number   10 9 8 7 6 5 4 3 2 1
Year   1999 1998 1997 1996

Typeset by Wearset, Boldon, Tyne and Wear.
Printed in Great Britain for Hodder & Stoughton Educational, a division of Hodder Headline Plc, 338 Euston Road, London NW1 3BH by Bath Press.

Contents

Acknowledgements

The authors would like to acknowledge the help and support of the following organisations in the preparation and illustration of this book:

British Airports Authority (BAA)
British Nuclear Fuels Ltd
Employment Department Group
Employment Service
Inland Revenue
Kwik-Fit
Mercury Communications
Mobil Oil Ltd
National Centre for Vocational Qualifications (NCVQ)

Pegasus
Peugeot Talbot
Royal Bank of Scotland
Smith & Nephew plc
Thorne Erickson Communication Ltd
Torres
UK Passport Agency
Woolworths plc

UNIT 4   CONTRIBUTING TO A TEAM ACTIVITY

element 4.1
PLAN AN ACTIVITY WITH A TEAM

Performance criteria

A student must:

1   Check that s/he and other team members have an accurate understanding of the given objectives of the activity.

2   Agree actions which will meet the overall objectives.

3   Contribute to identifying the **resources** which are necessary.

4   Contribute to identifying which team members are going to carry out different parts of the activity.

5   Contribute to identifying actions to deal with **anticipated problems** and maintain **health and safety**.

6   Contribute to producing a realistic team plan for the overall activity.

7   Agree and produce a realistic plan which provides details of own role in the activity.

RANGE

Resources: finance, people, materials, equipment, information

Anticipated problems: given, identified by the team

Health and safety associated with: oneself, other people, materials, equipment

INTRODUCTION

This element, as with the other elements that make up this unit, is a practical one. You will have to carry out the three main stages (plan, undertake and review) in dealing with a problem or an activity. In this element, we will focus on the planning of the activity. This means that we will be looking at the things that you should do, the things that you should consider and the ways in which you can split up the work within the team to make the best use of the skills you have and the time available to do the job.

We have provided you with a framework for a complete activity for this unit, but your tutors may choose to use an activity taken from one of the other units of the Foundation course. If this is the case, they will have to make sure that you follow the procedures and stages detailed in this unit at the same time as making sure that you cover the performance criteria of the other unit.

As we have said, this element covers the planning of the activity, the next covers the actual carrying out of that activity and the final one looks at the way in which the activity was handled and gives you a chance to review what you have done.

We have detailed the activity in the element assignment section of this element, so you will have to refer to the activity to make sure you follow all the planning procedures needed to cover this element. We will be giving you advice on how to plan the activity properly throughout the element.

4.1.1 Check that s/he and other team members have an accurate understanding of the given objectives of the activity

You will either be using the activity detailed in the element assignment or an activity related to one of the other units of the Foundation programme. Regardless of the nature of the activity, you must first make sure that you understand exactly what you have to do.

There are two parts to making sure that you understand the activity:

▼ **decide what has to be done before you can start the activity and what you need to know**
▼ **think about what will be expected of you by the time the activity is over**

The individual tasks and questions that are detailed in the element assignment will help you with this; read them and make sure you understand them. If you do not understand them now, you will not be able to plan the activity. Are you clear about what needs to be done and the evidence that will have to be produced to prove that you have carried out all of the tasks? If you are unsure, ask your tutor now. Later will be too late!

4.1.2 Agree actions which will meet the overall objectives

One of the best ways to agree the actions that you will undertake is to discuss the objectives of the activity as a group. No doubt there will be some disagreement about how you will carry out the various activities, but this is just a natural part of discussion. The important thing is to have the same ideas about what is required of you.

Figure 4.1.1 Apprentices at Kwik-Fit are encouraged to involve themselves in team activities.

Talk about the activity together, make sure that all members of the group contribute to the discussion and provide some suggestions and ideas. Remember, if you have a good idea about how you should do something and do not say anything, then you only have yourself to blame later if things go wrong.

You must produce an overall action plan that will cope with all the demands of the activity. You should, after the discussion, fill in the group action plan that is used by your centre. In the next two performance criteria, you will have to identify the resources that you will need as well as how you are intending to split the work between you. You may want to start thinking about this as you draw up a list of the things you have to do.

4.1.3 Contribute to identifying the resources which are necessary

There are very few activities that do not need resources. Exactly what you do need will depend on the activity itself. In this performance criterion, we have concentrated on the resources you will need to carry out the activity detailed in the element assignment. Obviously, if you are doing something different, the resources will be different too.

RESOURCES

Resources basically fall into the following categories:

▼ finance
▼ people
▼ materials
▼ equipment
▼ information

For the purposes of this assignment, you will need to consider all of these, but before we look at them in any great detail, let us draw up a basic list of needs. The most basic things that you will need for this activity are:

▼ paper and pens
▼ graph paper
▼ flip-charts and overhead projector sheets
▼ access to a photocopier
▼ use of a computer
▼ a map of your centre

This is only part of the list; you will be able to come up with other ideas and needs which will depend on how you are intending to carry out the activity. Do not be influenced by what we have suggested; you might not need some of them in the end. It might be a good idea to decide what you will definitely need, then have another list of things that would be useful but not absolutely essential. Most of the basic resources will be provided by your tutor or will be available somewhere within the centre.

Finance

Although your centre will be providing the majority of the resources for this assignment, you should keep a record of the cost of each item you use. You will have to ask your tutor for the cost of photocopying, overhead transparencies and flip-charts, for example. You should keep a detailed list of the costs of not only the physical items you use, but also those of telephone calls and other services. At the end of the activity, you should be able to provide your tutor with a full list and total of all expenses.

People

When we think about people involved in an activity, it is natural to consider only the main team members. You should make a list of the people that you think you will have to talk to, or use the skills of, to carry out the whole of the activity. Librarians, technicians, friends and family may all be useful sources of help and advice and you should not forget them.

Materials and equipment

Throughout your course you will have been using various materials and equipment, and using your knowledge of these you should list the things you will need to carry out this assignment. It is always a good idea to think about what you will need before starting a particular piece of work, since

Figure 4.1.2 Large organisations might also include video-conferencing facilities as important equipment for assisting team activities. With this system, individuals or groups situated thousands of miles away can engage in team activities via cameras, satellite links and monitor screens.

relying on things that may not be available when you need them will cause problems later. The typical items that fall into this category are:

▼ **photocopiers**
▼ **staplers**
▼ **envelopes**
▼ **paper**
▼ **overhead projectors and transparencies**
▼ **flip-charts and marker pens**
▼ **computers and printers**
▼ **folders**
▼ **paper clips**
▼ **rulers and pens**

The list seems endless. Your centre should be able to provide you with the majority of the materials and equipment that you will need, but some of them you will own anyway. Some lucky people have computers at home and will be able to do some work away from the centre.

Information

Apart from the information that you will find in this book and the sister volume *Foundation Business*, you will be able to use the library as a main source of books, articles and other materials.

If your centre has computers with CD-ROM drives, then they may have encyclopedias and other useful sources of information available. You will be able to look things up and get print-outs of articles and features.

As we already know, people are a very useful source of information and they will be able to give you up-to-date material. If they do not know about a topic themselves, they may be able to point you in the right direction.

4.1.4 *Contribute to identifying which team members are going to carry out different parts of the activity*

Trying to decide who will be responsible for the various parts of the plan is one of the hardest things to do. All of you will want to do the interesting parts and no one will want to do the boring bits. However, try to think of all of the parts of the plan as being as important as each other. Most activities involve a lot of routine tasks and someone has to carry these out. If you feel strongly that you should carry out a particular part of the plan, explain to the other members of the team why you think you are best suited to this job. If you cannot decide who should do each task, the fairest way is to put all of your names onto small slips of paper and fold them up. Get someone else to draw the slips of paper one at a time. The first person drawn can then pick one of the tasks. Continue like this until all of the tasks have been allocated to team members.

Some of the tasks will need more than one person to carry them out. Try to work with a team member who has different skills to the ones you have. Some people are good with words, others with numbers; some of us can draw, others are good on the computer. We are all different. Most of us have a skill that we are proud of, so this is a chance to use that skill for the benefit of the whole team.

If you are still unsure about how to divide up the various tasks that make up the whole activity, then jot down all the things you think you are good at. Compare your list with those of the other team members. With a bit of thought and discussion between you, you will be able to decide on the ideal person for each task.

If you really want to get the most out of the

activity, then you could choose a task that you are not very good at. The only way to learn is to try, so this could be another way of splitting up the tasks if all else fails.

4.1.5 Contribute to identifying actions to deal with anticipated problems and maintain health and safety

ANTICIPATED PROBLEMS

Even the best plans do not always work perfectly. No matter how well you have planned something, you might still forget one little thing that could upset the whole plan. This is very common and even the most expert planners will forget the odd thing once in a while.

Alongside your list of tasks that make up the plan, you should now begin to identify any problems which might come up. Think about your plan – what are you relying on? Do certain things have to be done before you can get on with the main parts of the activity? What about the resources you think you will need – what will you do if you cannot get them?

It is all very well to recognise what might go wrong, but you must also decide what you will do if things do go as badly as you have feared. You should always have a back-up plan to cope with situations like this. Hopefully you will not need to use the back-up plan, but you never know!

Against each of the problems that you suspect might get in the way of completing the task, you should also have your solution. Your tutor might be able to offer you a form or sheet that is ideal for this. If you want to create one for yourself, then the headings should look something like this:

Anticipated problem	First solution	Second solution

By the time you have completed this list of potential problems, you should be ready for almost anything!

Given problems

On the face of it, the whole of the assignment, related activities and tasks are a set of problems to be solved, and deciding on a way of dealing with the assignment is the first of these. It is important to get this right, as you might end up wasting time later. If you do find you have approached the assignment in an inappropriate way, you will have to identify a way in which you can get back on track as quickly as possible. In order to test your planning and ability to cope with problems as they arise, your tutor may decide to put other problems in your path as you get on with the work in hand. There is no way of predicting what these may be, only time will tell whether your plan is good enough to cope with them.

Problems identified by the team

Hopefully, by now, you will have correctly identified the potential problems that might crop up in the course of the activity. You should also have planned how you will handle these. If not, then you should really think about reviewing the plan and spend some time devising a better back-up strategy if things go wrong. Your tutor will be keen for you to have a good reserve plan and will probably not let you start the activity properly until you have done this.

Figure 4.1.3 No matter how experienced you may be at problem solving or in your job, there are times when you need to seek assistance (courtesy of the Employment Service).

HEALTH AND SAFETY

You do not need to know all about particular health and safety laws, but you should be aware of the potential hazards you might face in the course of any complicated activity, drawn out over a period of time.

For a full description of the various health and safety related dangers, hazards and problems, refer to Unit 5. This unit looks at health and safety in much greater detail.

Health and safety associated with oneself

We are sure you do not need to be reminded about the hazards that constantly surround us. Nearly everything can pose a threat if treated in the wrong way. In a work environment you will be expected to take care of yourself and not to take risks. There is no reason why you should not adopt the same approach during your course.

Equally, if you intend to collect information from outside your centre, perhaps from local businesses or members of the public, never go anywhere on your own. You cannot guarantee that people are what they seem. There are, unfortunately, people that could and would do you harm if they were given the opportunity. Do not let them have the chance. As the old saying goes, there is safety in numbers. This is not to say that all of the team should descend upon a local business and insist that they all attend meetings and meet people. A group of two or three is fine and would be sufficient to avoid this potential danger.

Health and safety associated with other people

Just as you can put yourself in a dangerous position, others can put you at risk too. If they are not careful with materials and equipment, you might be affected by their actions.

Always make sure that you follow instructions regarding the handling of equipment and materials in your centre carefully. Not only should you be aware of what you should and should not do, but you need to make sure that other people are not doing things that could put you at risk.

Health and safety associated with equipment and materials

Although most equipment and materials are not dangerous if used sensibly, there is always the possibility that something might go wrong accidentally. Remember that electricity is dangerous and lethal in certain circumstances; and that equipment like guillotines and staples are designed for office use and not as toys. No doubt you will have been warned about the dangers that surround you in the workplace; be aware that many of these dangers are with you now.

4.1.6 Contribute to producing a realistic team plan for the overall activity

As far as the requirements of the element are concerned, you should compile the following:

▼ a full action plan for the whole of the activity, along with a back-up plan to deal with the possible problems that you might encounter along the way
▼ an agenda for the initial meeting and other meetings that you will have in planning the activity
▼ an activity schedule, listing the activities and how long you expect them to take (approximate times are fine for this)
▼ an individual list of tasks and duties that are to be performed by each member of the team
▼ individual and group targets, which should include what has to be done by the end of each session, day or week by both the team as a whole and each of the individual team members

This may sound like a lot of work before you have even started the activity itself. Remember that everything you plan and organise now will help you later. Not having thought the activity through will cause problems and delays later.

The schedule and targets will help you to assess whether your actions are going according to plan. You should always slightly over-estimate the time that you think will be needed. If you under-estimate, the activity will be behind schedule and you will be putting unnecessary pressure on yourselves. You will be given a date for the completion of the whole of the assignment. If you work back from that, you will be able to allocate time for each part of the activity accordingly.

4.1.7 Agree and produce a realistic plan which provides details of own role in the activity

If you have now completed all of the above planning, you will have a good idea of your own role

---

BUSINESS CONNECTION

PC 4.1

We have now looked at all the major ways of planning an activity with a team. To test your memory and skill, complete the following business connection by turning finance into schedule. The last letter of each word or phrase is the first letter of the next word or phrase. To help you we have put in the first and last letter on each line, but you will have to do the rest.

```
F I N A N C E
E . . . . . . . T
    T . . M
M . . . . . . . S
S C H E D U L E
```

in the activity. In order to double-check that you have listed all the things that you will have to do, individually, as your part of the work, it is a good idea to create a separate action plan of your own. In this plan, which should run alongside the main team plan, you should write down (in order) all of the activities for which you are personally

responsible. Your centre will be using a particular form for this, which will be either designed by the centre or one that is recommended by the awarding body. In any case, you will be expected to complete this before moving on to the activity proper.

assignment

ELEMENT 4.1

PC 4.1.1–7

In order to cover all of the aspects of this unit, we have created a series of activities that can be based on the college or school that you are attending. There are lots of things to think about and do, so you must begin by thinking about how you will plan the activity between the members of the team. Remember that you will often have to work as a member of a team at work, as very few tasks (apart from very basic and simple ones) are carried out individually.

Ideally, the team should have at least three members, perhaps more if the scope of the activity is increased.

Before we look at the activity itself, let us recap on the requirements of this element alongside the performance criteria that make up the element itself. This will give you a format to aim for when you construct your overall team plan:

- *PC 4.1.1*
  Describe the main aims of the activity.
- *PC 4.1.2*
  Describe the actions and tasks that will have to be undertaken in completing the activity.
- *PC 4.1.3*
  List and describe the resources that will be needed and where these can be obtained.

- *PC 4.1.4*
  Identify who will be responsible for each of the actions and tasks that make up the activity as a whole.
- *PC 4.1.5*
  Identify the actions that will be undertaken in the face of potential problems.
- *PC 4.1.6*
  As a final check that you have covered all of the planning tasks, consider the following points:
  - *have all the options been considered within the timescale you have been given?*
  - *have all the resources been identified and are they available in the quantity, quality and time available?*
  - *does everyone in the team understand exactly what their jobs are?*
  - *does each individual member of the team have a clearly defined role?*
- *PC 4.1.7*
  Create an individual action plan which describes your own actions throughout the whole of the activity.

You will need to keep a log outlining your contribution to the team planning exercise. You should also keep a log of all of the actions that you have to undertake personally. Remember that this log must be accurate as the assessor will need to verify the account as a true record of what you have done.

the activity

As we mentioned, this activity is designed so that you can follow it through in the three elements of this unit. You will not see any performance criteria against the tasks in this assignment as the planning stage that we have already looked at relates to these.

scenario

Your school or college is keen to make the best use of the leisure facilities at the centre. It believes that the sports facilities are not being used as much as they could be, particularly by groups and individuals in the community. To this end, you been have asked to carry out a survey which investigates the leisure pursuits of the students and staff at the centre as well as the views of the local community. As a second major set of tasks, you are to arrange publicity for the leisure facilities at your centre and work out the costs of inviting the local press and prominent members of the local community to an event to promote the facilities.

tasks

1 *Design a questionnaire that asks the students, staff and members of the public about their leisure activities and whether they would like to use the facilities at your centre. You may wish to ask your tutors*

about the probable costs of hiring the facilities so that you can mention this on the questionnaire. You should try to get at least 50 questionnaires filled in by people of different ages and statuses.

2 *After you have collected this information, you should collate the results and put your findings into a format that can be easily understood. You should present your findings to your tutors in an oral presentation supported by visual aids and summaries. As part of this presentation, you should clearly state which you consider to be the most popular leisure activities.*

3 *You should also suggest charges for hiring the facilities and propose a way in which this money could be collected. Alongside this, you will also have to create a way of recording the bookings so that you can keep track of the times available for hire and those times for which the facilities have already been booked.*

4 *The final task is to organise a launch party for publicising the availability of the facilities. In order to do this you must undertake the following tasks:*

- *draw up a list of at least 50 people to invite – these should be representatives of local sports and leisure groups, journalists and reporters and other local business people*
- *working from the following costs and assuming that 50 people will attend, calculate the total cost of the event:*
  - *buffet costs £5.00 per head*
  - *printing the invitations costs £10.00*
  - *postage costs 19p per invitation*

element 4.2

UNDERTAKE A ROLE IN A TEAM ACTIVITY

Performance criteria

A student must:

1 Carry out the activities in the agreed individual plan and the agreed team plan.
2 Make the best use of available **resources**.
3 Maintain **health and safety**.
4 Co-operate effectively with others as required by the plans.
5 **Respond** to **problems** promptly and in the correct way.

RANGE

Resources: finance, people, materials, equipment, information

Health and safety associated with: oneself, other people, materials, equipment

Respond: taking action to resolve the problem, reporting the problem to person(s) responsible

Problems: anticipated, unexpected

4.2.1 Carry out the activities in the agreed individual plan and the agreed team plan

Having planned the activity, the main point of this first performance criterion is to make sure that you have carried out the activities which you have agreed and written down in your individual and team plans.

It is possible that some people will not have done everything that they were supposed to do and that others may have taken it upon themselves to do things that they were not asked to.

Bearing in mind that you will have been observed and monitored whilst you were preparing your individual and team action plans, your tutor will be aware of what you proposed to do and what you have achieved.

Your tutor will be looking out for the following:

▼ **whether you have fulfilled the promises made in your plans**
▼ **whether you have made the best use of resources available**
▼ **whether you have considered health and safety throughout the series of tasks**
▼ **whether you have co-operated fully with one another throughout the activity**
▼ **whether you have correctly and promptly responded to problems as they have arisen**

As we said in Element 4.1, the exact nature of the tasks which you are undertaking will depend upon the type of activity you have been given to carry out. Remember that your tutor will be looking at you individually and as a group and although you may be performing well yourself, this does not necessarily mean that the group is performing as well as it might do. Since the whole purpose of this unit revolves around being able to operate as a team member, you should bear this in mind throughout your actions from now on.

Monitoring and comparing actual behaviour with the agreed plans will help to ensure that all the tasks are carried out. You can do this by simply jotting down the initials of the person or persons undertaking various tasks against each of the tasks and then checking to see which individuals were supposed to be carrying out these tasks. Another thing that you might want to think about is how roles (or tasks undertaken) in the group are sometimes transferred from one individual to another without anybody really noticing that it has happened. Providing there is a good reason for this and that the work is shared out fairly, then as long as you note this and can explain the reasons why in Element 4.3, this may be acceptable to your tutor. It is, however, a good idea to avoid swapping roles as this can lead to confusion and, at worst, some of the tasks being overlooked or carried out twice.

You may wish to use the following headings to keep track of what has been done, by whom and how long it took them:

Task	Planned person	Actual person	Time taken

Beware that filling in a form like this may cause friction within the group, particularly if someone is not pulling his or her weight. If you all agree to fill in a form like this, it is possible that these sorts of problems might be avoided, as everyone will be aware that they are being monitored.

4.2.2 *Make the best use of available resources*

RESOURCES

As we have already listed the types of resources that you might need to carry out the team activity, we will not go into these again. Within your individual and team plans you will have identified the resources which you thought were necessary, and available. Since your tutor will be looking at how you used resources and whether you have made best use of what was available, you should make sure that you have used what you asked for in your plans and have not asked for items or information that you had not planned for. If you do not do this, it will show that your original plans were not sufficiently thought through.

In this performance criterion we will be offering you ways of monitoring your use of resources throughout the team activity. It will be your responsibility to list and account for any item, that is, materials, equipment, information or the help of someone in order to support your approach to the activity. Bearing in mind that you will have to review your activity in Element 4.3 you should keep a record of what you have and have not used as you will find it difficult to remember this information once the activity is completed.

Finance

As we discussed in Element 4.1, the use of almost anything has a financial implication. Photocopies are not free; neither are the running costs of machines and equipment. Every time you use paper or envelopes these will have to be replaced at a cost to your centre. Whilst you need not try to allocate costs to people's time when you ask them for assistance or information, you should, at the very least, list all of the consumable items

used during the activity such as paper, flip-charts and overhead projector transparencies. Your tutor will advise you about the cost of these items.

You may find the following headings useful in recording the consumable items which you have used:

Item	Used in task number	Cost per item	Total cost

You will have to calculate the final total which shows all expenses related to the activity at the bottom of the page.

People

As we know, you do not need to allocate costs to the time of any individual whom you have consulted. It would be a good idea, however, to list the individuals consulted and the questions you asked them, along with a brief summary of their response. The following headings may help you to do this:

Name of person	Information requested	Answer details

It is worth remembering that other group members may also be a valuable source of information, or may know someone who can help you with a particular problem. Since we all have different backgrounds and experiences, it is worth asking the group members first before attempting to gain information elsewhere. As we will see later in this performance criterion, when we look at information itself, you will always be credited for your ability to obtain information, from whatever source, and particularly if you are able to work out where or to whom you should go for that information.

Materials and equipment

Although you will have listed the consumable items or materials used in the activity when you completed your summary of expenses, you will also need to list the types of materials used, as well as any equipment that you may have required during the activity.

Again, it is a good idea to list the materials and equipment, cross-referencing them against the particular tasks and mentioning which member of the group used these materials or equipment and why. The following headings may help you to do this:

Equipment/ materials used	Used by	For task number	Problems found

We have added the last column to enable you to note down any difficulties which you encountered in using a particular piece of equipment or materials.

Information

If you are using our activity detailed in Element 4.1, then most of the information you need will have been collected by yourselves. Any problems which have arisen through the collection of that information have therefore been created by you. One of the problems you may have encountered is that you were over-ambitious, collected too much information and now do not know what to do with it all. On the other hand, you may not have collected enough and are now faced with the prospect of collecting more, or even considering the option of making it up in order to cover your lack of information.

The first problem is more easily solved than the second. If you find yourself with a mountain of information and do not think that you will be able to process it in the time you have been given for the activity, then, providing you can decide on the minimum amount of information that you need, you should consider only analysing the 50 or so questionnaires that we recommended in Element 4.1. You may ask yourselves 'how do we know whether the 50 questionnaires are a true reflection of the opinions of all of the people who filled in questionnaires?' The basic answer is that you do not, but there is no sure way of picking 50 that are, without going through all of the questionnaires you have collected. Since this is the basic problem, you will have to choose only a small selection. Assuming that you have been clever enough to keep your questionnaires in batches which either relate to individuals within your centre or individuals from the community, then obviously you should not just use one of those piles of questionnaires, but take some from each. In the final analysis there is no quicker or fairer way of choosing the questionnaires than to simply count out the top 25 from each pile.

Addressing the second problem of not having collected enough data poses an altogether different set of worries. Since your questionnaires are different from the other teams', you cannot even trade information as they may have had a different approach altogether to the one you used. Your tutor may not be happy with you trying to make any conclusions from a very small sample of questionnaires. The only alternative is to go out and collect more data. You will have to explain why you did not collect sufficient data in the first place, particularly if you had more questionnaires printed than you used. After all, in your team plan you did agree to have at least 50 questionnaires filled in and if this section is relevant to you, you have not fulfilled your action plan.

Faced with a pile of completed questionnaires, you must choose a way to process the data and obtain totals for each of the questions. If you have used questions which have only a limited number of answers, you need only add up the number of answers to fully process your data. The easiest way to do this is for one person to have a blank questionnaire and the other members of the team to have a pile of completed questionnaires each. Those with the completed questionnaires call out in turn the response to the question of the sheet in front of them. The person with the blank questionnaire can then use a simple tally method (卌) of counting the responses to each question.

For those of you that have used more open questions which have allowed individuals to express their own opinions in words, the processing of the information can be rather more lengthy. The best approach is to look through all of the questionnaires and highlight some of the more interesting responses and, at the same time, try to get a feel of the overall opinions of the people that filled in the questionnaires. You cannot hope to include all of the opinions and should try to cover the most popular ones.

The ideal questionnaire has features of both of the above approaches. The majority of the questions should be **closed** (which means that the people filling in the questionnaire can only answer yes, no, sometimes or maybe, for example). Some of the other questions can be more **open** (which means you leave space on the questionnaire for them to write their own opinion or statement).

Apart from the information that you will have collected from your questionnaires, there may be other things which you need to know to help you with the activity. If you are undertaking our series of tasks outlined in Element 4.1, then you will have had to discover the names and addresses of local people to invite to the event. Some of these names and addresses would have been easy to obtain. Others you may have had to ask for assistance in finding. Perhaps your librarian, tutor, friends or family will have been able to help you in this and you should note down the source of the information in each case. The following headings may assist you in doing this:

Again, use these headings as early in the activity as possible as you will find it very difficult to remember the details later. When you review the activity you will have to mention any problems that you encountered in collecting information and whether this had a bearing on your ability to complete the tasks and meet deadlines.

4.2.3 *Maintain health and safety*

HEALTH AND SAFETY

The main point of this performance criterion is to make sure that you have maintained health and safety throughout the activity and that your actions have not put yourself, or other members of the team, at risk. Rather than repeat what we have already said in Element 4.1, you will find under each section of this performance criterion a suggested set of headings which will help you record and monitor any potential health and safety concern that you and your team may have had during the activity. Again, a full description of health and safety considerations can be found in Unit 5.

Health and safety associated with oneself

As a result of the part you played in the team activity, you may have experienced health and safety concerns which you should note for future reference and for review purposes in Element 4.3.

Information sought	*From whom*	*Information obtained*	*Alternative source*

If you did not note any health and safety considerations associated with your own actions, then you should say so. The following headings may help you to log your health and safety concerns:

Problem encountered	Date	Action taken

to use the following headings to help you record these:

Problem encountered	Date	Action taken

Health and safety associated with other people

There is no way of predicting what you may or may not have encountered as a result of other people's actions during the activity. We did suggest some typical health and safety concerns, but you may well have experienced some unexpected problems. As in the previous range statement, you should note anything that has occurred from a health and safety point of view which is associated with other people. It may be useful for you

Health and safety associated with materials and equipment

This is the area in which you are more likely to encounter health and safety concerns. You will find a full description of the things to look out for in Unit 5.

If you have encountered any serious problems relating to materials or equipment you should, of course, report them to your tutor. Since the equipment should be regularly checked, your centre will want to know immediately if anything is faulty or dangerous. The following headings will be useful as a means of recording any faults or health and safety concerns you may encounter:

Equipment/materials used	Problem encountered	Date	Reported to

You will be expected to review the maintenance of health and safety throughout the activity in Element 4.3 and it is also worth bearing in mind that you will have to suggest ways in which health and safety can be improved within your centre in relation to all of the aspects covered in this performance criterion.

4.2.4 *Co-operate effectively with others as required by the plans*

Carrying out all of the tasks which you agreed in your own action plan is not sufficient to claim that the team activity was a success. You really must try to ensure that the whole team activity, including everyone's individual part in it, has been undertaken to the best of all your abilities.

Some members of the team will have worked far harder than others. Some may believe that they have undertaken more of the tasks and worked harder than anyone else. This may well be the case as it was almost impossible to predict just how much work would be involved in any individual task at the beginning. The main point about dealing with team activities is that you have all co-operated as much as possible and tried to sort out problems as and when they arose. By trying to agree on the best ways to approach problems and not bullying individuals within the team will show that you have operated well as a group. Remember that your behaviour towards one another and your approach to the activity in general will have been observed by your tutor throughout. Your tutor will be looking for evidence that will support your claims that you have worked well as a team. Give your tutor every opportunity to recognise your skills as a team and try not to show your weaknesses or an inability to co-operate.

Remember that co-operation also means helping with the workload of other members of the team who might be struggling. Perhaps they were given too much work or responsibility, or maybe they have had to wait for others to complete their tasks before they can begin work on their own. Co-operation is all about getting involved in the activity as a whole without wasting time arguing about whose responsibility certain things are. Just because you may have finished your part of the activity, you should not sit back and watch the other members of the team struggle to complete theirs.

Figure 4.2.1 At any level of an organisation teamwork and co-operation are essential for getting things done (courtesy of Mercury Communications).

4.2.5 **Respond to problems promptly and in the correct way**

RESPOND

Taking action to resolve the problem

Many problems that you encounter in the completion of this or any other activity will have to be handled by the team in the first instance. You cannot necessarily rely on the fact that someone else will sort out the problem for you. As problems arise, rather than attempting to solve them individually, you should try to discuss your difficulties as a team and arrive at the best solution for all of you. One of the other team members may have encountered a similar problem in the past and may be able, through experience, to offer the perfect solution to the problem.

If the action you are proposing to take to resolve the problem is acceptable and will not cause additional problems as a result, you may not have to refer to anybody else before taking this course of action. Remember, however, that some simple problems may not have simple solutions and you should think your actions through carefully before you do anything that will make the situation worse. If you are unsure about what course of action to take, it is probably better to ask the opinion of your tutor first.

For each problem, someone within the group will have to take the responsibility for seeing through the team's solution. You do not want to put that person in the position of having to deal with additional trouble because of the decision you have taken. If you cannot agree on a particular course of action, then you should go with the decision of the majority of the team or refer the matter to your tutor.

Reporting the problem to the person(s) responsible

In most cases the person to whom you should refer your problems is your tutor. He or she will be able to deal with most disagreements or problems that arise and suggest a range of options available to you which he or she will then expect you to choose from. Do not expect your tutor to give you the answer every time. Remember that your tutor will be looking at your ability to cope with problems and suggest and carry out different courses of action.

Some problems will be of a technical nature, which may involve faulty equipment or a lack of materials or resources. Your tutor may not be on hand to suggest solutions and you may have to refer to a technician, librarian or another member of your centre staff to help you. Unless the problem involves a health and safety matter, it will again be up to you to decide exactly which solution you will choose to solve the problem.

When handling problems you will be expected to make a note on a monitoring sheet (provided by the centre or awarding body), which details the problem and your solution. You should make sure that you have recorded the problem and solution so that you can refer to these in Element 4.3 when reviewing the activity and your actions throughout.

PROBLEMS

Anticipated problems

In Element 4.1 we suggested some of the problems that you might be able to anticipate. If you have created flexible individual and team action plans you will have thought about other ways of completing the activity if any of these problems arise.

If any of these problems do arise, this will be a good opportunity to show how good your action plan was in the first place and that you had anticipated certain situations arising and have worked out ways of getting around them. Again you should record the fact that these anticipated problems arose and the fact that your suggested solutions worked in reality. If your suggested solutions did not work then you can count these as unexpected problems.

Unexpected problems

One example of an unexpected problem is the sickness of a team member. Having spent a considerable amount of time working out the team plan and allocating specific tasks to individuals within the team, the prospect of having to carry out the activity without one of the members of the team will be disheartening. Sickness can never be anticipated and your tutor will be looking at the way in which the remainder of the team deals with this problem and accepts responsibility for the tasks that have been allocated to the absent team member. Once again, make sure that any unexpected problem is noted and the way in which the team dealt with it is identified.

BUSINESS CONNECTION

PC 4.2

We have now looked at all the major ways of undertaking a role in a team activity. To test your memory and skill, complete the following business connection by turning co-operate into safety. The last letter of each word or phrase is the first letter of the next word or phrase. To help you we have put in the first and last letter on each line, but you will have to do the rest.

```
        C O - O P E R A T E
E  •  •  •  •  •  •   •  •  •  •  •  M
        M  •  •  •  •  R
        R  •  •  •  •  •  •  S
        S A F E T Y
```

assignment

ELEMENT 4.2

PC 4.2.1–5

 ince you will be performing the tasks related to each of the performance criteria during the team activity, there is no specific element assignment. In order to help you think about the kind of things that your tutor will be looking at, we have created a number of personalised questionnaires for you to complete to assess your own abilities, strengths and weaknesses. Where possible we have linked these questionnaires with the performance criteria of this element, although some of the questionnaires cover more than one performance criterion, as well as core skills.

We will start with an analysis of your own strengths and weaknesses. By doing this you may be able to begin to realise your own abilities.

task	1	PC 4.2.1

Answer the questions, using the following responses:

- **always**
- **sometimes**
- **occasionally**
- **never**

1. Are you able to work long hours?
2. Do you find problems a challenge?
3. Can you come up with good ideas to solve problems?
4. If you started an activity and were struggling would you be prepared to keep going?
5. Are you able to keep going with an activity or problem until it is completed, regardless of how you feel about it?
6. Would you always put your own duties before anything else, including your leisure activities and your family?
7. Do you consider success to be measured in terms of how much praise you get?
8. Are you able to cope if you are unsure about how to carry out a particular task?
9. Do you consider yourself to be self-confident?
10. Are you able to take criticism?
11. Do you tend to ask for feedback on your performance so that you can do better next time?
12. Do you feel that your success or failure relies on others too much?
13. Do you tend to be a leader in certain situations?
14. Are you good at finding the right person or source of information to help you achieve what you want?
15. Do you have the ability to realise that in certain circumstances you may need help?
16. Do you set high standards for yourself?
17. Do you take risks rather than being cautious?
18. Are you healthy?
19. Do you have the ability to pass jobs on to others?
20. Are you able to identify which decisions are important and which are unimportant?
21. Do others think of you as a survivor?
22. Do you find coping with problems a real difficulty?
23. Do you respect other people's views and opinions?
24. When others express an opinion or offer advice or information, are you able to accept what they say?

If you have answered these questions with mainly **always** or **sometimes** responses, then you are probably a good leader.

task | **2** | PC 4.2.4

Decision making, problem solving and information seeking are important elements in working as part of a team.

Answer the following questions by stating one of the following:

- **I agree**
- **I neither agree nor disagree**
- **I disagree**

1. I want to control the tasks set me.
2. I want to be involved in everything.
3. I find it impossible to pass on a job to someone else.
4. I hate being uncertain about things.
5. I do not trust other people's ability to do a job.
6. I hate asking other people for favours.
7. I like to be alone when I have things to do.
8. I always check and change other people's work.
9. I would rather stop doing what I am doing than let someone else undertake a task that I think I should be doing.
10. I lose interest in a task if someone else interferes in what I am doing.

If you have agreed with the above statements, then you are much more of an individual than a team worker. If you have neither agreed nor disagreed with the statements, then you may be either unsure of what you might do in certain situations, or it may not actually worry you whether you are working alone or as a member of a team. Those that have disagreed with the majority of the statements will be reasonable group workers.

task 3 PC 4.2.1–5

Time management involves the constant checking of what needs to be done and people, as well as physical items such as paperwork, need to be taken into account.

*Answer the following statements with a **true** or **false** response:*

1. *I have identified my strengths in relation to time management.*
2. *I have identified my weaknesses in relation to time management.*
3. *I know where and how I waste my time.*
4. *I know why I allow my time to be managed badly.*
5. *I am able to decide which tasks should be done first.*
6. *I can quickly process and decide on the importance of information.*
7. *I understand the reasons behind my time wasting behaviour.*
8. *I can use a variety of different methods to manage my time.*
9. *I can cope with other individuals who may try to stop me from getting on with the tasks in hand.*
10. *I am able to control my time.*

*If you have responded **true** to the majority of these questions, then you have already begun to manage your time effectively. If you have responded **false** to some of these statements, then you may have to consider making stricter rules for yourself and others.*

task 4 PC 4.2.5

Decision making is also an essential skill in business. We all make decisions on a daily basis, but we may not recognise them as such. Without first deciding how, when and why you will make the decision, you cannot expect to find yourself in a position to make that decision.

Problems will often arise without notice and these will have to be dealt with. Your initial reaction might be to panic, but this is not an effective way to deal with a problem.

*Answer the following questions with a **yes** or **no** response:*

1. *I can identify the nature and sources of problems before they happen.*
2. *I have already examined the possible solutions before I make a decision.*
3. *I have clear ideas that help me arrive at a solution.*
4. *I am able to compare possible solutions and choose the right one.*
5. *I can put into action and then monitor the results of my decisions.*
6. *I am able to foresee a problem arising.*
7. *I never make a snap decision.*
8. *I would rather think about the problem at length than risk making a wrong decision.*
9. *I do not find decision making stressful but it is challenging.*
10. *If I manage information correctly then decision making is relatively easy.*

*If you have answered **yes** to the majority of these questions, then you do understand the decision-making process and are reasonably able to solve problems. If you said **no** to the majority, or some, of these statements, then you are perhaps being a little more honest with yourself. There are only a handful of even highly experienced managers who could claim that they always make the right decision and are invariably able to solve problems effectively.*

task 5 PC 4.2.2

Following on from decision making and problem solving, the collection and handling of information is yet another key skill. The information that you are able to obtain, handle and process will be vital in establishing your ability to communicate within a group.

*Again answer these questions with a **yes** or **no** response:*

1. *I know what information I need.*
2. *I know from whom or where I can obtain this information.*

3 I do, of course, know why I want it.

4 I am aware of the deadline involved.

5 I know how I want the information to look.

6 Once I have the information I know what I have to do with it.

7 I can look at the information and know what is valuable and what is useless.

8 I can process the information and present it in a clear and logical way.

9 Once I have tackled the information I can draw clear conclusions from it.

10 I know how to use the information and to whom it should be given.

If you have answered **yes** to the majority of these questions, then you understand how to handle information. If you have a mixture of **yes** and **no** responses, or mainly **no** responses, you should not consider yourself a failure in this respect. A cautious user and handler of information might see things that the more confident handler might miss.

| t a s k | 6 | PC 4.2.4–5 |

The use and development of communication skills is an important consideration when attempting to establish relationships with others.

Answer these questions with a **true** or **false** response:

1 I can use a variety of communication methods.

2 I can listen effectively.

3 I am able to make myself understood by others.

4 I have better communication skills than other members of the team.

5 I do not have any trouble in communicating with different people in different circumstances.

6 I know the right questions to ask to get the information I need.

7 I am able to understand what people are really saying to me.

8 I appreciate that I need to listen as well as talk.

9 I am able to communicate well in written form.

10 I am able to present information in a variety of different ways.

If you have responded **false** to a number of these statements, then you should consider how these communication aspects may be improved.

| t a s k | 7 | PC 4.2.3 |

Health and safety concerns are important in everything we do. In many situations they will not be something we consider, but we should all be aware of the health and safety of ourselves and others, not least in the working environment.

Answer the following questions with a **true** or **false** response:

1 I would never put myself in a position where I felt unsafe.

2 I would never use equipment that I had not been instructed to use.

3 I find it hard to understand why people get hurt at work.

4 I do not believe that electrical equipment is necessarily dangerous.

5 People who get hurt at work deserve it because they are probably being careless.

6 Simple pieces of equipment do not really have health and safety problems at all.

7 If I saw something dangerous I would definitely avoid it.

8 I have noticed dangerous things and have reported them.

9 If I saw something dangerous at my centre I would know who to report it to.

10 I know all there is to know about health and safety laws.

If you have answered **true** to the majority of these questions then you are probably a little over-confident; you should think more carefully as you are probably overlooking things that may be more dangerous than you think. Several **false** replies will show that you, along with the majority of people, think about health and safety but are not always sure whether you are at risk or not.

element 4.3

REVIEW THE ACTIVITY

Performance criteria

A student must:

1 **Review** the extent to which the overall objectives of the activity were met.
2 **Review** use of **resources**.
3 **Review** whether responses to **problems** were effective.
4 **Review** maintenance of **health and safety**.
5 Provide clear and constructive **feedback** to others on their performance.
6 Respond constructively to **feedback** from others.
7 Make and record suggestions for **improvements** in the way similar activities are tackled in the future.

RANGE

Review: of the team's overall performance, of individual team members' performances; through team discussions, through discussions between individual team members and teachers/tutors

Resources: finance, people, materials, equipment, information

Problems: anticipated, unexpected

Health and safety associated with: oneself, other people, materials, equipment

Feedback: on success in undertaking the activity, on aspects of performance which may be improved

Improvements to: the team's performance, the student's performance, the use of resources, the responses to problems, the maintenance of health and safety

4.3.1 *Review the extent to which the overall objectives of the activity were met*

This element aims to ensure you have met all the performance criteria of not only this element, but also of the other two elements in this unit. Your tutor will have reviewed your progress regularly and given you some feedback on your performance so far. This element gives you as an individual, the team undertaking the activity and your tutor the opportunity to look at the activity in detail and review your performance throughout.

In the element assignment you will be asked to produce a log which outlines your performance in the team review of the activity. In order to help you to do this we will look at some of the skills needed to write a log.

A good way to get started is to make a list of your good and bad experiences and ideas. In other words you can list things under headings like:

▼ I was good at . . .
▼ I was bad at . . .
▼ I felt . . . went well
▼ I felt . . . went badly

When writing your log, you should consider the following:

▼ do not 'waffle', keep to the point; after all you only need write a summary
▼ some things may occur to you as a result of your tutor's comments. Did you agree with what was said at the time?
▼ be yourself and do not feel that you have to hide things; be honest
▼ write exactly what you want to say and do not be frightened of the comments you might get back as a result
▼ try to be positive, productive and useful; after all, how else will you be able to progress and improve?
▼ write the log as if you were writing it for yourself and not for your tutor; this may help you to show your real thoughts and feelings

REVIEW

Review of the team's overall performance

The activity that formed the basis of this unit will have involved planning, carrying out and completing a series of tasks involving teamwork. One of the problems that your tutor will always face in assessing teamwork is the part actually played by individual members of the team. Hopefully, if you have followed our advice throughout this unit, you will have made it clear at each stage exactly what your contribution was and whether you undertook tasks beyond those which you had been allocated. If you have logged your contribution it will not necessarily matter that your tutor did not actually see you do it; you are providing evidence that you have completed the task.

When working as a group there is always the tendency for some members of the team to concentrate on certain tasks at the expense of other aspects of the assignment. This is why many assignments often ask you to repeat tasks or to follow them through a series of stages to completion.

Review of individual team members' performances

Your tutor will obviously have some comments to make about your performance during the activity but, at the end of the day, it is your own opinions which really matter. Provided that you have logged as evidence the various situations and occasions that you felt were important during the activity, you can make your own valid conclusions about your own performance. In other words, you are saying 'next time I will . . .'

You will have an opportunity to give your own opinion in the discussion sessions that make up part of this performance criterion and in the feedback sessions of performance criteria 4.3.5 and 4.3.6. Obviously the more you think about and remember now, the more valuable your contribution to these sessions will be.

Review through team discussions and discussions between individual team members and teachers/tutors

It can be extremely useful to get feedback from someone like your tutor who has watched you undertake an activity. As we will see in performance criterion 4.3.5 when we look at feedback, some people find it difficult to tell you how you actually performed, but even more people find it difficult to accept what is being said about them. The main point of this performance criterion is to try to decide whether the team as a whole performed well and met the objectives of the activity.

Perhaps it would be a good idea to begin by thinking about what we actually mean by the word discussion. This is not necessarily an opportunity for you to make accusations against other team members for not having worked hard enough during the activity but, if you feel that the team's overall performance was hindered by some of the team members not pulling their weight, then you should say so. They will probably be aware of this and your tutor will probably have noticed it anyway. To help you, here are some questions you may wish to think about when reviewing the team's performance during any discussions you have:

▼ **why did we decide to approach the activity in the way that we did?**
▼ **what could we have done to make the activity easier for us?**
▼ **did we take everyone's opinion into account when we planned the activity?**
▼ **what should have been done that was not done?**
▼ **were all the team members happy with the workload allocated to them?**
▼ **were all the team members happy with the end result of the activity?**
▼ **how could our performance be improved if we were asked to complete this activity in the future?**

4.3.2 *Review use of resources*

RESOURCES

It is possible that some of the resources you hoped to use and that you had noted in your individual and team plans were not available when, where and in the quantity that you needed them. Although it will not help you now, if you can highlight the resource problems which you encountered during the activity, your tutor will be in a better position to ensure that these problems are not encountered by others in the future.

As we will see in this performance criterion, your tutor will discuss with you the resources available, how they were used and whether you should have used them in a different way. We will begin by looking at finance.

Finance

As we suggested earlier in this unit, a record of the costs of all the consumable items used in the activity will help you here. Although you will not have been given a budget as such, your tutor can get a better idea of the costs of the activity for each team by seeing your cost totals. If you had been asked to stay within a particular budget at the beginning of the activity, then you would now have the opportunity to compare your actual spending with the recommended amount.

As with all other resources, you should also consider whether you actually needed to use these resources and whether your money was well spent. Different members of the team and, indeed, your tutor, may have very different views on this. If you have spent money on items that were not really needed, then you did not consider the financial side of the activity carefully enough.

People

Again, a list of the sources of your information and guidance will be useful here. Hopefully, you did not take up any particular individual's time too much in trying to get the activity completed. You probably used your tutor as the main source of advice and information and he or she will have an opinion about whether you relied on them too much. Other individuals, who may not be able to give direct feedback on how much you used them during the activity, may also have views that are valuable. It may be a little harder to obtain these opinions, but your tutor may be in contact with them.

If you bear in mind that the more you actually do on your own, the more you can claim that the end result of the activity was because of your own actions, you will learn that it is not always advisable to seek other people's help all the time.

When reviewing people as a resource you should also consider whether the advice and information they gave you was actually useful at all. Did you explain to them what you really needed and did you get from them what you expected? Your experiences in this activity may well have an impact on who you ask and how often you ask for help in the future.

Materials and equipment

As far as materials and equipment are concerned, you may have discovered that the items you detailed in your action plan in Element 4.1 did not actually prove to be useful. Perhaps they were not available at the time you needed them or in sufficient quantity or quality. You may have felt that your performance in this assignment was hindered by shortcomings in materials and equipment but, as you will discover, this can occur in the workplace and individuals often have to undertake tasks without the support they were expecting. You may wish to consider some of the following questions to help you assess and review your use of materials and equipment:

▼ did we make sure that the materials were on hand and of the right quality and quantity before we actually needed them?
▼ when we had to use equipment did we know exactly how to operate it?
▼ were there times when a lack of materials meant that tasks were not completed on time?
▼ were there times when confusion over the operation of and the availability of equipment meant that tasks were not completed on time?
▼ were there materials and equipment that we had requested which were not available when needed?
▼ were there materials and equipment that we had not requested which we found we needed and consequently wasted time obtaining?

Again, your tutor will have noted your use of materials and equipment throughout the activity. If certain materials and equipment were suggested as being useful in completing the activity, you may wish to think about whether this advice was, in fact, relevant or useful in the event. Finally, you could compare your use of materials and equipment with that of other teams. To this end you might ask yourself the following questions:

▼ did other teams identify materials and equipment that you did not?
▼ if so, did this make their job easier or harder?
▼ what influenced your choice of materials and equipment?
▼ do you think you could have carried out the activity more efficiently if you had requested a different set of materials and equipment?

Information

Knowing where to get information is only one part of using information itself; once you have obtained the information, you still need to know how to use it effectively.

In your activity you may have collected a large amount of information and, in completing the activity, either decided not to use it or found that you did not have time to use it. This could have been as a result of not obtaining the information as early as you should have done. Bearing in mind that a great deal of information is not found in the desired format, your information will have had to be processed by you in some way in order to make it useable. If you were using our assignment detailed in Element 4.1 and had constructed a questionnaire which was both focused on the information that you needed to collect and in a format that included closed questions, then the information should have been easy for you to process. But, if you found yourself in a position of not being able to use that information, then you should consider the fact that your questionnaire was possibly poorly designed. Obtaining information from individuals or from books, articles and magazines is never an easy job. In most cases the information is not written in an easy way to either understand or use, nor is it necessarily up-to-date. Faced with information in this state there is often a temptation to ignore it. In terms of reviewing your use of information, perhaps you should think about the following questions:

▼ **were you able to collect all the information that you wanted?**
▼ **how much time did you spend collecting this information and was it worth the time spent?**
▼ **how much time did you spend trying to make use of information that you had collected?**
▼ **were there times that you needed information and had to pause whilst it was being collected?**
▼ **do you think you should have used other forms of information collection to have made this aspect of the assignment easier?**
▼ **did you find yourself with information that you did not use at all?**

It is also worth remembering that information seeking and information handling are grading criteria for your award. Basically, these grading criteria or themes look at how you identify and use information sources. You will have been expected to do the following:

▼ *identify information needs –* **independently identify the information you need for the various tasks**
▼ *identify and use sources to obtain information* **– independently identify and collect various information and identify where this information can be found**

4.3.3 *Review whether responses to problems were effective*

PROBLEMS

No matter how skilled or experienced you are in tackling tasks and assignments, there will always be times when problems prevent you from successfully completing your task.

In this performance criterion we will be working on the problems that caused difficulty in the completion of your assignment. A good action plan should provide solutions to potential problems, but these are anticipated problems. As their name suggests, you will not have been able to suggest solutions for any unexpected problems.

Anticipated problems

As we know, a good action plan will have considered potential problems and your tutor will have encouraged you to think about different ways of tackling various tasks during the activity to avoid these. It is sensible to think of more than one way of carrying out any task, but this is not always possible, as we sometimes need to have carried out certain tasks before others may be attempted. If, for example, you encountered problems in collecting information, it would be impossible to process it or analyse it. You may wish to think about some of the following questions when reviewing the way you dealt with anticipated problems:

▼ **did you anticipate all of the potential problems (if you did not, then were these unexpected problems or not?)**
▼ **what were your main anticipated problems? Did they relate to people, materials, equipment or information?**
▼ **could you have avoided an anticipated problem by attempting a different way of handling the assignment?**
▼ **if you had to carry out this activity in the future would you now be more aware of anticipated problems than you were this time?**
▼ **how many of the anticipated problems were a result of the team's actions?**

Your tutor will have been assessing your ability to switch from one set of actions to another during the course of the activity. He or she will have looked at how smoothly you managed to work around an anticipated problem and dealt with any unexpected problems.

Unexpected problems

In this part of the performance criterion we consider the problems that arose that were beyond your control. You may wish to think about the following questions:

▼ **although unexpected when you wrote your action plan, how many of the unexpected problems became anticipated problems the further you got into the assignment?**
▼ **how many of the unexpected problems should have really been anticipated problems and you just failed to recognise them as such?**
▼ **were the unexpected problems harder to handle as a result of the fact that you had not considered ways of getting round them in your action plan?**
▼ **how many of the unexpected problems were a result of your own actions and how many were a result of others' actions or the non-availability of**

materials and equipment?
▼ **were there any unexpected problems that you could not cope with?**
▼ **how many unexpected problems in this activity would be anticipated problems in a future activity?**

Your tutor will not have expected you to be able to look into the future. Although you will have identified some anticipated problems in your action plan, you will also be assessed on your ability to handle the unexpected and cope with the problem with the minimum of difficulty.

4.3.4 *Review maintenance of health and safety*

HEALTH AND SAFETY

Health and safety associated with oneself, other people and materials and equipment

We have already outlined the possible health and safety considerations in both Elements 4.1 and 4.2. You should now think about any health and safety matters which came up during the activity.
Consider the following:

▼ **were you responsible for any act that put yourself in danger during the activity? If so, why did you do this and how will you avoid this situation next time?**
▼ **were you responsible for any act that put other people in danger during the activity? If so, why did you do this and how will you avoid this situation next time?**
▼ **was another person responsible for any**

act that put a member of your team in danger during the activity? If so, why did he or she do this and how will you avoid this situation next time?
▼ do you consider that the whole of your team was aware of health and safety implications during the activity? If not, how could you ensure that everyone is aware next time?
▼ are there any materials or equipment which you would avoid in the future for health and safety reasons? If so, have you reported them?

4.3.5 Provide clear and constructive feedback to others on their performance

4.3.6 Respond constructively to feedback from others

We have put these two performance criteria together since, essentially, they are linked aspects of the review process. Obviously the content of feedback will vary according to the work carried out. Bear in mind that constructive feedback is not always necessarily positive. The review process is intended to contribute towards your learning and improvement in your performance. Feedback will take the form of comments, opinions and suggestions, as well as offering other members of the team the opportunity to comment.

FEEDBACK

Feedback on success in undertaking the activity and aspects of performance which may be improved

We can often accept feedback and criticism from tutors which we would not accept from other members of the team. Although at the time it may not seem like it, even criticism can be positive. In order to make sure that any feedback is valuable it is worth thinking about the following:

▼ how do you know that something happened if you do not have evidence of it? In other words, if something was important enough to log when it happened, then you will have evidence that it happened, even if the individuals involved cannot remember the incident
▼ did you take other team members' feelings into account when you did something? This refers to situations when you might have been rather too bossy or perhaps lazier than you should have been. You should consider how the other team members felt when you were behaving like this
▼ can you step back and actually criticise yourself? Although you may not notice certain things that you have done, you will probably have been thinking about others that are important to discuss with the rest of the team now
▼ were there more positive things about the activity than negative ones? Did you hate the activity and find it impossible to work with the other team members? Or did you keep too quiet at the beginning of the activity, particularly when it was planned, and as a result feel that the way in which the activity was tackled was all wrong?

4.3.7 **Make and record suggestions for improvements in the way similar activities are tackled in the future**

IMPROVEMENTS

Improvements to the team's performance and the student's performance

Your tutor may have his or her own ideas about how to approach this part of the performance criterion. If this is not the case, or you would like to suggest possible improvements, then you might want to consider the following steps:

▼ **individually think about and write down at least two occasions when you had problems in carrying out the activity. One occasion should be when you handled the situation well and one should be when you handled the situation badly. What were the outcomes of these two occasions?**

▼ **in pairs, describe the two situations to one another. Listen to your partner's description of how he or she handled the situation and try to suggest ways in which the problem could have been solved**

▼ **in your teams, describe the situations you have been talking about, as well as your proposed solutions to them, and see if the rest of the team agree with what you have suggested**

Improvements to the use of resources

Having reviewed your use of resources, you are now in a position to make valuable comments in response to your tutor's feedback. Provided that you can justify your use of resources throughout the activity, you will be able to answer any queries or criticisms which may be levelled at you. Remember that any suggestions in the improvement of your use of resources is meant to be constructive. Listening to these suggestions will put you in a much better position when you use resources for your next activity. Make sure that this feedback session is a two-way process where you explain to your tutor the shortcomings of any resources, so that he or she is able to address these and make sure the same problems do not occur next time.

Improvements to the responses to problems

In reviewing your list of responses to anticipated and unexpected problems, you may already have identified a way in which you, as a team, could have improved these. On the other hand, you may not be able to think of better ways to approach them. Bearing in mind that solving problems which you encounter whilst undertaking an activity yourself can be more difficult than if you are watching someone else face a problem, your tutor may have noticed and be able to suggest a better way of handling a situation. Although tutors will not have been able to put themselves in your position or know what you were thinking or considering as a team, do listen to their advice and guidance.

Improvements to the maintenance of health and safety

As we will see in Unit 5, there are various ways of reducing the common risks to individuals in the workplace. In relation to your assignment, think about the following as potential improvements to the maintenance of health and safety:

▼ **were there situations that could have been prevented?**
▼ **were there situations when health and safety equipment should have been available?**
▼ **were there situations when health and safety problems arose as a result of someone not following the correct procedure?**
▼ **were there situations when health and safety problems arose which could**

have been avoided had you been suitably trained?
▼ **were there situations when a health and safety problem arose as a result of problems with equipment or materials?**

If you have answered **yes** to any of these then there is room for improvement in health and safety. You should immediately inform your tutor if there is a hazard. Your tutor may have noticed certain behaviour or use of equipment and materials that he/she will report back to you. Listen to this advice and consider the ways you, as a team, could have dealt with them.

BUSINESS CONNECTION

PC 4.3

We have now looked at all the major ways of reviewing an activity. To test your memory and skill, complete the following business connection by turning finance into safety. The last letter of each word or phrase is the first letter of the next word or phrase. To help you we have put in the first and last letter on each line, but you will have to do the rest.

```
      F I N A N C E
    E • • • • • • T
  T • • •   • • • • • • S
    S • • • • • S
      S A F E T Y
```

WORDSEARCH

How many of the words listed below can you find? They run forwards and backwards across and up and down the grid.

```
H  E  A  L  T  H  A  N  D  S  A  F  E  T  Y  O  P  F
I  O  G  M  G  N  V  B  X  E  I  O  T  A  M  E  S  O
I  R  R  E  A  L  T  H  M  V  O  I  N  S  E  T  E  Y
M  M  E  M  B  E  R  O  F  I  L  I  K  K  O  P  C  T
O  P  E  O  P  L  E  F  O  T  T  H  E  S  I  N  R  L
U  Y  I  M  E  S  C  A  L  C  N  T  U  V  W  Y  U  N
I  N  N  M  E  A  S  L  E  E  S  N  O  I  T  P  O  S
S  U  G  G  E  S  T  I  O  J  N  S  F  O  R  N  S  F
I  O  A  M  T  E  A  M  O  B  J  E  C  T  I  V  E  S
I  N  C  Z  Q  R  P  N  J  O  T  I  M  E  D  O  R  N
W  L  T  W  O  R  L  D  S  M  E  S  E  N  E  N  Y  L
F  F  I  N  A  N  C  E  A  A  L  A  S  T  A  S  T  Y
I  N  O  B  J  T  A  R  G  E  T  S  M  N  S  D  I  L
I  B  N  I  B  N  T  E  A  M  P  L  A  N  J  E  V  R
I  N  O  I  T  A  M  R  O  F  N  I  T  A  M  E  I  J
O  N  E  A  C  T  I  O  N  P  L  A  N  X  L  R  T  O
T  I  M  E  S  C  A  L  E  D  A  Y  N  O  L  G  C  L
I  P  G  O  L  T  N  E  D  U  T  S  I  J  K  A  A  L
```

ACTION PLAN	INFORMATION	SUGGEST
ACTIVITY	MEMBER	TARGETS
AGREED	OBJECTIVES	TASKS
AGREEING ACTION	OPTIONS	TEAM OBJECTIVES
FINANCE	PEOPLE	TEAM PLAN
HEALTH AND SAFETY	RESOURCES	TIMESCALE
IDEAS	STUDENT LOG	

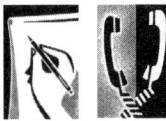

assignment

ELEMENT **4.3**

PC 4.3.1–7
COM 1.1, 1.2, 1.3

Assuming that you have followed our advice from the beginning of this unit, you will now have a detailed log which outlines your performance throughout the activity. In this part of the unit you are expected to undertake a review of your performance and evaluate your contribution. Your tutor will be responsible for some of the aspects of this element, particularly those relating to feedback. Your review should match the performance criteria of this element and we have broken down the content of your review in task form below.

Your review should take the form of a log sheet, provided by your tutor, which is an accurate record of your performance. Remember that this will have to be verified by your tutor or assessor.

Your log will be compared to the notes and observations made by your tutor throughout the activity so it is essential that your log is accurate.

| **task** | **1** | PC 4.3.1 |

Comment on your performance against the roles and tasks which were allocated to you as part of the overall activity. Also, mention whether your actions allowed the overall objectives of the activity to be met.

| **task** | **2** | PC 4.3.2 |

Comment on whether you think that the resources needed were used effectively.

| **task** | **3** | PC 4.3.3 |

Comment on whether you believe that your solutions to problems were effective.

| **task** | **4** | PC 4.3.4 |

Comment on whether you felt that health and safety was maintained throughout the activity.

| **task** | **5** | PC 4.3.5–6 |

Give feedback to other members of the team on their performance and respond to feedback given to you by other members of the team and your tutor.

| **task** | **6** | PC 4.3.7 |

Write a list of suggestions for improvements in your performance that you will take into consideration when you are asked to tackle similar activities in the future.

element 5.1

IDENTIFY KEY FACTORS IN SAFE WORKING

Performance criteria

A student must:

1 Describe and give examples of **common hazards** to people in the workplace.

2 Describe and give examples of **common risks** to people in the workplace.

3 Identify **ways to reduce common risks**.

4 Identify the **key regulatory requirements** for safe practice in the workplace.

RANGE

Common hazards when using: materials, machinery, tools, equipment

Common risks: injury, fire, contamination

Ways to reduce common risks: prevention, health and safety equipment, procedures, training

Key regulatory requirements: codes and practices, Health and Safety at Work Act, Control of Substances Hazardous to Health

5.1.1 *Describe and give examples of common hazards to people in the workplace*

COMMON HAZARDS

The cost of accidents in the workplace and health problems related to work can be very high. Perhaps one of the easiest ways to measure this is in money terms. From an employer's point of view, the following costs may occur as a result of accidents and health problems in the workplace:

▼ **having to pay for temporary staff to replace those employees who have fallen sick or have been injured at work**
▼ **the loss of work and disruption to other employees if one of their colleagues is off work**
▼ **the time and money that will have to be spent in training staff to replace those who are off work**
▼ **the payment of welfare benefits to those who are off work**
▼ **the payment of compensation claims to those who have been injured or have fallen sick as a result of hazards and accidents in the workplace**

On the employee's part, there are also costs to consider:

▼ **even if the employee receives sickness benefit, this will not be as much as a regular wage**
▼ **if the employee is badly hurt or is permanently sick, then he or she may never return to work**
▼ **the costs of having to go to hospital, clinics and the purchase of prescriptions**

There is no doubt that many accidents and hazards could be avoided if we all paid attention to the working environment in which we operate. We can, perhaps, begin by looking at the main differences between dangers, risks and hazards:

▼ **a danger is the potential exposure to a hazard**
▼ **a risk is the chance of being hurt**
▼ **a hazard is a situation that may result in someone being injured or damaged**

PC 5.1.1
COM 1.1

`00:20`

Discuss these questions as a group:

• *can someone deliberately cause an accident?*
• *do accidents normally mean that someone is injured?*
• *do accidents usually mean damage to property?*
• *do accidents normally mean damage to the environment?*

Common hazards when using materials

There are a number of things to consider when you are handling and using materials in the workplace. The types of hazards and potential problems that might crop up will depend upon the sorts of materials that are being used, but here are some of the general rules:

▼ materials should be stored in easily accessible places, particularly if they are heavy or bulky
▼ materials should also be stored in places where it is dry and safe
▼ materials that are not being used should be put away again as soon as possible
▼ materials should never be left in a place that will cause an obstruction to others
▼ materials should always be kept in containers which are designed for them and not others
▼ materials need to be disposed of if they are out of date or become useless as they might become a hazard if they are left lying around

---

FIGURE IT OUT

PC 5.1.1
COM 1.1

00:15

*A*s a group, think about the kind of materials that you use either at your centre or, perhaps, when you are working on placement or during your part-time job. What types of hazards, related to these materials, should you be aware of?

Common hazards when using machinery, tools and equipment

Probably the most important thing to remember when you are using machinery, tools or other equipment is that they are powered by electricity. We will look at this aspect first:

▼ make sure that you always use the closest power point when plugging in a machine, tool or piece of equipment
▼ remember that trailing wires and flexes can cause accidents if they are left where people have to cross
▼ never overload an electrical socket when you could use another one; it is very unwise to plug several pieces of equipment into the same socket using a multi-adaptor
▼ if there is anything wrong with the machine, tool or piece of equipment, never be tempted to try to mend it yourself; always report the fault to your supervisor or a technician
▼ the same point should be remembered when you spot a broken socket, plug or a loose wire; never try to mend these yourself
▼ always switch off the machine if you see that there is something wrong with

it; never mess around with machines, tools or equipment if they are still plugged in

▼ when you have finished using a machine, tool or piece of equipment, always turn it off and unplug it. Make sure that you always unplug at the end of the day without fail

There are some general points to remember when using machines, tools and equipment:

▼ always follow the manufacturer's instructions
▼ never try to use a machine, tool or piece of equipment for something that it is not designed for
▼ if the machine is bulky and not meant to be moved, never try to move it; it

has been placed there for a reason
▼ always read the instructions related to the piece of equipment before you start to use it
▼ make sure that you can see what you are doing; never try to use machinery in poor light
▼ always use the protective equipment provided for the job; never even turn on the machinery before you have put this protective equipment on
▼ make sure that you know the safety rules regarding the machinery before you attempt to use it
▼ never try to use a piece of equipment that you have been told not to touch or have never received any instructions or training for

---

FIGURE IT OUT

PC 5.1.1
COM 1.1

00:15

*A*s a group, try to remember any times when you could have had an accident as a result of equipment. You can consider instances at home, work or the centre. Have any of you actually hurt yourselves? What precautions would you take in the future?

5.1.2 Describe and give examples of common risks to people in the workplace

COMMON RISKS

In this performance criterion, we have included the risks that people face in the course of their work. There are so many that we could not possibly mention all of them, but these are the main worries.

Injury

The word **injury** covers the majority of accidents that happen in the workplace. The main injuries that could occur fall into the following categories:

▼ *eye injuries* – eyes are very delicate and can be injured by flying particles, dust, chemicals, molten metal, gases and radiation
▼ *ear injuries* – loud noises can affect your ears, even if you are exposed to them for only a short period of time
▼ *head and neck injuries* – hair can get tangled in machinery; your face can be splashed by chemicals or you could get hurt in extreme temperatures
▼ *hand and arm injuries* – hands and arms, often the parts of the body that are in direct contact with machinery, can be damaged by crushing, burns, cuts, chemicals, electric shocks, falling objects or friction
▼ *feet and leg injuries* – slipping is the most obvious way to receive an injury, but injuries can also be caused by stepping on sharp objects, falling objects, heavy weights and chemical splashing

▼ *body injuries* – the heat and cold of certain situations may damage the body, as can chemicals, pressure and falling objects

Fire

The risk of fire is a concern in most workplaces. After all, we all use electrical equipment and this can be a source of fire hazards. Here are some general things to think about in relation to fire. Maybe you can see why these are important to remember:

▼ **make sure that you know what the fire drills are and that you practise the evacuation at least once a year**
▼ **make sure that you read all of the fire notices that are displayed around the workplace**
▼ **make sure that you know where the fire equipment is and how to use it in an emergency**
▼ **make sure that the fire exits are always clear and not blocked by boxes or equipment at any time**
▼ **make sure that anything that could catch fire (this is known as inflammable material) is stored away**
▼ **make sure that any inflammable materials or objects are stored out of direct sunlight. Sunlight could cause them to catch fire**
▼ **make sure that you do not smoke in areas that have been designated no-smoking areas, as there may be very good reasons for this**

Contamination

Contamination means exposure to chemicals or other dangerous items that could cause long-term illness or injury. You may have heard of asbestos, a white or grey material which was often used for ceilings in offices, chosen because it was light and fire resistant. The problem, as was discovered much later, was that the dust got into people's lungs and caused an unpleasant disease in the long term. Some people have even died as a result of inhaling lots of the dust. Breathing in any dust, gases or other vapours might cause long-term illness.

  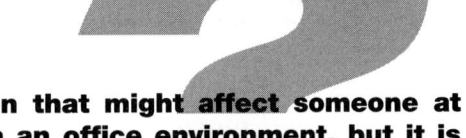

finding out

PC 5.1.2
COM 1.1

Find out the different types of contamination that might affect someone at work. You may not find very many examples in an office environment, but it is likely that you will find some for factories.
Compare your findings with those of the rest of the group.

5.1.3 *Identify ways to reduce common risks*

WAYS TO REDUCE COMMON RISKS

Prevention is the best cure, it is said. In this performance criterion, we will be looking at some of the ways in which risks can be reduced. You will also find useful information in the other two elements of this unit.

Prevention

In every organisation, beyond the part that all employees should play in the prevention of risks and hazards, there will be certain individuals who have a specific duty to ensure that risks are minimised. No prevention scheme is completely fool-proof and so everyone must keep their wits about them at work to avoid the possibility of dangers becoming disasters.

Health and safety equipment

Amongst the most common types of health and safety equipment are the following:

▼ **personal protective equipment, such as helmets, visors, masks and harnesses**
▼ **ventilation**
▼ **fire extinguishers**
▼ **safety warning signs**
▼ **first-aid equipment**

We will now look at these in more detail.

Personal protective equipment

When dealing with toxic or otherwise dangerous materials or substances, protective clothing and equipment should be worn. It is also worth remembering that loose clothing can be caught in machinery.

39

FIGURE IT OUT

PC 5.1.3
COM 1.1

00:30

*I*n the following circumstances, certain sorts of protective clothing and equipment are usually worn. Why is this so? What is the reason for wearing this equipment and what might happen if it is not worn?

- *why are reinforced boots worn on a building site?*
- *why is it not advisable to wear high-heeled shoes in a factory?*
- *why should machine operators wear gloves?*
- *why is it law to have protective guards on most pieces of machinery?*

Compare your thoughts with those of the rest of the group.

Ventilation

Good ventilation is essential in all workplaces and especially those where hazardous fumes and smoke are created as a result of the processes used. This is not a simple question of having windows open or doors kept ajar. Extractor fans and machinery to circulate the air can ensure that sufficiently good air quality is maintained at all times.

Fire extinguishers

Materials used to combat fire include the following:

▼ **water**
▼ **carbon dioxide**
▼ **powder**
▼ **foam**
▼ **halon**

Fire blankets can also be used to smother fires, and are particularly useful if a person is on fire. Buckets of sand are also still available in some workplaces.

finding out

PC 5.1.3
COM 1.1

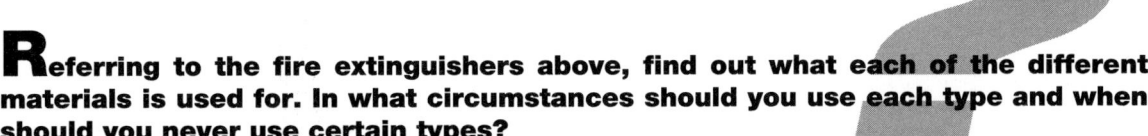

Referring to the fire extinguishers above, find out what each of the different materials is used for. In what circumstances should you use each type and when should you never use certain types?

Collect this information and compare it with the findings of the rest of your group.

Safety warning signs

These should always be clearly marked and put in places that can be seen easily by the employees or other people visiting the organisation. Signs should never be covered or blocked from view for any reason. In addition to this, it may be necessary to put specific signs next to certain machines and equipment to make sure that the users understand the potential hazards associated with them.

finding out

PC 5.1.3
COM 1.1

As a group, visit the various areas in your centre that have machinery or equipment and make a list of all of the safety warning signs that you can find. Are they all up to date and clearly visible? Make sure that you tell your tutor if you find any that are wrong.

First-aid equipment

Certain people in every organisation are trained to be first aiders. These people should know how to deal with basic first-aid situations and be on hand to help if there is an accident. Under the Health and Safety at Work Act, the employer is required by law to make sure that qualified first aiders are available. Normally, basic first-aid equipment is available in most organisations and this includes the following items:

▼ **bandages**
▼ **plasters**
▼ **splints**
▼ **antiseptic**
▼ **safety pins**

finding out

PC 5.1.3
COM 1.1, 1.2

Can you think of other things that you would find the first-aid box? What things should not be in there? How would you report the fact that certain items are missing and who would have the responsibility to make sure that they are replaced? Write a list and then compare your list with those of the rest of the group and check with your tutor that you are correct.

Procedures

As we will see in the remainder of this unit, there are different procedures for different sets of circumstances. The exact way that things should be done will depend upon the organisation itself.

Training

In the workplace or the centre in which you are studying, it is important that you make sure you attend any training sessions which cover the following:

▼ **machinery**
▼ **equipment**
▼ **tools**
▼ **safe practice in the workplace**
▼ **employee welfare**
▼ **training and information or guidance to any of the above**

You should also make sure that you are aware of the following:

▼ **fire exits**
▼ **fire drills**
▼ **fire evacuation procedures**
▼ **other rules and regulations of the organisation that refer to health and safety**

5.1.4 *Identify the key regulatory requirements for safe practice in the workplace*

KEY REGULATORY REQUIREMENTS

Every organisation and workplace will have its own particular set of requirements and there are a number of key pieces of health and safety legislation aimed at making sure that neither you, nor any other person, is at risk in the workplace. We will look at some of the most important ones at this point, but you will also find some mentioned later in this unit.

Codes and practices

Although you are not expected to remember all of the rules and regulations that relate to health and safety in the workplace, always try to remember the ones that relate to you and the work that you are expected to carry out. As long as you make sure that the main health and safety considerations are covered, then you can help to make sure that both you and others are not threatened by your actions.

Above all, if you see anything that could be considered a hazard, it is your responsibility to make sure that a supervisor is made aware of it. Also, you should check that anything you have noticed and reported is put right as quickly as is practically possible.

As an employee or student, it is your responsibility to follow these general rules in the workplace:

▼ **gangways should be kept clear**
▼ **fire exits should be kept clear**
▼ **fire doors should be kept shut and never propped open**
▼ **all filing cabinet drawers should be closed after use as, if left open, cabinets can topple over and might fall on someone**
▼ **cigarettes should be put out carefully and you should always observe the smoking rules of the organisation**
▼ **electrical items should be unplugged at the end of the day**
▼ **any adaptors or electrical wires should not be trailing along the floor in case someone trips over them**
▼ **faulty equipment should be reported to the appropriate person immediately upon discovering the fault**
▼ **items should not be stacked too high on shelves or in cupboards**
▼ **frayed or damaged carpets should be mended or covered until the repairs have been carried out**
▼ **first-aid equipment should be in an accessible place and always replenished after use**
▼ **unguarded fires should never be used in the workplace**
▼ **employees should be familiar with the use of fire extinguishers and the fire drill should be well-known throughout the organisation**
▼ **valuable items should be locked safely away at the end of the day**

All organisations are required to have a safety policy and must do everything possible to avoid accidents and fires. This is normally achieved by making sure that:

1 All employees receive a written safety policy.
2 All employees have a copy of the safety handbook.
3 All employees attend regular training sessions.

Health and Safety at Work Act

The Health and Safety at Work Act of 1974, also known as the HASAWA, sets out the responsibilities of employers and employees to ensure the following:

▼ **that there are safe working practices used in the workplace**
▼ **that the workplace is non-hazardous**
▼ **that the workplace is as healthy as possible**

The particular responsibilities of the employer are:

▼ **that the workplace is kept as safe as possible**
▼ **that all of the equipment used in the workplace is safe and regularly serviced**
▼ **that any hazardous substances or materials are stored in such a way as to avoid potential danger**
▼ **that the employees have sufficient welfare facilities in the workplace**
▼ **that employees can easily exit if there is a problem and evacuation is necessary**
▼ **that the employees are provided with up-to-date and relevant training and supervision on a range of health and safety matters**

For the employees, the HASAWA could not be more clear. Basically, they must take responsibility for their own areas of work as well as their own actions in the workplace. They should also immediately report any potential hazard to the employer or a safety representative.

Control of Substances Hazardous to Health

These Regulations have been introduced to make sure that organisations control the use of chemicals and other substances that could cause harm to people. It also states that the employer has to make sure that employees handling these substances are fully aware of the dangers that they present to them. A good example of the types of substances involved are solvents that can be extremely harmful if they are inhaled.

BUSINESS CONNECTION

PC 5.1

We have now looked at all the major ways of identifying key factors in safe working. To test your memory and skill, complete the following business connection by turning fire extinguisher into training. The last letter of each word or phrase is the first letter of the next word or phrase. To help you we have put in the first and last letter on each line, but you will have to do the rest.

```
F I R E   E X T I N G U I S H E R
          R  .  .  .  S
S . . . . . . . . . . . . . . . S
          S . . . . . . E
          E . . . . . . T
          T R A I N I N G
```

assignment

ELEMENT 5.1

PC 5.1.1–4
COM 1.1, 1.2, 1.3

In order to complete this element assignment (which could be completed along with the assignments of the other two elements of this unit), it might be a good idea to base your research around a work placement. Failing that, you can look at the centre in which you are studying. As you will have to compare two different working environments for this assignment, your tutor may be able to arrange a visit to a workplace or ask a safety officer to come in and talk to you.

| task | 1 | PC 5.1.1–2 |

For two different workplaces, provide a description of common risks and hazards to people. You should give one hazard and one risk per workplace.

| task | 2 | PC 5.1.3 |

Identify ways in which the common risks that you referred to in Task 1 could be reduced.

| **t a s k** | **3** | PC 5.1.4 |

Identify the key regulatory requirements for safe practice in the workplace.

| **n o t e s** | |

Useful sources of information for this element assignment are:

- *The British Safety Council*
- *The Royal Society for the Prevention of Accidents (ROSPA)*
- *Her Majesty's Stationery Office (HMSO)*
- *A Guide to the Health and Safety at Work Act (1994) (HR(R)4)*
- *The Essentials of Health and Safety at Work – a Booklet for Small Firms*

The last two items on this list can be found at Citizens Advice Bureaux and libraries.

element 5.2

INVESTIGATE COMMON ACCIDENT AND EMERGENCY PROCEDURES

Performance criteria

A student must:

1 Describe the **main reasons for accident and emergency procedures**.

2 Identify and give examples of **common accidents and emergencies** in the workplace.

3 Describe **emergency procedures** for **shutting down** equipment.

4 Describe **safe evacuation procedures** for **common emergencies**.

5 Describe **how to summon assistance** in case of accidents and emergencies.

6 Describe **how to report** accidents and emergencies.

RANGE

Main reasons for accident and emergency procedures: to protect people, to protect the workplace

Common accidents and emergencies: medical emergencies, fire, equipment malfunction, electric shock, contamination, security alert

Emergency shut-down procedures: when to shut down, how to shut down

Safe evacuation procedures: appropriate to the equipment and materials used, appropriate to the condition of oneself or others, appropriate to the workplace

How to summon assistance: operating appropriate equipment, verbally

How to report: verbally, in writing

5.2.1 Describe the main reasons for accident and emergency procedures

MAIN REASONS FOR ACCIDENT AND EMERGENCY PROCEDURES

What would you do in the event of an accident? You have probably thought about this before, but never actually been in a situation where you have had to do anything. It is important to be aware of the procedures to deal with all types of accident before they actually happen and not just to hope that they will never happen.

The purpose of this element is to look at the actions you should take in the event of an accident and what you should do to prepare yourself for almost anything. Some accidents may never happen, but you cannot be sure of this.

To protect people

Any number of things in the workplace could put people in danger. Employees and other individuals must be an organisation's first priority. Remember that premises, equipment and other items are replaceable; people are not. It is therefore important to make sure that people are safe before looking at the damage or danger to premises. Never put yourself at risk for the sake of possessions or property, and only tackle a problem if there is little or no risk to yourself or other people.

To protect the workplace

Protection of the workplace must not be at the risk of endangering yourself or others. Fire extinguishers, alarms and other equipment are designed for you to protect or save the premises from danger. As we will see, you should always make sure that you know how to use the equipment that is available and never try to use something for which you have not received training. There are other 'in-built' systems that can help to protect the workplace, including sprinklers, fire alarms and smoke detectors, but these will only be effective if they are all working correctly.

5.2.2 Identify and give examples of common accidents and emergencies in the workplace

COMMON ACCIDENTS AND EMERGENCIES

It is often said that accidents occur as a result of 'failures of control'. What does this mean? There are two answers:

▼ the organisation has not made sure that there are physical safeguards in place
▼ the organisation has not set up effective safety control systems

On the whole, organisations are keen to improve their safety record and many take the following steps:

▼ setting practical goals for health and safety that everyone can understand
▼ encouraging the employees to work together in a safe manner

▼ encouraging the employees to meet the safety goals within the limits available to them

▼ making sure that the employees use the available resources to the best effect

▼ making sure that the employees accept responsibility for health and safety

▼ making sure that ways are developed so that health and safety can be measured against a particular standard

Medical emergencies

There are literally hundreds, if not thousands, of medical emergencies that could occur in the workplace. Here is a brief list and explanation of some of them (where needed):

▼ *airways and breathing problems* – suffocation, choking, drowning, hanging, strangling, throttling, hyperventilation (unnaturally fast and deep breathing), asthma (breathing difficulty)

▼ *circulation problems* – shock, fainting, anaphylactic shock (a massive allergic reaction), heart disorders, including angina pectoris (narrowed arteries), heart attacks

▼ *wounds and bleeding* – from the head, ear, mouth, chest, abdomen, eyes; loss of limbs, nosebleeds

▼ *bites and stings* – from animals, insects, and exotic creatures (such as snakes) if you work in a zoo or as a vet

▼ *burns and scalds* – including electrical burns, chemical burns, sunburn, flash burns to the eyes

▼ *unconsciousness* – head injuries, concussion, skull fractures, convulsions, epilepsy (disturbance of the brain), hypoglycaemia (caused by low blood sugar)

▼ *cold and heat* – frostbite, hypothermia, heat exhaustion, heatstroke

▼ *bone, joint and muscle injuries* – face and jaw, upper limbs, collar bone, elbow, forearm or wrist, hand and fingers, ribs, spine, pelvis, hips and thighs, knees, ankle, foot

▼ *poisoning* – from gases, drugs, plants and food

▼ *foreign bodies* – in the eye, ear, nose; swallowed or inhaled

▼ *other situations and conditions* – fevers, headaches, toothaches, abdominal pain, vomiting, diarrhoea, hernia, cramps, hysteria, allergies

We will be looking at how to deal with certain medical emergencies later in this element. There are, however, a great number of medical problems that you will not be able to help with; either the problem will not be apparent, or will be so complicated or serious that you will have to call in expert help.

---

finding out

PC 5.2.2
COM 1.2

Spend some time looking at a basic first-aid book. This will tell you more about some of the conditions we have mentioned above.

Figure 5.2.1 Mobil's Coryton plant has its own fire appliances and fire fighters.

Fire

Fires will start in the following conditions:

▼ **if there is an ignition (like a spark or a flame)**
▼ **if there is a source of fuel (such as wood, petrol or clothing)**
▼ **if there is oxygen (air)**

It is therefore important to keep inflammable items away from any sources of ignition and to keep all fire doors closed.

Every workplace will have its own procedures for dealing with fire and you should make sure that you are aware of these as an employee or student. It will be your responsibility to help others if a fire does break out in your workplace. Most procedures will insist that you activate a fire alarm and/or contact the emergency services, but stress that you should not attempt to tackle a fire yourself.

Equipment malfunction

Obviously, lots of things can (and do) go wrong with machinery. If the machinery is regularly ser-viced it is less likely to cause a problem, but do not be surprised if a regularly serviced machine does malfunction. This could happen because there is something wrong with the machine, that is, it is faulty in some way or because the operator has used the machine to do something it is not capable of doing.

In either case, the potential injury to the operator will depend upon the machine itself. The operator could, at worst, be killed or could suffer slight or long-term injury.

Electric shock

Electric shocks can cause severe burns and scarring and, in extreme cases, death. All employees should treat electrical items with care. Before we look at some of the more common accidents, let us recap on some general safety rules:

▼ **always make sure that you understand the instructions before attempting to use an electrical item**
▼ **always switch off the machinery or electrical appliance before plugging it in**
▼ **always make sure that you report any damage or fault that you find, including to the cables**

Contamination

There are various regulations that are aimed at protecting the individual from the dangers of substances that might contaminate at work. Remember, some of the substances are so common that you might not think they are dangerous. Here is a check list to consider:

▼ **make sure that you follow the organisation's safety procedures in dealing with substances**
▼ **read the hazard warning signs and labels on the containers. These should tell you if the substance is dangerous and likely to cause you injury if it touches your skin or is inhaled**
▼ **make sure you know what you should do if any of the substance spills onto your skin or clothes**

▼ never take clothes or protective equipment home with you if it is stained or soaked by hazardous substances

▼ never transfer hazardous substances into smaller containers that do not have the right labels on them. Unlabelled containers are a potential hazard to all who might come in contact with them

▼ make sure that you work in a dust free environment; continued exposure to dusty air can damage your lungs and in time other parts of your body

Security alert

Security alerts and threats to the premises of an organisation can come from both inside and outside the company. We will begin with those that come from the outside:

▼ *robberies* – thieves entering the premises to steal property or information. There is always the possibility that they will resort to violence if they do not get what they want

▼ *burglaries* – thieves entering the premises to steal property or information or do damage

▼ *fire-raisers* – also called arsonists, who will attempt to set fire to the premises

▼ *bombers and bomb threats* – individuals who leave explosives on the premises to either threaten a company or make a political statement

▼ *vandals* – who enter the premises with the intention of damaging or wrecking the building or the machinery

▼ *activists* – who enter the premises to do damage to the site or tamper with goods to make a political point

▼ *spies* – who enter the premises to steal organisations' secrets, information or machinery to sell to competitors

Although most organisations never suffer from any of these, there are many that have had such problems. For your part, if you do not recognise someone on the premises, you should challenge them or contact security.

Security alerts can also occur as a result of the actions of someone within the organisation. In this category we should consider the following:

▼ *theft* – of goods, products and machinery by employees

▼ *forgery* – when an employee falsifies a document or a cheque

▼ *fraud* – when an employee attempts to deceive the employer for his or her own gain

It is often said that no matter what security precautions the organisation has taken, if the problem comes from within the organisation then all security measures are useless.

5.2.3 *Describe emergency procedures for shutting down equipment*

EMERGENCY PROCEDURES AND EQUIPMENT

There are very few jobs, these days, that do not involve the use of machinery or equipment. In the workplace, we should not just think of machines in terms of large pieces of equipment that can be found in a factory, as many office workers also use other types of machinery and equipment. No matter what our situations, we all need to consider the health and safety aspects of using this equipment.

When to shut down

Machinery should always be shut down if there is a chance that the equipment will be dangerous. Domestic current, as found in homes and offices, can cause death or serious injuries through faulty plugs, frayed cables or defects in the machinery itself. In an emergency, always unplug the machine or turn it off at the mains, but never try to do this if it means that you are putting yourself in danger. Remember that the passage of electrical current through the body may stun, stop breathing or affect the heart itself. Electricity will also burn where it enters and leaves the body.

Never, ever handle electrical appliances when your hands are wet, or when standing on a wet floor; this will substantially increase the chances of getting a shock.

How to shut down

If an accident involves a casualty, never approach the casualty until the electricity has been turned off, and keep at least 18 metres away.

The following procedures should be followed:

▼ **break the contact by switching off the current. This may be achieved by turning off the machine, pulling out the plug or wrenching out the cable (after having switched off the electricity at the mains)**

▼ **if you cannot reach the cable, socket or mains, stand on dry insulating material (such as a wooden box or a pile of newspapers) and, using a long stick or broom handle, move the casualty away from the source of the electricity**

---

finding out

PC 5.2.3

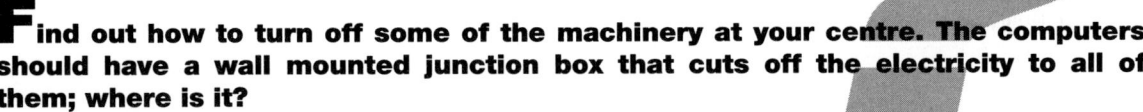

Find out how to turn off some of the machinery at your centre. The computers should have a wall mounted junction box that cuts off the electricity to all of them; where is it?

5.2.4 *Describe safe evacuation procedures for common emergencies*

SAFE EVACUATION PROCEDURES

Quick, clear thinking is the key to ensuring that panic and resulting additional dangers are avoided in the evacuation of a building or the vicinity of an accident.

In the case of fire, remember that it can spread quickly. You must warn anyone that could be at risk and then alert the emergency services immediately. Always try to be calm, even if people are panicking around you.

Safe evacuation procedures appropriate to the equipment and materials used

If materials or equipment become dangerous, whether as a result of fire or any other problem, you should make sure that as much of the material as possible is moved away from the source of danger. It is also possible that this will lead to the evacuation of the area. It is always better to be safe than sorry and no one should be put at risk if there is a problem.

Employers or the people who install equipment will instruct on safety procedures and evacuation should it be necessary.

FIGURE IT OUT

**PC 5.2.4
COM 1.1**

`00:10`

***W**hat would you do in the following situations?*

- *a computer screen has exploded and pieces of glass are all over the room*
- *a hot water tap has ruptured and there is scalding-hot water spraying all over the room*

Compare your solutions with the suggestions and remedies offered by your tutor.

Safe evacuation procedures appropriate to the condition of oneself or others

Assuming that you respond quickly enough, there should not be any reason to worry about injuries at this point. If the worst has happened and people are hurt, then you should do your utmost to move the casualties from immediate exposure to danger. The injured should be your priority, provided that you do not put yourself in danger as a result.

Safe evacuation procedures appropriate to the workplace

Without putting yourself at risk, you should try to follow the steps given below:

▼ **make sure that everyone is out of the building or at least out of immediate danger**

▼ **make sure that you shut all doors behind you; this is a way of double-checking that a room has been cleared, and in the event of a fire it will help to stop it spreading**

▼ **look out for notices that give you the location of the fire points and assembly points. The fire exits will also be marked – make for these and do not deviate from the route that is shown unless the route is blocked**

▼ **make sure that you are familiar with the guidelines in operation at your workplace and follow these instructions in the case of an evacuation**

5.2.5 *Describe how to summon assistance in case of accidents and emergencies*

HOW TO SUMMON ASSISTANCE

If you do see an accident or are involved in an emergency situation, try not to panic. This may be very difficult if you see that someone is hurt or that the premises are damaged or in danger. If it is possible and you are trained, use first aid on the person who is injured. Once you have done this, raise the alarm and make sure that the emergency services are called. Finally, you should make sure that the area is clear of people in case it is still dangerous, and so that any injured people are not upset by them.

FIGURE IT OUT

PC 5.2.5
COM 1.1

`00:10`

*W*hat would you do in the following situations?

- a man's eye has been hurt, but he does not want to make a fuss and says that it is only a little sore
- a woman has just slipped on the floor – she is not really hurt, but tells you that this is the third time this has happened

If you are called to, or witness, an accident, you should try to follow this procedure:

▼ **take in as much information about the accident as quickly as you can**
▼ **identify any dangers to yourself, the injured person or others around you**
▼ **look around to see if there is anything nearby that can help you**
▼ **decide whether you can handle the situation or whether you need specialist help**

Operating appropriate equipment

If the situation calls for the use of firefighting equipment, you should know where it is and how to use it. Never use equipment that you are unsure about; not only do you run the risk of hurting yourself, but you may also make the situation worse.

If the situation involves machinery, make sure that you turn it off immediately; not only will an operating machine be dangerous in itself, but it could catch fire and make the situation even more dangerous.

Summoning assistance verbally

Not all accidents will need the emergency services and we will be dealing with these in the next section of the element. If you do need to call for help, make sure that you try to do this without causing too much panic. If people are injured you may have to tell them that you are leaving them for a few minutes to get help. Try not to alarm them, especially if they are in shock, as this could cause more unnecessary pain and worry.

Once you have found help, explain what has happened calmly and slowly so that the people understand. If they need to find help or call someone, return to the scene of the accident and stay with the injured person.

If you need to call the emergency services, follow the steps outlined below:

▼ **give them your telephone number**
▼ **tell them exactly where the accident has occurred**
▼ **tell them the nature and seriousness of the accident**
▼ **tell them the names, ages and sexes of the injured people if you know them**
▼ **tell them about any hazards that they**

might encounter when responding to the accident
▼ do not put the telephone down until the control officer clears the line

5.2.6 *Describe how to report accidents and emergencies*

REPORTING ACCIDENTS

All organisations require their employees to report accidents in the workplace and these are usually recorded in an accident book. The main reasons for this are:

▼ to make sure that any insurance claims can be made – if a person is hurt at work they will have to prove that it happened there and not somewhere else
▼ to make sure that additional precautions can be taken in the future – an accident might reveal risks that had not been considered before

How to report verbally

If you are reporting an accident or emergency situation to the emergency services, here are some points to remember:

▼ when you dial 999, you will be asked which service you need
▼ you will then be put through to the control officer
▼ if there are any casualties ask for the ambulance service; they can pass the message on to the other services if necessary
▼ the control officer will need to know the exact details of the accident, which will include:

– the number of casualties
– any hazards that may be encountered by the services

Remember that if you are unsure about the location of the accident, it is possible for your call to be traced.

If you witness an accident at work and it is not serious enough to have to call the emergency services, then it should be reported at least verbally to your superior. Your manager will have the responsibility of making sure that action is taken to avoid this situation occurring again.

How to report in writing

If you are involved in an accident, you may be expected to fill in an accident report form. This will detail the nature of the accident and give a full explanation of the situation as and when it happened. We will now look at the questions which might appear on a typical accident report form:

ACCIDENT REPORT FORM
Employee's name ....
This is your own full name, or the name by which you are known at work.

Employee's address ....
....
This is your home address; you should include your full address and post code.

Particulars of accident
Date ....
Time ....
Department ....
In this part of the form, you should put the date and time of the accident. You should also put in the name of the department in which it happened (if not appropriate, then put your own department down).

Treatment needed ....
....
You should now detail the treatment given at the scene of the accident, and who it was given by.

Hospital treatment ....
....
....
If known, you should write down the nature of
the treatment given in hospital.

Nature of injury ....
....
State exactly what physical injuries were sus-
tained.

Treated by ....
State who treated you at the workplace and/or
the hospital.

Witnessed by ....
....
Were there any independent witnesses who saw
how the accident came about? If so, who were
they?

Description of accident ....
....
....
Describe exactly what happened and how the
accident occurred.

Activity undertaken at time of accident ....
....
....
....
What were you doing immediately before the
accident took place? You should describe this in
detail.

**Was the person authorised to do this activ-
ity?** ....**YES/NO**
This is an important question and has a
bearing on who was to blame for the accident.
If you were not authorised to carry out the activity that caused the accident, then the employer
may not be liable for the injuries.

Was the accident caused by machinery?...........
YES/NO
Another important question; did a machine actually cause the accident? The employer and the
safety inspectors may want to know whether the
machine was safe to be used.

Was the machine in operation? ....**YES/NO**
If the machine was being used at the time and if
this caused the accident, it is important to find
out whether the machine itself was faulty or
whether it was being operated incorrectly.

Were the protective guards being used? ....
YES/NO
Legally, they should have been, but many operators do not bother with the guards that are meant
to protect them. This is a breach of the health and
safety regulations and you could be held responsible for the injuries.

Signed ....
Make sure your signature can be read. If it is hard
to read, then print your name (again, because you
have written it down already at the top of the
form) and date it.

BUSINESS CONNECTION

PC 5.2

We have now looked at all the major ways of investigating common accident and emergency procedures. To test your memory and skill, complete the following business connection by turning common accidents into safe evacuation. The last letter of each word or phrase is the first letter of the next word or phrase. To help you we have put in the first and last letter on each line, but you will have to do the rest.

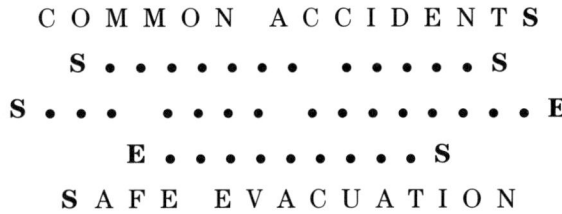

```
C O M M O N   A C C I D E N T S
    S . . . . . . .   . . . . . . S
S . . .   . . . .   . . . . . . . . E
    E . . . . . . . . . S
S A F E   E V A C U A T I O N
```

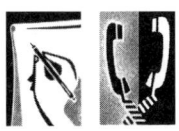

assignment

ELEMENT 5.2

PC 5.2.1–6
COM 1.1, 1.2, 1.3

This assignment is an ideal activity to undertake whilst on work-placement and will give you the chance to see how different organisations deal with accidents and emergencies. If this is not possible, then the centre in which you are studying is a useful place to investigate the procedures needed for this assignment. As an alternative, you could ask friends or family if they will tell you how accidents and emergencies are handled at their places of work, or better still, speak to the safety officer at their organisations.

You will need to look at two different organisations throughout this assignment.

| task | 1 | PC 5.2.1 |

Describe the main reasons for accident and emergency procedures in the two identified organisations.

| task | 2 | PC 5.2.2 |

Identify and give examples of common accidents and emergencies from both organisations to include the following:

- *medical emergencies*
- *fire*
- *equipment malfunction*
- *electric shock*
- *contamination*
- *security alert*

| task | 3 | PC 5.2.3 |

Describe the emergency procedures for shutting down equipment.

| task | 4 | PC 5.2.4 |

Describe the safe evacuation procedures for common emergencies.

| task | 5 | PC 5.2.5 |

Describe how you would summon assistance in the case of accidents and emergencies.

| task | 6 | PC 5.2.6 |

Describe how you would report accidents and emergencies.

element 5.3

CARRY OUT SAFE WORKING PRACTICES

Performance criteria

A student must:

1 Describe **safe working practices**.
2 Describe the **main reasons for following safe working practices**.
3 **Prepare for safe working**.
4 Demonstrate **safe working practices** in carrying out tasks.

RANGE

Safe working practices: appropriate (to sector, to task, to workplace), for the reduction of risk (when using machinery, tools and equipment), for working with others, for handling materials and components, for maintaining the workplace

Main reasons for following safe working practices: safety of oneself, safety of others; security and maintenance (of materials, of machinery, tools and equipment, of premises)

Prepare for safe working: checking equipment and materials (condition, that safety equipment is in place and working), availability of safety clothing, availability of safety equipment; checking that alarms and sensors are operating correctly, checking that the workplace is in a safe condition

5.3.1 **D**escribe safe working practices

SAFE WORKING PRACTICES

If accidents are to be prevented, then it is important that the right approach and attitude is adopted at all times and that precautions are taken whenever possible to avoid accidents.

Safe working practices appropriate to sector, task and workplace

The main responsibility for making sure that safe working practices are adopted lies with the employer. Whether you work in an office, shop, factory or any other workplace, it is essential that you build up safe working practices to avoid accidents. The following are examples of common accidents that could occur at any time and in any place:

▼ **people tripping over things left on the floor**
▼ **people slipping on wet or over-polished floors**
▼ **people bumping into things because the work area is too cluttered**
▼ **people injuring themselves on sharp edges or corners of furniture**
▼ **things being stacked too high and falling on people when they try to get them down**
▼ **sharp tools or equipment that cause injury when they are picked up**
▼ **people hurting themselves when moving through blocked passageways**

Figure 5.3.1 British Nuclear Fuels not only makes sure that its working environment is safe, but also regularly tests grass and soil samples for radiation around its premises (courtesy of BNFL).

Safe working practices for the reduction of risk (when using machinery, tools and equipment)

Some of the tasks we undertake can cause temporary or long-term injuries. One of the most common examples of this is known as RSI, or Repetitive Strain Injury, and occurs as a result of repeated movements or having to work in an uncomfortable position. The main causes of this injury are:

▼ **incorrect posture**
▼ **having to work too hard and for too many hours at a time**
▼ **having to make repeated movements, particularly awkward ones**

▼ having to sit awkwardly with your arms or head in a difficult position

▼ not resting enough between periods of work

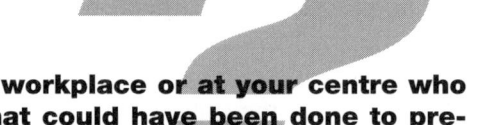

finding out

PC 5.3.1
COM 1.2

Find out whether there are any people at your workplace or at your centre who suffer from RSI. How have they suffered and what could have been done to prevent this happening? Make a list of your findings.

Safe working practices for working with others

Training is essential to ensure that all staff know how to carry out their duties and operate machinery safely. It is important that you are confident in not only your own abilities, but also in those of others; there is no point in you taking precautions when others are making the activity dangerous. Everyone, regardless of his or her position in the organisation, should follow all health and safety guidelines and company rules. An organisation will not ignore breaches in health and safety rules just because the person responsible is a senior manager.

Safe working practices for handling materials and components

In the first performance criterion of this element and in Element 5.1, we have seen that any material or component can be a source of danger. All of these have to be treated with care and consideration as even the most innocent materials, if used incorrectly, can be a potential hazard.

Chemicals, in particular, must be handled properly. Mishandling can cause leaks, poisoning, chemical plant failure, fires and other major accidents.

The most common injuries are caused by the inhalation of gases and corrosive chemicals that cause burning. Organisations at risk will have oxygen masks available that can be used in case of accidents.

Safe working practices for maintaining the workplace

In order to make sure that the workplace is a safe place within which to operate, regular checks should be made. We can identify these as falling into the following areas:

▼ **general office safety**
▼ **fire prevention**
▼ **hygiene**
▼ **machine safety**
▼ **control of dangerous substances**
▼ **transport and handling of goods**
▼ **general maintenance**

Here are some check lists that you could use for inspection of the various areas that we have mentioned above:

Focus study

Fire Prevention Check list

Item | **yes/no** | **details and remarks**

- Are the fire extinguishers clearly accessible?
- Have the fire extinguishers been inspected recently?
- Are the fire alarms working?
- Are all of the fire doors clear?
- Have the sprinklers been checked recently?
- Have the fuse boxes been checked recently?
- Has the fire alarm been checked recently?
- Are all the inflammable materials and liquids labelled?
- Are all the inflammable materials and liquids stored correctly?
- Do all of the employees know what to do in the event of a fire?

General Office Safety Check list

Item | **yes/no** | **details and remarks**

- Are there any obstructions?
- Has all equipment been positioned safely?
- Are the floors clean and dry?
- Are the offices reasonably clean?
- Are the waste paper bins full?
- Are the filing cabinets covered with paper and files?
- Are the exits and entrances clear?
- Is there good ventilation?
- Are there cables lying on the floor?
- Are the power points overloaded?
- Are there any sharp edges that could injure people passing by?

Hygiene Check list

Item | **yes/no** | **details and remarks**

- Is the area regularly cleaned?
- Are the toilet facilities clean?
- Is the protective clothing regularly cleaned?
- Are hot water and soap available?
- Are there clean towels or disposable towels available?
- Is there any sign of mice, rats or insects?

Now that we have looked at some sample check lists for maintaining safe practices in the workplace, try the following activity:

5.3.2 Describe the main reasons for following safe working practices

MAIN REASONS FOR FOLLOWING SAFE WORKING PRACTICES

Safety of oneself and others

All employees need to be clear about the responsibilities that they have towards operating in a safe and careful manner. In addition, they must be aware of the procedures if things should go wrong. Employers, as we have seen, must make sure that they have taken every precaution to implement safe systems (a safety policy) and that everyone has been correctly trained.

It is easy to get hurt, or hurt someone else, in the workplace if you do not take care. Except in the case of genuine accidents, you will be held responsible for injuries you cause to someone else and, in extreme circumstances, legal action may be taken against you.

Security and maintenance (of materials, machinery, tools, equipment and premises)

Security is a major problem for most organisations. Large organisations will usually have their own security staff who patrol the building when it is not being used. Smaller organisations are normally linked to the emergency services, or patrolled from time to time by a private security organisation.

It is important that all employees follow the security rules of the organisation in which they work. The key things to remember are:

▼ **to lock away all cash, valuables and legal documents in safes, locked cabinets or other secure places**

Safety of self and safety of others

Mobil Oil's Target Zero Safety Suggestion Scheme aims to reduce the potential for accidents and provides rewards for anyone whose idea is judged a winner.

The scheme, which operates within their Fuel Operations Division, asks any of the 250 employees to submit, in writing, their ideas to their supervisor. The ideas then go before a management panel and, if any of the suggestions are considered to be valid, an appropriate award in Argos vouchers is made.

safety Mobil update

Figure 5.3.2 Mobil Oil's Safety Update bulletin offers suggestions and incentives to employees to be accident and safety conscious (courtesy of Mobil Oil).

▼ **to arrange for safes, in particular, to be accessible to only a small number of people**
▼ **to fit security doors that prevent entry to the building by unauthorised persons**
▼ **to make sure that all external doors are secure**

The following are examples of practices used to keep equipment and property secure:

▼ *identity cards* **– which can include the photograph of the owner. Temporary passes should be given to all visitors. Careful use of this system will ensure that all areas, particularly high security ones, are secure**
▼ *automated systems* **– remote controlled doors can offer considerable security and include key features such as:**
  – a buzzer for visitors to push
  – an intercom through which those inside the building speak to the visitor in order to ask who it is and the purpose of the visit
  – a button which will release the door when pressed, to allow the visitor to enter
▼ **a closed-circuit television camera, through which the person inside the building can view the visitor**

Employees may simply use a key pad on the side of the door to gain entry to the building and do not have to go through all of the procedures outlined above.

As far as maintenance is concerned, all machinery, equipment and tools should be checked at regular intervals. It is very important that an appropriate expert makes sure there is no potential danger attached to the use of any items. There should be a sticker, card or sheet on the item which states the last time the machinery was checked by a recognised inspector.

5.3.3 *Prepare for safe working*

PREPARE FOR SAFE WORKING

As we already know, it is important to make sure you do everything in your power to ensure a safe working environment at all times. In this performance criterion, we will be looking at the things you can do to make sure you work in the safest conditions.

Checking equipment and materials (condition, that safety equipment is in place and working)

Before you use anything in the workplace it is sensible to check that the equipment or materials are in a reasonable condition and that any safety equipment is available for use if needed.

Most of us do not check whether the machinery or equipment we are using is working correctly every time we use it. Yet, this is a simple precaution and definitely worth taking. We have all heard tales of people who have been hurt as a result of not ensuring that their equipment is safe.

Refer back to the potential dangers regarding machinery and equipment that we discussed in Element 5.1 for further details.

With regard to safety equipment, as opposed to safety clothing, it is important to check that there are fire extinguishers and/or other appropriate items available should they be needed. You should, of course, also know how to use them, what to do if the situation gets out of control, how to get out of the area and how to raise the alarm.

Availability of safety clothing

If you are in a position where you have to wear safety clothing or use protective equipment, you will probably be doing a potentially dangerous job. It is therefore essential that you wear or use the equipment provided properly. Always use safety clothing or equipment if it is provided and do not be tempted to use any of the following excuses:

▼ **it is too much trouble to put on**
▼ **there is not really a hazard to worry about**
▼ **vital time might be lost in putting on the clothing**
▼ **the clothing would not be of any use in the event of an accident**
▼ **the task will only take a few minutes so it is hardly worth the effort of putting it on**

Unfortunately, these excuses are all too common. The result is that people get hurt at work when they could have avoided it, by using the safety clothing provided.

Availability of safety equipment

It is an employer's responsibility to make sure that there is sufficient equipment of the right sort available in the case of an accident and to ensure that it is also regularly checked and serviced. For the employee's part, he or she should know exactly where the safety equipment is kept. If the equipment is damaged or otherwise unsuitable, it should be replaced as soon as possible. If an employer fails to do this, you should report it to the employer immediately. If this does not work, you are perfectly within your rights to report your employer as this means health and safety laws have been broken.

Checking that alarms and sensors are operating correctly

Alarms are systems designed to detect intruders or fire. The two basic types are sensors that can detect heat and smoke and sensors or detectors that can sense an intruder. When alarms or sensors are set off, it usually means there is a problem, although these can sometimes be triggered by accident. Alarms and sensors rely on the following:

▼ **they must be placed in the right position**
▼ **they must be on and set**
▼ **once they have gone off someone must be alerted or told that they have been set off**
▼ **the appropriate person must respond to the alarm or sensor and know what to do next**
▼ **the person who is alerted must then inform the appropriate person or authority expected to deal with the situation (the police in the case of an intruder and the fire service in the case of a fire)**

Some areas in an organisation might also be fitted with a personal alarm that can be used in the event of attacks or other serious problems. If there are security guards at the workplace, they will be given radios so that they can be reached wherever they are on the premises. There will also be a contact number that can be dialled if you need to inform someone, such as the police, a security guard or the alarm company, of an emergency or security problem.

Setting alarms and sensors will depend upon the system used by the organisation. Broadly speaking, the following points should be remembered:

▼ **intruder alarms are activated when the premises are empty, provided that they have been set**
▼ **an intruder may be detected by heat sensors, foot pads or connectors that are fitted to doors**
▼ **smoke detectors are usually fitted to the ceiling and make a buzzing sound if they pick up the presence of smoke**

These systems will normally alert the police or alarm company who, in turn, will contact the key holder (the person responsible for the security of the building when it is empty).

finding out

PC 5.3.3
COM 3.1, 3.2

Using the check lists provided in **PC 5.3.1** and the ones that the group was asked to create, carry out a safety survey of the workplace or the centre in which you are studying. Remember that you need to be thorough and truthful and must make sure that you have checked everything that could be a hazard or danger.

If you do discover something, use the following form to report it to the appropriate member of staff.

Checking that the workplace is in a safe condition

> **REPORT FORM**
> **Notification to the employer of conditions and working practices that are considered to be unsafe or unhealthy and of arrangements for the welfare of all employees at work to be considered.**
>
> Date and time of inspection ....
>
> Particulars of matter notified ....
> ....
> ....
> ....
>
> Person reporting ....
>
> Action to be taken ....
> ....
> ....
> ....

In normal circumstances, an employer must make sure that immediate action is taken to sort out the problem that has been identified and this will also be the case if you have discovered a genuine hazard or danger. We will return to this in the last performance criterion of the element.

5.3.4 *Demonstrate safe working practices in carrying out tasks*

As this performance criterion is a practical one, the only way of really testing your understanding and ability to figure out what to do in certain circumstances is to actually be in the workplace. For practice, however, work through the following activities. We have given some suggested answers after the activities, but do not look at these until you have decided what you would do.

FIGURE IT OUT

PC 5.3.4
COM 1.1

`00:10`

*T*wo people are painting the walls of a building when the scaffolding suddenly gives way and they both fall about 15 metres to the ground. They both appear to be seriously injured.

   What should you do? Discuss this in pairs, then present your solution to the rest of the group.

We hope that the way you suggested dealing with this situation was something like this:

1   Try to give first aid to the two people.

2   Make sure that someone has called an ambulance.

3   Clear the area in case the rest of the scaffolding falls down.

FIGURE IT OUT

PC 5.3.4
COM 1.1

00:10

S *omeone is using an electric drill, but the wiring is faulty and the person gets a severe electric shock. The drill falls onto a metal table and the operator collapses.*

What should you do? Discuss this in pairs and then present your suggestions to the rest of the group.

What was the right thing to do? The procedure is a little more difficult this time:

1 Switch off the power or you might get a shock too.

2 If you know how, use first aid to resuscitate the person (help them start breathing again).

3 Get medical help.

FIGURE IT OUT

PC 5.3.4
COM 1.1

00:15

S *ome poisonous and inflammable liquid has been spilt on two of your work-mates. It is all over their clothes. You see what has happened and must act fast.*

What should you do? Talk about the procedure in pairs, then put your suggestions forward to the rest of the group.

There are two options here:

1 If the liquid is not giving off toxic fumes, your workmates should be unaffected and therefore able to get out of the area themselves, but will need to take off their clothes and be checked for injuries by a medical expert

2 If they cannot get out of the area themselves, it is a priority to get them out somehow and you would need help with this. Once they are clear, you should give first aid and call for medical help

FIGURE IT OUT

PC 5.3.4

00:30

*U*sing one of the three previous examples, fill in the following accident report form (you can make up any details that you do not have).

ACCIDENT REPORT FORM
Employee's name ....
Employee's address ....
....
Particulars of accident ....
....
Date ....
Time ....
Department ....
Treatment needed ....
....
Hospital treatment ....
....
....
Nature of injury ....
....
Treated by ....
Witnessed by ....
....
Description of accident ....
....
....
Activity undertaken at time of accident ....
....
....
Was the person authorised to do this activity?...
YES/NO
Was the accident caused by machinery?...
YES/NO
Was the machine in operation?..
YES/NO
Were the protective guards being used?...
YES/NO
Signed ....

BUSINESS CONNECTION

PC 5.3

We have now looked at all the major ways of carrying out safe working practices. To test your memory and skill, complete the following business connection by turning handling materials into security and maintenance. The last letter of each word or phrase is the first letter of the next word or phrase. To help you we have put in the first and last letter on each line, but you will have to do the rest.

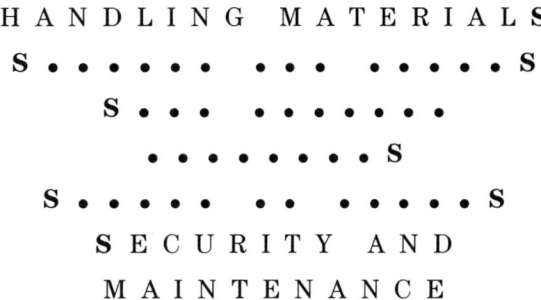

```
H A N D L I N G   M A T E R I A L S
S . . . . . .   . . .   . . . . . S
      S . . .   . . . . . . .
          . . . . . . . . S
  S . . . . . .   . .   . . . . . S
      S E C U R I T Y   A N D
      M A I N T E N A N C E
```

WORDSEARCH

How many of the words listed below can you find? They run forwards and backwards across and up and down the grid.

```
O  L  S  H  I  J  H  M  N  P  W  S  S  C  O  D  E  S
O  R  E  G  U  L  A  T  O  R  Y  W  H  O  P  I  L  G
B  V  C  O  P  L  Z  G  H  O  I  P  U  M  N  A  E  H
Q  W  U  M  N  G  A  I  T  C  L  K  T  O  P  T  C  M
G  H  R  M  G  L  R  G  H  E  A  L  T  H  Y  S  T  G
O  R  I  S  K  S  D  M  N  D  I  L  I  O  N  R  R  N
Q  E  T  M  N  E  S  L  O  U  G  H  N  I  O  I  I  Y
M  J  Y  Q  I  E  R  S  T  R  E  F  G  L  I  F  C  O
E  V  A  C  U  A  T  E  L  E  D  D  D  O  T  I  S  A
P  O  L  I  T  I  C  M  N  S  I  T  O  L  A  L  H  L
R  M  E  D  I  C  A  L  T  O  W  N  W  I  N  F  O  R
A  I  R  M  A  D  I  C  A  L  O  U  N  F  I  F  C  L
C  F  T  I  N  O  I  T  C  N  U  F  L  A  M  U  K  Y
T  I  N  J  U  R  Y  T  O  W  N  R  I  S  A  E  N  D
I  R  C  E  C  N  A  T  S  O  I  S  S  M  T  I  O  N
C  E  C  N  A  T  S  I  S  S  A  H  E  A  N  E  A  T
E  L  E  C  T  R  A  P  A  S  S  A  F  E  W  O  R  K  E
S  A  F  E  T  Y  S  I  G  N  S  O  F  F  C  O  I  N
```

ASSISTANCE	HAZARDS	REGULATORY
CODES	HEALTH	RISKS
CONTAMINATION	INJURY	SAFE WORK
ELECTRIC SHOCK	MALFUNCTION	SAFETY SIGNS
EVACUATE	MEDICAL	SECURITY ALERT
FIRE	PRACTICES	SHUTTING DOWN
FIRST AID	PROCEDURES	

assignment

ELEMENT 5.3

PC 5.3.1–4
COM 1.2

Work through all the following tasks.

task **1** PC 5.3.1

Describe the various sorts of safe working practices appropriate to the normal conditions in which you work (this can include your centre if necessary).

task **2** PC 5.3.2

Describe the reasons for following the safe working practices you have mentioned in Task 1.

task **3** PC 5.3.3–4

In the form of a log, outline your preparation for safe working and your performance in carrying out two different tasks following these safe working practices.

SCHEDULING AND BOOKING

element 6.1

PRODUCE A SCHEDULE FOR A VISIT

Performance criteria

A student must:

1   Plan the **timings** for a visit and allocate them on a **schedule**.
2   Identify **resources** available for the visit.
3   Identify **constraints** which need to be taken into account
    when planning a **schedule**.
4   Identify and give examples of **reasons for being accurate**
    in preparing a **schedule**.
5   Produce a **schedule** for a visit to a business organisation.

RANGE

Timings: day, date; length of time available, start time, finish time

Schedule: name of organisation, place of meeting, person (people) to meet, arrival time, meeting point, how time is spent, refreshments, departure time, travel information

Resources: equipment, premises, refreshments, people, transport

Constraints: health and safety, security, confidentiality, other people visiting

Reasons for being accurate: quality of service, efficiency, reliability

6.1.1 *Plan the timings for a visit and allocate them on a schedule*

TIMINGS

When planning a schedule, whether it is for a visit you are making or for one someone else is making, the timings involved are very important. Considerations that have to be taken into account are whether or not enough time has been allocated for the journey, for the visit itself and whether the times arranged are convenient for all concerned. It is a good idea to confirm the timings involved in any visit with the person or organisation being visited, as well as with those who are visiting, *before* the visit. This confirmation can be made in the following ways:

▼ *verbally* – **by telephone or in person, although by confirming in this way you will have no written evidence to show that you have, in fact, confirmed the details**
▼ *in writing* – **by letter**
▼ *by telecommunication* – **by sending a fax or an electronic mail message**

If you are responsible for arranging a schedule for a visit, you should start by making a list of things to do. You can use the following headings as a guide to the steps you will need to take to ensure that the visit is successful.

Day and date

The first place to start when arranging a schedule is with the day and date of the visit. Diaries should be checked at this stage to make sure that no other meetings or visits have been arranged for that date.

The person or organisation being visited should

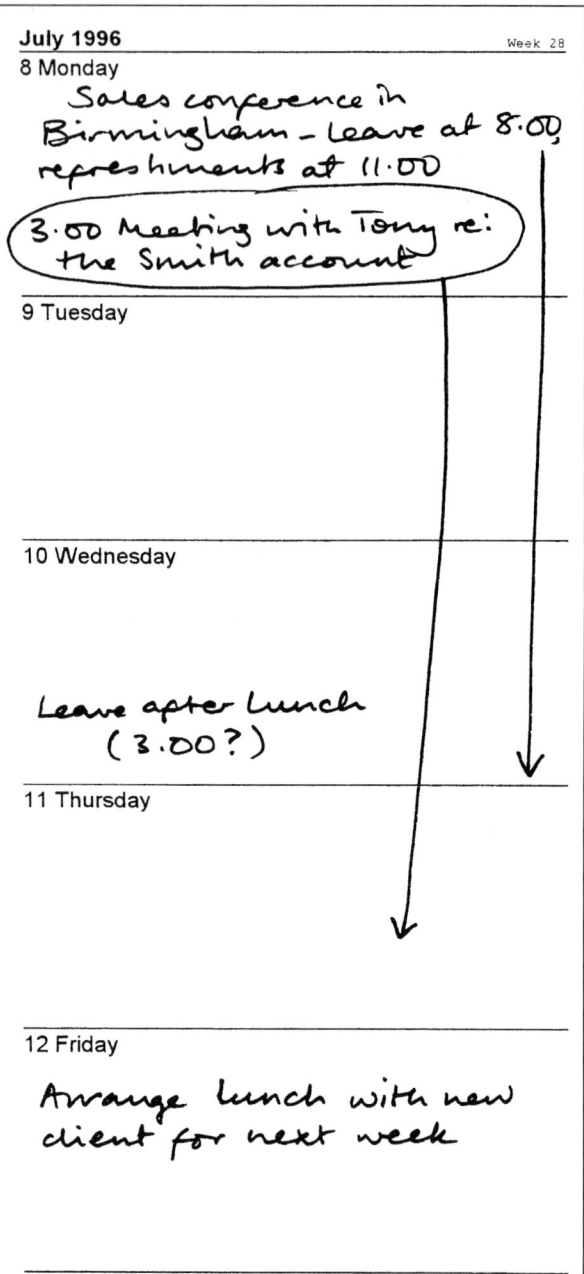

Figure 6.1.1 A page from a diary.

be contacted to find out whether the day and date is convenient.

Once these have been provisionally booked, an entry can be made into the diary so that nothing else is booked which will clash.

When thinking about the day and date of a visit, other considerations should also be taken into account, such as:

▼ **the amount of traffic likely to be encountered on the journey – this could differ from day to day and at different times of the year**
▼ **the ease with which the visitors will be able to park their cars if they are**

driving to the meeting place – this can also differ from day to day and at different times of the year in some towns or cities

Considerations like these will affect schedules because extra time will be needed for travelling to the meeting point to ensure that visitors do not arrive late or flustered.

FIGURE IT OUT

PC 6.1.1
COM 1.1

00:10

Thinking about the town or city in which you live, what considerations would you have to take into account when arranging a schedule, particularly with regard to the day of the week and the time of the year? Do you think that you would have to consider extra traffic problems, maybe on a market day? Discuss this first in pairs and then as a group.

Length of time available

When booking an appointment with a person or organisation, it is important that it is clear to both parties involved exactly how much time is to be put aside for the visit. If this is not clear at the outset, confusion could occur on the day. It would be unfortunate for a visitor to have travelled a long distance or for a long time to what he or she thought was to be an all-morning visit, only to find out that the person being visited thinks it is only for one hour.

In addition to this consideration, it should also be confirmed that the visit will allow enough time for all the discussions or meetings to take place. It would be unsuitable, for instance, to book a visit to an exhibition to last one hour if there is obviously at least two hours' worth of exhibition to see.

It is important to take the length of time available and the length of time needed into consider-ation and to try to make the two as flexible as possible. Again, the length of time that the visit is likely to take should be confirmed to the person or organisation concerned in one of the ways previously mentioned.

Start and finish times

The time the visit will start is of prime importance. Whether the visit is one that you are arranging for yourself or for another person, it would be inefficient and embarrassing for all concerned if you or the visitor were to arrive late. When arranging the start time, make sure that enough time is allowed for travelling and parking or, if the journey is being made by train, that the visitor has time to travel from the railway station to the venue itself.

If the venue is some distance from the home

town or workplace, then an overnight stay might be needed if the start time is early in the morning. We look at arranging accommodation in Element 6.3.

The finish time is equally important, firstly so that everyone involved knows when they are likely to be free, and secondly so that travel arrangements can be made for the homeward journey.

Again, the start and finish times should be confirmed with the person or organisation concerned at the time of booking.

FIGURE IT OUT

PC 6.1.1
COM 1.2
IT 1.1, 1.2, 1.3

`01:00`

*I*magine that you have arranged a visit to a business organisation of your choice. You now need to confirm this in writing by means of a letter. Word process a letter to the organisation concerned – we will leave the details of the visit and the timings up to you.

SCHEDULE

When planning a schedule (which is a version of an itinerary, covered in Element 6.3), it is important that the people taking part in the visit have all the information they will need. Being thorough in the planning and preparation stages will help to ensure that the visit is successful. Visitors should be aware of each of the following before they leave for their visit.

Name of organisation

The people involved will obviously need to know the name and the address of the organisation they are intending to visit. Bear in mind that the visit may not be at the postal address of the organisation concerned, but at another venue.

Place of meeting

If the meeting is not being held at the postal address of the organisation concerned, then the people visiting will need to know the venue. This venue should be stated clearly on the schedule so that there is no confusion on the day.

Person (people) to meet

The names of the people the visitors are expected to ask for when they arrive at the venue should also be stated clearly. These may not be the people they will be visiting, but could be a receptionist or gatehouse person who regularly greets visitors and then directs them to the people concerned.

Arrival time and meeting point

As we have already mentioned, embarrassment can be caused if someone arrives late for a meeting or is delayed because of details which are unclear. The schedule should show clearly where the meeting is being held, who to report to and at what time.

How time is spent

Whether you are planning a schedule for someone who is visiting you or for someone going on a visit, the person will obviously need to know what the proposed activities are likely to be. Find out as much information as you can in the planning stage and list this information on the schedule. If workshops are being held during the day then list their start and finish times. If different departments of an organisation are being visited at different times during the day, then list the expected start and finish times for each one.

By knowing how the visit is expected to run, visitors will see that it has been well planned and that they are getting the most out of the time.

Refreshments

When scheduling, make sure that you allow some time for 'breaks'. Show the times when refreshments will be served so that visitors are relaxed and know when they can expect a break. Also, if you are planning the visit to your own organisation, be sure that visitors are aware of the location of the toilets so they can visit them during the refreshment breaks if necessary.

Departure time

You will have indicated on the schedule the proposed departure time for the visitors. If you are entertaining visitors at your own business organisation, try to keep to this time whenever possible. Visitors may have long journeys ahead of them and will not want to be kept too long after the expected finish time.

Travel information

If your visit involves a lot of travel for several people, then be sure to give them as much useful information as possible when sending them the schedule. This could include:

▼ **a road map which shows clearly the location of the venue**
▼ **a street map which gives more detail of how to get to the meeting point**
▼ **directions on how to get to the venue from the railway station (if necessary)**
▼ **details of the meeting point and to whom they should report on arrival**

FIGURE IT OUT

PC 6.1.1
COM 1.2

00:45

*U*sing the letter of confirmation that you wrote in the previous activity, now draft a schedule for this visit. Make sure you cover all the headings listed above and make the information clear.

6.1.2 *Identify resources available for the visit*

RESOURCES

If you are arranging a schedule for a visit to your own organisation by other people then, in addition to the arrangements we have already covered, you will need to consider what resources they require whilst attending. Your visitor may be coming to your organisation to give a talk to a group of people, or to show some slides or a video to members of staff.

When planning the schedule for the visit you need to consider the resources visitors will require once they arrive and the best location within the organisation for them to use as a venue. The following list of headings will help you to consider these resource requirements:

Equipment

If visitors need specific equipment for a talk or presentation, they will not be expected to bring it with them, but will expect the organisation concerned to provide it. The equipment could include any of the following:

▼ **an overhead projector and screen**
▼ **a video or slide projector**
▼ **a computer software package**

Premises

If equipment is being used, then a suitable room will have to be arranged for the visitor. It would be useless to provide a video in a room with no electric sockets or no blinds to shut out the light.

The size of the room is also important, particularly if a large number of staff is going to be involved in the meeting or presentation. Suitable premises (rooms or buildings) should be booked for the time required to ensure that visitor(s) have the use of the appropriate resources or equipment and the audience is comfortable and not too cramped. The temperature of the premises should also be considered. If the room is too small it may not only be too cramped, but also too hot. If this is the only room available, then it would be a good idea to arrange for the heating to be turned off for the duration of the meeting.

Refreshments

To ensure that the visit runs as smoothly as possible, refreshments should also be regarded as a resource requirement. During coffee and lunch breaks visitors and members of staff often continue to talk about business, and strong and lasting working relationships are often formed in these situations. When arranging the refreshments for your visit you should consider the following points:

▼ **the time the refreshments will be served**
▼ **where the refreshments will be served – if possible, it is usually better to serve coffee and lunch in a different room to the one in which the meeting is taking place. This gives the people concerned a chance to relax and talk informally**
▼ **what refreshments will be served**
▼ **who will serve the refreshments**

People

People are also resources and are known as the organisation's human resources. When planning the visit it may be necessary to list those people the visitor may need to see and to make sure that they are available at given times during the day.

Transport

As we mentioned earlier, a visitor will need to know how to get to your organisation. If he or she is driving, send a map which gives clear directions. If he or she is travelling by train, a company car could be sent to the railway station to collect and bring him or her to the organisation.

Whatever transport arrangements are made, be sure to notify the visitor of the arrangements in advance and give the timings of all the transport details.

---

finding out

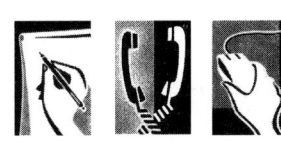

PC 6.1.2
COM 1.1, 1.2
IT 1.1, 1.2, 1.3

Working in pairs, imagine that you are expecting a visitor to the place in which you are studying this course. Your visitor is going to give a talk to a group of 45 students about career opportunities in your nearest large city, and is travelling from there to see you all. This careers advisor will be showing a video and will need an overhead projector and screen. The visit is to last for the whole morning and your timetables have been cancelled for that time.

Using the headings in this performance criterion, plan and word process a schedule for this visit, making sure that all the necessary resources will be appropriately arranged.

6.1.3 Identify constraints which need to be taken into account when planning a schedule

CONSTRAINTS

Constraints are those things which make it difficult, or impossible, to plan something. They can also be additional considerations which have to be taken into account. For the purposes of this performance criterion, constraints should be regarded as additional considerations. The following headings are the additional considerations which should be taken into account when arranging a schedule for a visitor to your organisation.

Health and safety

In the previous performance criterion we mentioned the resources that a visitor may require and, more specifically, equipment and premises. If you are studying Unit 5, then you will know that health and safety is an important consideration in all aspects of the working world.

When people visit an organisation their health and safety has to be virtually guaranteed. This is the case even if someone is just visiting for one morning or one day and not on a regular basis.

When arranging your schedule for a visit you must also consider the health and safety requirements of visitors, particularly if they are using any equipment within your organisation.

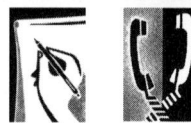

FIGURE IT OUT

PC 6.1.3
COM 1.1

00:20

*R*eferring to the previous activity when you arranged a visit for a careers advisor, now discuss in pairs what health and safety requirements that visitor would have. What would your organisation need to ensure? How can you make sure you do everything you can to keep the visitor safe at all times?

Security and confidentiality

Another constraint which must be considered by any organisation receiving visitors is security and confidentiality of information.

Naturally, an organisation would not want a visitor to be allowed to wander around its premises without supervision, or to be allowed to gain access to information which might be of a confidential nature and useful to competitors.

In order to overcome some of the security and confidentiality problems, organisations usually have a strict set of rules which must be followed when people visit their premises. These might include:

▼ **visitors reporting to reception or the gatehouse keeper before being allowed any further into the building. The receptionist will keep a log which details the name and business address of visitors, the time they arrive and the time they leave**
▼ **visitors being accompanied on their journey to the meeting point**
▼ **visitors being issued with a badge which tells everyone that they are merely visiting the organisation and not working there**
▼ **making sure that members of staff of the organisation know what the policy is regarding visitors and security and confidentiality of information and that**
they are updated at regular intervals on this procedure
▼ **using passwords and codes for access to safes, files and computers within the organisation**

Other people visiting

In large organisations it is possible that several visitors will meet at the organisation in order to go to different rooms with different groups of people. If this is the case, then there could be a constraint on the resources the organisation has available for these visitors. In such cases, the planning of schedules is even more important so that equipment is available in a room for those who need it and not lying useless in a room where it is not required.

Other people visiting could also cause problems if more than one visitor needs to see the same member of staff. The diary of the member of staff will have to be arranged carefully so that he or she can allow some time for each visitor.

Another resource which has to be considered when this constraint is in force is refreshments. If there are a number of meetings going on at the same time, the organisers should make sure that there is enough crockery and appropriate groceries (tea, coffee, milk, biscuits etc.) to go round. Extra provisions might have to be hired or bought to allow for this. As far as the scheduling is concerned, if different groups of visitors to the organisation are direct competitors, they will not want to take their refreshments at the same time.

In this case, the refreshment breaks for each of the meetings could be staggered so that they do not coincide, or the refreshments could be taken in a different room.

6.1.4 Identify and give examples of reasons for being accurate in preparing a schedule

REASONS FOR BEING ACCURATE

You already know how important it is to be accurate. During your course you will have found it is important to be accurate in spelling, grammar, calculations and the taking and passing on of messages.

Being accurate is also important when making arrangements, particularly if people from outside the organisation are involved. This accuracy is important for the organisation you are working for, but it is also important for you and your reputation of being reliable and efficient.

Quality of service

If an organisation is to continue to grow and develop, then the service it is seen to provide should be efficient and reliable. The term, 'service', applies to all contact the organisation has with others. These others may be customers, suppliers or visitors. If the arrangements made for these people run smoothly, then the service the organisation is providing is regarded as being of quality.

It is not only the organisation that should be seen to provide a quality service; you, as an individual, are providing a service as well. Whether you are making arrangements for a visitor to your organisation or for a colleague who has to travel to another organisation, you are providing that service and it should be seen to be a quality one. If you can prove that the quality of the service you are providing is good, then you are much more likely to do well in your career.

Efficiency and reliability

If the organisation regularly makes arrangements for its members of staff to visit other organisations, or for visitors from other organisations to attend meetings at its premises, then this must be done efficiently. The organisation does not want to gain a reputation of being inefficient and incapable of organising events. If the organisation is seen to be efficient then this will help its growth.

In much the same way, you, as an individual, need to show that you can be efficient. Nobody will expect you to get everything right the first time, but they will respect you for getting it right the second and each and every other time. This will soon work to your benefit because you will be given more important work to do and you will be able to prove how efficient you can be. Efficiency is not something that comes overnight. It is something that has to be worked at.

Organisations and individuals have to be reliable in order to be efficient. Reliability means having the right paperwork available at the right time and being in the right place at the right time. It is not possible to be fully efficient if you are not being reliable.

6.1.5 Produce a schedule for a visit to a business organisation

This performance criterion is a practical one. You must produce a schedule for a visit to another organisation. You may be able to plan a visit to a

79

local business organisation, or you may be given a role play exercise by your tutor.

We have covered all the areas you need to consider in the previous sections of this element, and we have provided an end of element assignment for your portfolio evidence. For the purposes of this performance criterion, you should carry out the following activity.

---

finding out

PC 6.1.5
COM 1.1, 1.2
IT 1.1, 1.2, 1.3

In a previous activity we asked you to draft a schedule for a visit to another organisation. You should now word process this schedule and ensure that you have covered all the considerations we have mentioned in this element. Your finished product should be checked by your tutor and he or she will assess it for you.

BUSINESS CONNECTION

PC 6.1

We have now looked at all the major ways of producing a schedule for a visit. To test your memory and skill, complete the following business connection by turning meeting point into schedule. The last letter of each word or phrase is the first letter of the next word or phrase. To help you we have put in the first and last letter on each line, but you will have to do the rest.

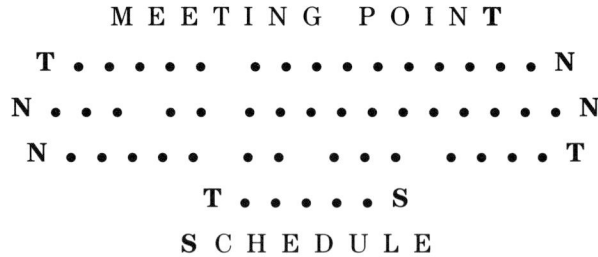

MEETING POINT

T • • • • •   • • • • • • • • N

N • • •   • •   • • • • • • • • • N

N • • • • •   • •   • • •   • • • • T

T • • • • • S

SCHEDULE

assignment

ELEMENT 6.1

PC 6.1.1–6
COM 1.1, 1.2
IT 1.1, 1.2, 1.3

In order to prove your competence in this element, you are required to prepare a schedule for a visit to a business organisation of your choice. Your tutor might make some of these arrangements for you, or perhaps you know of an organisation you would like to visit and which you can contact yourself. If no such organisation is available, then a simulated visit can be created.

You are to prepare a schedule which should include all of the following:

task 1 PC 6.1.5

The first part of your schedule should include a brief introduction to the organisation.

task 2 PC 6.1.1, 6.1.5

The second part of your schedule should state the times of arrival and departure for the visit, the meeting point and the person (or persons) you have to meet.

task 3 PC 6.1.2–5

The third part of your schedule should state the timings of the individual activities and any refreshments that have been arranged.

task 4 PC 6.1.2, 6.1.5

The fourth part should state any relevant travel information which has been arranged.

task 5 PC 6.1.3, 6.1.5

The final part should state any constraints which have been taken into account during the preparation of the visit.

notes

Your schedule should be word processed and you should list any resources which were required.

element 6.2

MAKE A BOOKING

Performance criteria

A student must:

1   Identify the **booking requirements** of a specified person.

2   Make a booking that meets identified requirements.

3   **Confirm** that requirements can be met.

4   Complete all necessary **documents and records** clearly and accurately.

5   **Confirm** the booking with the appropriate person.

RANGE

Booking requirements: time, date, place (room, area), equipment, people, services, transport

Confirm: right time, suitable place, right equipment, right services (refreshments, access to toilets)

Documents and records: bookings log, reservation slips, diary, letter of confirmation

6.2.1 *Identify the booking requirements of a specified person*

BOOKING REQUIREMENTS

This element is a practical one. Using the information that we have outlined in Elements 6.1 and 6.3, you must now make a booking following all of the headings given below.

Date

Finding out the correct date for the booking is extremely important since nearly all of the other information and booking details will rest upon the availability of accommodation, equipment, people, services and transport on that day. Remember that when you make a booking you need to know not only the departure date (if applicable), but also the dates of particular events or meetings that will occur during or as a part of the main booking.

FIGURE IT OUT

PC 6.2.1

00:05

An individual needs to visit London on the last Monday of June this year. What is the date?

Time

It is essential that you ensure that each of the days involved in the booking is accurately timetabled and scheduled. Individuals making the booking may have to be at a particular place at a particular time, so you will have to make sure that they have sufficient time between each of the events for travelling. Equally, individuals will not wish to arrive after a long journey and be expected to give a presentation or attend a meeting without having had the chance to freshen up or have some refreshment.

PC 6.2.1

00:05

An individual needs to arrive in Birmingham at ten o'clock in the morning for a meeting at twenty to eleven, but must leave Birmingham by three in the afternoon. What are these times using the 24-hour clock?

Place (room, area)

Taking into account the fact that a group of people will need more room or area than a single individual, you must make sure that you have booked adequate space for them both for their meeting or event and their overnight accommodation.

PC 6.2.1

00:10

An individual needs to meet someone in a city that neither knows. List at least five places that are common to most cities as potential meeting places.

Equipment

If specific business equipment is required, such as overhead projectors, video screens, presentation boards or slide projectors, this must be included in the booking. It is possible, however, that visitors will need more sophisticated equipment that is not generally available at a conference or hotel venue and, in these instances, local organisations may have to be contacted to provide telecommunications equipment, computers and other materials.

PC 6.2.1

00:05

A representative of an organisation needs to attend a trade fair and must be able to carry all the equipment he or she needs. There will be display boards provided, so what must the representative take?

People

There are two aspects to consider here. These are:

- the individuals within the group who have made the booking may have specific needs, such as some may be vegetarian, others may need rooms on ground floors as they are disabled

- the individuals who are providing services to the group may have specific needs themselves

PC 6.2.1

00:05

If a group of sales representatives are due to have a meeting at a local hotel and there are no support staff available from the organisation to go with them, where would you obtain individuals who could take minutes of the meeting and run errands for the group?

Services

Individuals may require services on their way to the location, or once they get there. These will include regular refreshment breaks, access to toilet facilities or, in some instances, more specialised needs such as crêches, direct telephone lines, video conferencing or presentation materials.

PC 6.2.1

00:05

How would you find out which services are available at a particular hotel before confirming a booking with them?

Transport

Not only will the group or individual need transport to and from the location, but they may also require transport once they get to their destination. This might be necessary if they need to visit a number of places close to the hotel or main venue. It is also worth considering that the transport should be appropriate to the needs of the individual or group: it is not worth booking a coach for a small number of people, or a car for a large group. You should choose transport which is big, comfortable and flexible enough and available on demand.

FIGURE IT OUT

PC 6.2.1

`00:05`

*W*hich would be the most appropriate form of transport for people in the following situations:

- an individual who needs to attend a meeting in a town 200 miles away
- an individual who needs to take a range of samples from his or her organisation to show to a group of potential customers
- a group of 10 people who need to attend a conference in a city 300 miles away

6.2.2 Make a booking that meets identified requirements

Again, as in the previous performance criterion, this is a practical one. In the activity below, we have given you some information to help you research the requirements of the booking. Alternatively, your tutor may give you some other information from which you can make your booking. The booking we require you to make is for a visit to a European Union country.

FIGURE IT OUT

PC 6.2.2
COM 1.1, 1.2, 1.3
AON 1.1, 1.2, 1.3

A group studying at your centre are to make an educational visit to Paris. This will be a one-week trip and you are to make the necessary enquiries and arrangements. They will be travelling by coach and ferry and you should make the booking through a company that specialises in student travel. The group will need to stay in a hotel in the centre of Paris on a bed-and-breakfast basis. Included in the amount you are prepared to pay will be excursions to some of the following places:

- *Euro Disney (a one-day visit by coach)*
- *Versailles Palace (a half-day visit by coach)*
- *the Eiffel Tower*
- *the Louvre*
- *Montmartre area (and the Sacre Coeur)*
- *a half-day coach tour of the sights of Paris*
- *the Opera House*
- *a boat trip along the Seine*
- *the Notre Dame*
- *an opportunity to spend free time shopping*

In order to complete this activity you should contact several tour operators and ask them to send you copies of their brochures. From these brochures you should identify those who provide a coach trip to Paris and compare their costs and facilities provided. You should then work out how much it would cost each student to participate in the visit and draw up an itinerary for the whole trip, including the excursions which can be fitted in during the time in Paris itself.

Remember that you will require the coach to stay with the group for the whole of the visit so that the excursions can be carried out using the coach. The hours that the coach driver is allowed to drive will have to be taken into consideration here.

You should also remember that ferry crossings will have to be booked, so adequate time will have to be allowed for the coach journey from your centre to the port.

Those students who are involved in the visit will require passports and E111 forms. You should write a list of the necessary documentation which will have to be taken with you.

6.2.3 Confirm that requirements can be met

CONFIRMATION

Whenever arrangements are made for bookings or itineraries, it is important that these are confirmed in writing. This confirmation may take the form of a memorandum or letter or, alternatively, it may just require a note to be placed on the desk of the person who asked you to carry out the task. When confirming a booking, remember to include all the necessary information. We have given details regarding the considerations to be taken into account when making a booking throughout this unit. The following headings will help you to remember what information is needed when confirming the booking.

The right time

The person for whom the booking is being made

will want to know that this has been done for the right time. This means the correct date and a suitable time for either the meeting or the visit. When arranging the time it will be necessary to allow for any travelling that has to be made, as well as leaving some leeway for any delays that might be encountered.

A suitable place

When confirming the place or venue of the visit, make sure that you have picked somewhere suitable. The venue will have to allow for the number of people involved and will also have to be the most convenient in terms of travel from railway stations or airports and for car parking facilities.

The right equipment

If the person requesting the booking has asked you to arrange for equipment or materials to be available at the venue, then you should confirm that these arrangements have been made. It would be very embarrassing if the person were to arrive at the venue only to find that the equipment he or she needed had not been provided.

The right services (refreshments, access to toilets)

When confirming the time and venue of the visit you should also include details about facilities and services available both at the venue and during the journey itself. The traveller will want to know what time refreshments will be available, as well as where and when toilet stops can be made.

6.2.4 Complete all necessary documents and records clearly and accurately

DOCUMENTS AND RECORDS

As with all tasks which are carried out by individuals within an organisation, it is necessary to record the fact that something has been done when making a booking. Naturally, it is vital that this information is recorded accurately and clearly. When confirming a booking, you should always keep a copy of any documentation for yourself or for the file so that the information can be retrieved at a later date if required.

If bookings are made on a regular basis, then it may be useful to keep a log of these. Certainly, when providing evidence that you have made bookings for this unit, it would be useful to include a log of that information in your portfolio of evidence.

Bookings log

A bookings log is simply a list of the requirements that have been met. As you will see in Figure 6.2.1, this can be a very simple form which is completed each time a booking is made. It will provide evidence that the booking has been made and by whom.

Reservation slips

A reservation slip may be required by the organiser of the meeting or visit to confirm that the person attending actually requires the place. A copy of the reservation slip should be kept so that you have written confirmation that you made the booking.

LOG OF BOOKINGS MADE

DATE	BOOKING FOR (PERSON)	DEPARTURE DATE/TIME	ARRIVAL DATE/TIME	TRAVEL BY (MODE)	DESTINATION	MADE BY

Figure 6.2.1   A bookings log.

Diary

Naturally, any booking you make should be entered in your own diary, as well as that of the person who requested you to carry out the task. As soon as the booking is made and confirmed, even if this is only over the telephone, you should enter the details in the diaries. This will avoid any double-booking and will act as a reminder, to both yourself and the person concerned, that this event is taking place on that particular date.

Letter of confirmation

As we have already mentioned, it is always advisable to write a letter of confirmation for any booking you make. This letter may be to a hotel or, on the other hand, it may be to confirm attendance at a meeting. You should always file a copy of this letter in case any problems are encountered in the future.

6.2.5 *Confirm the booking with the appropriate person*

This is another practical performance criterion. You will need to carry out the following activity to provide evidence for your portfolio. Alternatively, your tutor may give you some activities to complete in order to prove competence in Element 6.2.5.

FIGURE IT OUT

PC 6.2.5
COM 1.1, 1.2, 1.3
IT 1.1, 1.2, 1.3

00:40

*U*sing the activity you completed in Element 6.2.2, when you made a booking for the visit to Paris, word process a letter to the tour operator that you have chosen to provide the service for you. In addition, word process an itinerary for your tutor, including a list of documentation which you think will be required for the visit.

BUSINESS CONNECTION

PC 6.2

We have now looked at all the major ways of making a booking. To test your memory and skill, complete the following business connection by turning documents and records into suitable place. The last letter of each word or phrase is the first letter of the next word or phrase. To help you we have put in the first and last letter on each line, but you will have to do the rest.

D O C U M E N T S   A N D
R E C O R D S
S • • • • • • S
S • • • • • R
R • • • • • • • • • S
S U I T A B L E   P L A C E

assignment

ELEMENT 6.2

PC 6.2.1–5

In order to prove your competency in this element, you need to have made a booking. This booking can be real or a role play, but should be for a specified person. You may have used the booking in the *Figure it out* activity in Element 6.2.2. Whatever booking you made, your tutor will have observed you making the booking and will have recorded his or her comments. This observation check list should be kept by you as evidence that the booking was made and that you were competent in the following areas:

- *being able to identify the booking requirements of a specified person*
- *being able to make the booking by completing all the necessary documentation and records clearly and accurately*

- *being able to confirm the booking accurately*

When you confirm the booking in writing or electronically, be sure to keep a copy for your portfolio.

notes

The booking can be for a room at a venue or accommodation or an area of a building for any of the following:

- *a seminar*
- *a meeting*
- *a conference*
- *a trade fair*
- *a holiday*
- *travel arrangements for a visit*
- *accommodation arrangements for a visit*

element 6.3

PREPARE TRAVEL ITINERARIES

Performance criteria

A student must:

1   Locate travel **destinations** on a map and identify the countries concerned.
2   Establish what the **traveller's needs** are.
3   Select suitable routes and **means of travel** which meet the **traveller's needs**.
4   Check transport times using a **timetable**.
5   Prepare **travel itineraries**, including necessary **stops**, and present them in an effective way.
6   Prepare the **itineraries** clearly with highlighted copies of **timetables**.

RANGE

Destinations: major cities, within the European Union, outside the European Union

Traveller's needs: route, time (of year, of day), type of transport (public, private hire road transport), individual's personal requirements

Means of travel: air, rail, car, taxi, coach, ferry

Timetable: bus, rail, coach, air, ferry

Travel itineraries: people, number of people in party, date of travel, destination, means of travel, point of departure, time of departure, details of stops, point of arrival, time of arrival, overall travel time, overall cost

Stops: refreshment breaks, transport connections

6.3.1 *Locate travel destinations on a map and identify the countries concerned*

DESTINATIONS

In this performance criterion we will be asking you to locate various travel destinations. Not only will you have to find the city involved, but also name the country in which it lies.

The remainder of this performance criterion is of a practical nature and we will set you a number of tasks. You can use the map printed in this book, or a larger one provided by your tutor. Bear in mind that the map will be blank apart from the borders between each country.

Major cities

You will have to find a number of cities both within and outside the European Union. Remember that major cities are not just capital cities: Birmingham, Manchester, Leeds, Glasgow and Norwich are examples of major cities, none of which are capital cities. You will need to find some major cities that you may not have heard of before, but you will need to mark only the rough location of each of these cities.

Within the European Union

At the time of writing, there are a number of countries which make up the European Union. Possibly, by the time you read this book, others may have joined. To make things simple, we will list cities only in the more common or more well-known parts of Europe.

Figure 6.3.1 A world map.

PC 6.3.1
COM 1.1, 1.2

00:15

*M*ark *the following cities on a blank map of Europe and name the country in which they can be found:*

- *Copenhagen*
- *Dublin*
- *Bonn*
- *Marseilles*
- *Athens*
- *Frankfurt*

- *Milan*
- *Barcelona*
- *Brussels*
- *Rotterdam*
- *Dusseldorf*
- *Toulouse*

Compare your suggestions with those of the rest of your group.

Outside the European Union

There are hundreds of cities across the world that many people have heard of, and others that are not quite so well known. With the changes in the Middle East and Central Asia, there are new destinations that have only just become accessible to the business traveller.

PC 6.3.1
COM 1.1, 1.2

00:15

*M*ark *the following cities on a blank map of the world and name the country in which they can be found:*

- *Harare*
- *Tokyo*
- *San Francisco*
- *Bogota*
- *Melbourne*
- *Auckland*

- *Cape Town*
- *Tunis*
- *Tel Aviv*
- *Quebec*
- *Buenos Aires*
- *St Petersburg*

Compare your findings with those of the rest of your group.

6.3.2 *Establish what the traveller's needs are*

TRAVELLER'S NEEDS

Before preparing a travel itinerary find out from the travellers their exact requirements and needs. They may have a preferred route, perhaps one that they have not used before, or one that they know and enjoy. They will certainly have a particular day or time of day in mind. Equally, they might have a preferred means of transport and may not want to travel in a particular way; for example, some people are frightened of air travel or ferries, and these kinds of needs must be taken into account. We will now look at some of the specific needs of a traveller.

Route

When considering possible routes to a particular destination, we are often faced with a number of alternatives. For destinations further afield, the quickest and most direct route is probably by air as, generally speaking, air routes are straight lines linking different airports. Isolated destinations are most difficult to get to and you might have to make detours, stop-overs or aircraft changes to reach them.

Even rail and coach travel offer a number of different routes. Travellers might not necessarily want to go direct from the point of departure to the destination; they might want to stop over and include an extra visit elsewhere *en route*.

Travelling by car perhaps offers the most flexible and personalised opportunity to meet the traveller's needs. If the traveller is the one driving the vehicle, then it is only necessary to offer him or her a series of alternative routes and allow them to choose. There are various computer programs which have been created to supply different routes, which include:

▼ **the quickest route**
▼ **the shortest route**
▼ **the scenic route**
▼ **the motorway route**
▼ **the A and B road route**
▼ **the route least likely to encounter hold-ups**

By using these programs you might see that the motorway route, for example, is not necessarily the shortest or, indeed, the quickest one. The choice of route very much depends upon the traveller's needs and a facility such as this can provide a variety of choices.

Time (of year, of day)

If we are considering a business traveller, then the requirements might be to be at a particular place at a particular time. In conjunction with the route, you will be able to work out whether the traveller will reach his or her destination at the appropriate time.

It is worth remembering that travelling at particular times of the year can involve additional complications. Travelling during the summer months will mean that the traveller will encounter much more traffic and probably slow-moving traffic too. If the destination is likely to be busy on a particular day of the week or year, such as a market day, then the traveller should be warned.

The final consideration is that foreign travel also involves a change in time. Many countries are ahead or behind the UK (the UK time is known as Greenwich Mean Time).

Type of transport (public, private hire road transport)

There will always be a particular type of transport which is the most appropriate or convenient by which to reach a particular destination. Even if there are several different options, some may have to be ruled out for a variety of reasons: perhaps the traveller gets air sick, cannot drive or the type of transport takes too long or leaves at the wrong time of day. All of these points have to be considered and are important features in deciding which type of transport will be the most appropriate. In some cases, however, travellers might be able to choose which type of transport they would prefer to use to get to their destination.

Basically, transport falls into two different categories; these are:

▼ **public transport – which includes coach, air, rail, ferry, bus and taxi**
▼ **private hire – which would include coach, car or bus. In some cases, organisations even charter their own aircraft**

If none of the above are appropriate for the travellers, then the only alternative left is for them to drive themselves.

An individual's personal requirements

There are some other constraints specifically relating to international travel which, although not listed in the performance criteria for the qualification, we feel it is necessary to cover here. If you are to arrange travel itineraries for anyone travelling to a European Union country or one further afield, then it is important that you are aware of these constraints, which include the following.

Health

Vaccinations and inoculations are required for some diseases in some countries. Travel agents and the Department of Health give advice on what is required by various countries. If the member of staff is travelling in the European Union, some countries provide limited health cover if the traveller has a Form E111 which is

Figure 6.3.2 This leaflet, issued by the UK Passport Agency, gives information to travellers regarding new health advice and updates.

available from the Post Office. A leaflet, *The Traveller's Guide to Health*, can be obtained from travel agents and the Department of Health and gives detailed information about how to ensure cover whilst abroad.

Insurance

It is advisable to take out travel insurance to cover medical fees, accident fees and loss of baggage whilst travelling. This insurance can be arranged directly with the organisations' insurance companies, or through an insurance broker or travel agent.

Passports

Full passports (those lasting for 10 years) are available from the Passport Office. Application forms and details of how to apply are available from Post Offices.

Foreign currency

When travelling to an international destination, it is usual to take some foreign currency with you. In addition, travellers' cheques either in pounds sterling or other currencies, particularly dollars, may be taken. When foreign currency is purchased from a bank, the bank will sell notes in the foreign currency. On return, any foreign currency left can be sold back to the bank, although foreign coins cannot be exchanged. Money can be exchanged in places other than banks, such as foreign exchanges in some travel agencies, on cross-channel ferries and at airports. Payments may be made abroad by credit card and Eurocheque.

Visas

A visa is not required for European Union countries, but for other visits enquiries should be made at a travel agent or the Embassy or High Commission of the country being visited. Regulations regarding visas are subject to change, so it is advisable to check well in advance if one is required.

Documentation

The people travelling may have to take documents with them for presentation when they arrive at their destination. The following might be included here:

▼ **briefing documents – these will provide any relevant facts and information relating to the visit. They might include a list of companies to be visited, general policies of the organisation or country concerned, the financial position of the organisation or future plans and personnel of the organisation**
▼ **speeches – if the traveller will be making a speech or presentation at a**

conference, he or she will need to be well prepared. In addition, some visual aids may also be required

▼ *sales literature* – when a visit is planned as part of a sales promotion the traveller will need to take supplies of sales literature, preferably in the language of the country being visited. This will have to be planned well in advance so that accurate translations can be made

▼ *specimens and samples* – sometimes the traveller will need to take actual samples of products the organisation produces. Care should be taken to ensure that these are packaged sensibly and that allowances are made for different voltage requirements in the case of electrical products

▼ *display equipment* – some marketing managers might have to take presentation material in the form of displays of the products produced by the organisation, or video tapes and equipment to show in their promotional programme

▼ *visiting cards* – depending on the status of the traveller within the organisation, he or she will carry a supply of visiting or business cards which are distributed to those individuals and organisations encountered during the visit. Managers should always have a supply of these cards to hand out as they represent the organisation and include all the necessary information for contact with the organisation

▼ *address and telephone lists* – wise travellers will always ensure that they have prepared a detailed list of all possible business contacts to be visited during their stay. By having an address/telephone list with them they will ensure that contacts can be reached quickly so no valuable time is wasted

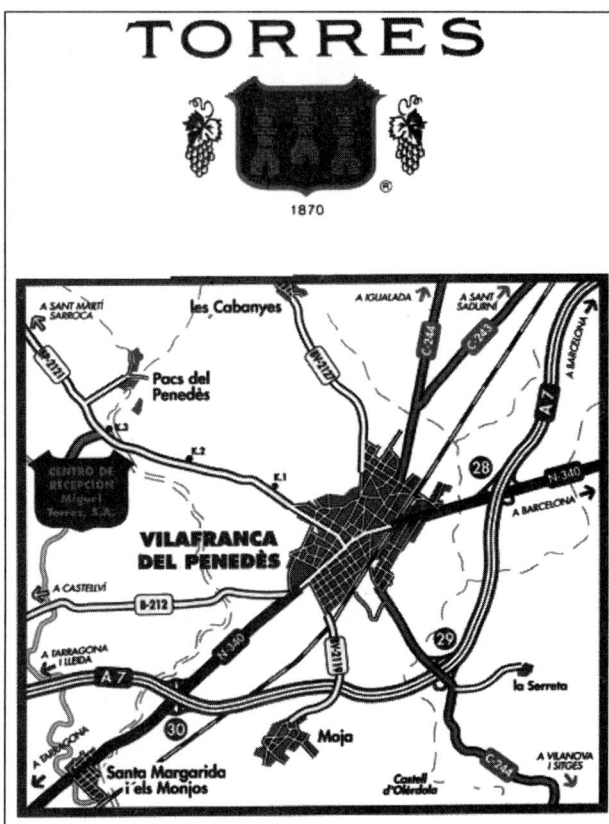

Figure 6.3.3 Torres includes a map when inviting customers to visit its vineyard.

When considering the needs of the traveller, it should be remembered that the people travelling may not be familiar with the area in which they are travelling. If this is the case, then it might be useful to provide them with a suitable map, including a street map, and perhaps a sketch map of the local area.

6.3.3 *Select suitable routes and means of travel which meet the traveller's needs*

MEANS OF TRAVEL

When deciding which means of travel to use, the needs of the traveller must be taken into account. The main consideration is whether the travel will be of a local, national or international nature.

Local travel normally means within the area near to the traveller's own office. It is often not necessary for the visit to be more than one day, which means that hotel accommodation is not always a requirement.

With national travel, a one-day visit is not always possible, so hotel accommodation may have to be booked for one or more nights.

Depending on the length of the visit, international travel can be much more complicated and involved than national travel. It is, however, possible to fly to The Netherlands and back in a day from the UK, making overnight accommodation unnecessary. In most cases though, an international trip will involve more arrangements with regard to travel and accommodation. In addition, other key considerations have to be taken into account, and we discuss these a little later in this element.

Air

Air travel is possible within the UK. For instance, regular services are provided daily from Norwich to Aberdeen, making it possible for someone to travel to Scotland from the South of England and back the same day. This method of transport is expensive, but not in terms of time. If a manager needs to be at a conference which will last only two or three hours, this method will allow him or her to be back in the office the following day, rather than still be travelling back.

Flying is probably the most convenient method of travel for international visits and is certainly the quickest. However, the location of airports might also involve rail or road travel. Air travel can also be very expensive, particularly for long-haul flights, and may involve long waits at airports for connecting flights. All these features should be taken into account when arrangements are being made.

Rail

If the venue of the meeting is convenient for the station and the train times allow it, this is one possibility, certainly for local and national travel. Sometimes, particularly in rural areas, connections cannot easily be made, or the service does not run very frequently.

If the journey is to be a long one, rail travel allows for members of staff to arrive more refreshed than if they had driven and also allows them time during the journey for working on papers etc. If several members of staff are travelling together, they might use the time to have pre-meeting discussions.

For international travel, travelling by train can be expensive, takes longer and might involve long waits for connections. Rail travel is therefore not as popular as flying. However, the opening of the Channel Tunnel has meant that the journey time from London to Paris has been reduced.

Again, travel by train might involve the hiring of a car once the country of destination has been reached in order to arrive at the meeting venue.

Car

This is probably the most convenient method of transport for local travel. An organisation might pay the expenses for staff members to use their own cars, or it might provide a company car or allow for a car to be hired. If road travel is considered to be the best option, then detailed instructions of the most appropriate route should be given to the member of staff who is making the journey.

Road travel is often the most economical method of transport, particularly if more than one member of staff is travelling. It does, however, mean that someone has to drive, making him or her more tired than the others. On the other hand, the petrol costs, or even the car hire costs, will probably be much less than the cost for four people to travel by train.

Although road travel is a popular and less expensive way to travel for a group visiting a foreign country on holiday, it is not so popular for international business trips. This is mainly due to the length of time road travel can take compared to air travel. Additionally, road travel to a country either within the European Union, or outside it, will involve crossing the Channel. This will increase the cost of the visit and, although the opening of the Channel Tunnel has made this crossing a quicker process, it is not necessarily a cheaper one.

Taxi

Taxis are readily available at most stations and airports. Indeed, in most major cities taxis can be found almost anywhere. It is the job of taxi drivers, after all, to know where potential customers will be, so areas with businesses tend to be well-served by this type of transport.

Travellers working on a tight schedule might have to pre-book taxis so that they can ensure that they are picked up at a particular place and at a particular time. This can be done some time in advance, but it is not difficult to organise a taxi at fairly short notice. In areas which are not served by taxis a mini-cab service will probably be available. Travellers will have to decide whether the comparatively high cost of using a taxi can be justified if there is readily available public transport at hand.

Coach

There are two ways of using coaches as a means of transport:

▼ *private coach hire* – in this case, the driver and coach is dedicated to the travellers' use only and is hired to carry them from the point of departure to the destination, making any requested stops or detours along the way

▼ *scheduled coaches* – there are a number of coach lines in the UK. These run regular and reliable services, linking towns and cities around the country. Careful planning can allow the traveller to 'coach hop' and reach remote destinations with the minimum of fuss. It is advisable to book ahead when using scheduled coaches; they are relatively cheap compared to rail or air travel and are often fully booked

Ferry

Compared to air travel, sea travel takes much longer. In addition to the added time factor, there is the consideration of transport to the venue once the country of destination is reached.

6.3.4 Check transport times using a timetable

TIMETABLE

Timetables are available for most methods of transport which offer services to the general public. There is no charge for timetables and they are readily available on request from stations, airports, ports, coach and bus stations, travel agents and the AA and RAC.

Bus

Rather like rail timetables, as we will see in the next section, bus timetables can be obtained in advance of the departure date. They will state where the starting point is and where the bus will terminate. A time will be given for the beginning of the journey and for all stops between this and the termination point. Remember that the times tend to be estimated and it is advisable to arrive at the stop at least five minutes before the bus is due.

Rail

The rail timetable for your local area and for connections to large cities can be obtained via a recorded message by telephone. Rail companies issue timetables which are revised twice a year for all the services they offer. They will also answer direct enquiries regarding the best routes, prices and times of trains. In addition, they will take advance bookings for tickets and seats, although the reservation of seats can incur an additional charge.

Coach

In a similar way to a bus timetable, coach operators will state the departure and arrival times of their scheduled coach services. The major difference between coaches and buses is that the coach tends not to stop at as many places as a bus. In fact, many coaches are non-stop and this is their appeal. Another major advantage of coaches is that they do tend to have refreshments and toilet facilities on board, as well as the capacity to carry luggage.

Air

Since many air operators offer a flexible and regular service to and from a variety of destinations, the traveller can become easily confused with the assortment on offer. The best thing to do is to approach a local travel agent which can pre-book the air flight. If this is not possible, then most operators will accept bookings via the telephone using a credit card. Some companies run regular services to certain destinations from major airports, which means that it is possible to literally 'turn up and take off'. The one thing that nearly all operators insist upon is that you pay before you board the plane. In many respects, air travel has become so easily available that it is really no different from getting on a train.

Ferry

Since the completion of the Channel Tunnel, ferry operators have begun to offer a far more flexible and regular service. This is the only way that they can hope to survive. It is a good thing for the traveller, since regular sailings mean that you do not have to organise your whole day around the departure or arrival of a ferry. On less popular routes, such as those to Ireland, Scandinavia and Holland, the ferry times are not quite as regular but are extremely reliable. It is a good idea to book ahead as once a ferry is full your only alternative is to wait for the next one.

6.3.5 Prepare travel itineraries, including necessary stops, and present them in an effective way

TRAVEL ITINERARIES

An itinerary is a summary of the details and plans for a visit, including all times, accommodation and methods of travel. If a visit is a particularly long and complicated one, the itinerary will be very detailed and might consist of many pages. In such a case, a briefer version containing only essential information could be printed onto cards so the traveller can carry this in his or her pocket for easy reference.

You may be required to make travel and/or accommodation arrangements for visitors to your organisation. On the other hand, your manager or another member of staff may have to travel during the course of his or her duties, and you may be asked to arrange the travel and accommodation requirements. This might involve making the arrangements for just one individual or, alternatively, for a large group. The travel may be by various methods and may involve arrangements for travel and/or accommodation within the UK, the European Union or to countries further afield. As always, attention to detail is the key factor when preparing itineraries. The following range statements list the main considerations.

People and number of people in party

The larger the group, the more difficult it is to arrange complicated and flexible travel itineraries. If there are stop-overs or visits involved, then you will have to check ahead to ensure that the intended stops can cope with the number of people in the group. If you are making scheduled stops, then there are a number of other things to consider, and these might include some of the following:

▼ **do the type of transport and the intended stops have facilities for disabled people?**

▼ **if it is going to be a long journey, is there entertainment available on the means of transport?**

▼ **if there is a chance of losing people on the journey, what can be done to avoid this?**

▼ **have the scheduled stops got facilities for refreshment and, if so, do any of the travellers have special dietary requirements?**

▼ **is the travel organiser going to assume responsibility for any paperwork that needs to be carried by the group?**

Date of travel and destination

Naturally, the location of a meeting will have an effect on the travel and accommodation requirements. Ideally, the accommodation should be as near to the venue of the meeting as possible, but other key considerations are the car parking facilities, the location of the railway station or airport, and the distance from these to the establishment in which the meeting is to take place.

For local and national travel, the following steps should be taken when producing an itinerary:

1   Agree the dates for travel and accommodation requirements with all those concerned and enter them in your diary.

2   Book any hotel requirements.

---

finding out

PC 6.3.5
COM 1.1, 1.2
IT 1.1, 1.2, 1.3

Word process a letter to the hotel of your choice enquiring about accommodation for two nights for two travellers. They will require breakfast but no evening meal and they each need a single room with bath. Find out the price for accommodation and ask the hotel to send any literature to assist the travellers in finding the hotel from the closest railway station.

ITINERARY

FOR SARAH BROWN

25 JANUARY 19..

Monday 25 January 19..

Depart:	Norwich	0930
Arrive:	London Liverpool Street	1105
Hotel:	Regent Palace Piccadilly Circus London Tel: 0171-273-6290	
Seminar:	At the hotel	

Registration	1230
Lunch	1300
Interpersonal skills	1400
Afternoon tea	1530
Plenary session	1545
Close	1630

Theatre:	The Adelphi Theatre 'Sunset Boulevard'	2015

Tuesday 26 January 19..

Seminar:	At the hotel	

Dealing with customers	0930
Coffee	1100
Role play exercises	1130
Lunch	1300
Aggressive callers	1415
Afternoon tea	1530
Plenary session	1545
Close	1630

Depart:	London Liverpool Street	1800
Arrive:	Norwich	2000

Figure 6.3.4 An example of a travel itinerary.

3 Arrange the meetings and appointments that the travellers will be required to attend during their visit.

4 Arrange any rail tickets, seat reservations or car hire.

5 Gather together any documents the traveller may have to take.

The list above will also apply to international travel, but the following will also have to be taken into consideration:

▼ **book any air tickets**
▼ **arrange any insurance requirements**
▼ **arrange any vaccinations or inoculations that may be required**
▼ **apply for any visas that may be required**
▼ **check that the passports of all those travelling are up to date and will not expire whilst the visit is taking place**
▼ **collect any information you can regarding the country being visited, including information about food, drink and places of interest**
▼ **arrange taxis or hire cars for transfer from the airport to the hotel and vice versa**
▼ **check with the AA and RAC for regulations regarding Green Card Insurance or an International Driving Permit if the traveller is driving**
▼ **confirm that the traveller has a Form E111 if appropriate**
▼ **order any travellers' cheques, foreign currency or a Eurocheque book from the bank or travel agent if required**

Means of travel

As we have seen, there are many different ways of travelling and before a firm decision is made about the preferred mode, it is a good idea to make a final check that none of the travellers has medical reasons for not travelling this way. If everyone is happy, you should include the means of travel on your itinerary and also state when and where there are changes to the type of transport used, if this is the case. For example, if you travel by coach to Dover *en route* to Paris, you will take the ferry across the Channel and get back onto another coach at Calais.

Point of departure and time of departure

You should clearly state on the itinerary exactly where the travellers should meet in order to begin their journey. Always make it an obvious place that cannot be confused with any other location. Make sure that you ask the travellers to arrive at the point of departure well before you actually need to leave: the rest of the itinerary could be affected and you might miss vital travel connections if somebody is late. Remember to state the time of departure by using the 24-hour clock. This will avoid any confusion, such as travellers arriving at 10 a.m. instead of 10 p.m.

Details of stops (refreshment breaks, transport connections)

It is important to assure travellers that they will not be travelling for any great length of time without a break and a chance to get refreshments. You should state on the itinerary when and where stops will be made and the lengths of stops, so that travellers can pace themselves and decide whether they should eat at a particular stop or just have a snack and a rest.

Point of arrival and time of arrival

The point of arrival is just as important as the point of departure, particularly if there will be someone waiting for the travellers at the other end of their journey. In these situations, you should always ask the person meeting the travellers to decide on a meeting point. He or she will know the local area and will be able to suggest a suitable meeting point that will not cause confusion or unnecessary delay.

Remember that the time of arrival should also be stated using the 24-hour clock and, if the point of arrival is in another country, you should always state the local time and not UK time.

Overall travel time

Naturally, this is one of the most important factors governing the method of transport to be used. If the visit is within the UK then it is often much quicker to travel by air than by train. However, the cost may not allow this. What must be ensured is that the travel can be arranged in the shortest amount of time so that members of staff are not spending any more time travelling than is absolutely necessary.

It must also be considered that the meeting will start whether the members of staff are present or not, unless they are key members of staff, in which case it would be embarrassing for them and irritating for others if they were very late. Ensuring that the time factor allows for some delays in transport is, therefore, also essential.

Overall cost

Travel is costly, as is accommodation. Although cost is an important consideration when making arrangements for travel and accommodation, it must be noted that the member(s) of staff have no alternative but to attend the meeting. For this reason, the most convenient method of travel and the nearest hotel are often more important than the cost.

With regard to accommodation, although members of staff would probably be quite happy to stay in a five-star hotel, it is not cost effective. When making accommodation arrangements the most convenient and reasonably priced hotel should be selected. If members of staff visit the same area frequently, they might well have a preference with regard to their accommodation. This makes life easier when arrangements are being made, as you know that they will be happy with the hotel, and that the organisation will not find the rates too excessive.

6.3.6 *Prepare the itineraries clearly with highlighted copies of timetables*

In order to complete this performance criterion and the element assignment, you will need to arrange two travel itineraries for two different journeys. This is a complicated task and it is probably the first time you have had to make these kinds of arrangements. You must consider where you will find the necessary information and who will help you with this. Most organisations do have a list of travel contacts, recommended hotels and preferred businesses that they have worked with before. As you probably do not have access to this information, you will need to find other organisations that will be able to help you put together a travel itinerary.

Travel agents

It is always wise to choose a travel agent which is a member of ABTA (the Association of British Travel Agents). This means that any arrangements you make or money you spend with them is protected to some extent by insurance. Organisations that make regular travel arrangements tend to carry out their business with one particular agent who will get to know them and appreciate the standards they demand. The services offered by travel agents are free as they receive a commission on the bookings they make from travel companies and airlines. Most provide a comprehensive travel service and can be good sources of information for all aspects of travel. They can normally be relied upon to have access to up-to-date information as they are linked via computer terminals to travel companies, as well as sea and airlines. A travel agent will also be able to offer help with rail and coach bookings and obtaining foreign currency and travel insurance.

Prestel

The Prestel service is available via most modern televisions. By looking at the appropriate pages (you can find out the right pages by using the index) you will find information regarding travel and flights. Each of the television stations has its own Prestel service, for example Ceefax or Teletext.

The AA and the RAC

The AA and the RAC both produce handbooks which are useful sources of general information and give advice on the requirements concerning international driving licences, in particular. They give details about obtaining Green Cards which are necessary in certain countries when travelling in one's own car. (A Green Card is for insurance purposes and is available through the organisation's own insurance company in the UK.) They supply books for overseas travel by road and book sea and air travel for their members, as well as giving advice on insurance cover requirements. They also produce guides which recommend hotels and restaurants within the UK, the European Union and countries outside the European Union.

A–Z guides

These are fully comprehensive street guides which cover all the major cities in the UK and internationally. They are a particularly useful reference book for those who have to arrange travel itineraries on a regular basis to several areas.

The Good Food Guide

This is published annually by the Consumers' Association and gives detailed information regarding restaurants throughout the UK and Ireland. There is a particularly large and detailed section on London.

---

finding out

PC 6.3.5
COM 1.1

Find the answers to the following questions using Prestel (if you have access to this facility):

- **how many flights leave London Gatwick for Athens on a Tuesday?**
- **what are the weather conditions in Bonn and Hamburg today?**
- **what is the exchange rate for the Japanese Yen today?**

Present your findings to the rest of the group and discuss how easy or difficult it was to obtain this information.

Airlines

Airlines produce timetables and brochures and you will be able to find out all you need to know about 'flight only' trips if you contact an airline directly. Airlines can be contacted either at the local airport or through their central booking offices which are usually based in London.

Rail companies

At the time of writing, finding out about the times of trains is comparatively easy as they are all handled by British Rail. It is possible that by the time you read this several new rail companies will have been created. The sensible thing to do if you require information is to contact the main local railway station, which will have recorded messages detailing the departure and arrival times of various trains to different locations, and will give an enquiry number which will allow you to find out prices and the best routes to different locations. You can, of course, order tickets and seats in advance using a credit or debit card, although it should be noted that reserving a seat does mean an additional charge.

The following guidelines should enable you to complete an itinerary without including any information which is not really relevant. Essentially, the itinerary should be produced for each traveller involved in the visit, and you should consider all of the following points:

▼ try not to make the itinerary too tight – allow the traveller some time to him or herself
▼ remember that when travelling abroad time differences will affect the itinerary
▼ allow time for delays in transport – holiday times and weather conditions can affect the time it takes to travel
▼ research national, religious or local holidays and festivals in the country being visited – this could affect the itinerary drastically
▼ always use the 24-hour clock when producing the itinerary
▼ allow for time at airports and ports and waiting for connections on the railways
▼ include in the itinerary all flight numbers as well as check in, departure and arrival times
▼ remember to indicate the correct airport terminal number
▼ include the name, address and telephone and fax numbers of each of the hotels where accommodation has been arranged
▼ suggest a time for contact with the office or home, particularly on long visits, or arrange a time when the traveller will be available to receive a telephone call
▼ keep a copy of the itinerary in the office for anyone who may require information as to where the traveller can be contacted

BUSINESS CONNECTION

PC 6.3

We have now looked at all the major ways of preparing travel itineraries. To test your memory and skill, complete the following business connection by turning transport into stops. The last letter of each word or phrase is the first letter of the next word or phrase. To help you we have put in the first and last letter on each line, but you will have to do the rest.

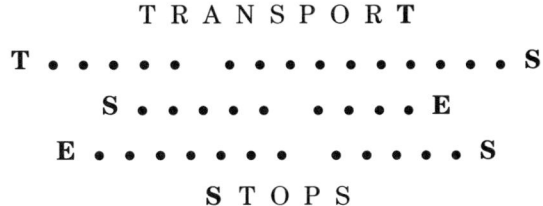

WORDSEARCH

How many of the words listed below can you find? They run forwards and backwards across and up and down the grid.

```
W E R T R M N O I T A N I T S E D L
P L M E A N S O F T R A V E L I M N
H G F N I S T U M P R W Z C V L G G
Q D H P L A C E M E A N C C H P O L
Z C B N T R O P S N A R T M M R O G
Q U A L I T Y O F S E R V I C E G E
P H I C H E D U L C Q R T Y U M O M
E R R E M G D H C H O O P Q C I L I
A Y S T A T N M E E T I N G I S N T
O C O A C H H L M D I C V B O E Q E
U N E R R Y S I D U M O P L M S P R
F E R R Y D I M E L E Q P W X Z O U
Q I N B V I R T U E O O S D A F G T
O C S P I L S N O I T A V R E S E R
Y I L K S R N B V C O Q L K T H G A
O F I T I Q R E T B N B O P A E R P
I F O O T J K F G T R U O O D L Q E
R E F R E S H M E N T S D A T O M D
```

AIR	FERRY	REFRESHMENTS
BUS	MEANS OF TRAVEL	RESERVATION SLIPS
COACH	MEETING	SCHEDULE
DATE	PLACE	TIME
DEPARTURE TIME	PREMISES	TRANSPORT
DESTINATION	QUALITY OF SERVICE	VISIT
EFFICIENCY	RAIL	

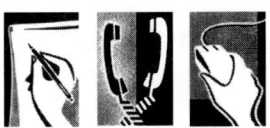

assignment

ELEMENT 6.3

PC 6.3.1–6
COM 1.1, 1.2, 1.3, 1.4
IT 1.1, 1.2, 1.3

For the purposes of this element you will need to carry out the following tasks and ensure you keep a record of all conversations and documents involved. Whenever possible you should try to word process letters and documents.

This assignment can be linked to the one carried out in Element 6.2, where you made a booking, but remember that your itineraries must follow an appropriate business format.

| **t a s k** | **1** | PC 6.3.1/5/6 |

You must produce two travel itineraries for two separate journeys. One of the journeys should be to a European Union country, which could include anywhere in the UK, and the other should be to a country outside the European Union. Each of the itineraries must include the following:

- the dates
- the calculated travel timings
- all necessary stops

| **t a s k** | **2** | PC 6.3.2 |

From the itineraries you have produced you should now compile a summary which states how the needs of the traveller were taken into account when the arrangements were made.

| **t a s k** | **3** | PC 6.3.4/6 |

You should produce highlighted copies of timetables which have been used in the compilation of the itineraries. In addition you should include a map which identifies the route(s) selected.

| **n o t e s** | |

You can, if appropriate, include an itinerary for your own personal travel arrangements, although you must present this in an appropriate business format. Any timetables you may require are obtainable from travel agencies and coach and rail travel centres.

element 7.1

DESCRIBE INFORMATION PROCESSING

Performance criteria

A student must:

1 Identify and give examples of **types of information** in a business organisation.

2 Describe the **main stages** involved in processing information in a business organisation.

3 Identify and give examples of the most common **methods of processing information** in a business organisation.

4 Identify and give examples of **ways to track information** during processing.

RANGE

Types of information: written, oral, visual, electronic; for a business organisation, within a business organisation, from a business organisation

Main stages: receiving information, collecting information, preparing information, distributing information, storing information

Methods of processing information: oral, written documents, word-processed documents, telecommunications

Ways to track information: references, filing, keeping copies, keeping logs

7.1.1 *Identify and give examples of types of information in a business organisation*

TYPES OF INFORMATION

In this element you will become aware of the variety of information that flows in and out of any business organisation. This information can come in to or go out of the organisation in many different ways and formats. In this performance criterion we look at these different pieces of information and the different formats they can take.

Throughout the element you will be asked to describe, process and present business information, as well as research and present, by means of a short verbal presentation, the information that you have gathered regarding the importance of legible and accurate documents which an organisation must produce and store for easy retrieval.

The term **business document** simply refers to any piece of paper that has been either received, or sent out by the organisation. Business documents include invoices, order forms, payment records, receipt records, and other documents such as letters, memos, notices and telephone messages.

Written information

In Performance Criterion 7.2 we give you some useful hints on ways to ensure that your written documents are accurate, legible and informative. In this performance criterion we look at the different formats in which written information can be presented. An organisation or an individual within an organisation might receive written information in the following formats:

▼ *letters* – these might be received from customers who are making an enquiry or complaint. In addition, letters might be received from suppliers who are requesting payment or further information from an organisation. Letters might also be received if a meeting has been arranged outside the organisation and employees are expected to attend or if instructions are to be given to an employee

▼ *memos* – these might be received by one individual within an organisation from another employee. The purpose of the memo could be to give information or to confirm a meeting. Memos are never received from another organisation; they are regarded as internal mail

▼ *notices* – again, this is an internal communication. Individuals within an organisation might receive information via a notice, either on a noticeboard or via a computer network

▼ *telephone message form* – if someone telephones an organisation with information or a request, then this information is transferred to a message form and passed to the person(s) concerned

▼ *pre-printed forms* – these can be orders from another organisation for goods required or invoices from another organisation requesting payment for goods

An organisation might request information using the following documents:

▼ *letters* – these might be sent to suppliers or customers in reply to information received or requesting information or goods. Letters could also be sent to give instructions to someone being employed to carry out a particular task for the organisation

▼ *pre-printed forms* – orders to another organisation or invoices requesting

ORDER FORM

TO			ORDER NUMBER	
			DATE	
DELIVERY ADDRESS		SPECIAL INSTRUCTIONS		
REF NO	QUANTITY	DESCRIPTION	UNIT PRICE	AMOUNT

Figure 7.1.1 An order form.

payment from another organisation
- ▼ *memos* – to another individual within an organisation asking for information, giving instructions or confirming meetings
- ▼ *notices* – an individual might request information from other individuals within an organisation by displaying a notice on the noticeboard or sending a notice via E-mail

We continue to look at these written forms of requesting and receiving information throughout this unit.

Oral information

We give detailed information regarding the ways in which to communicate well with other individuals in Element 7.2. In this section we look at the different ways information is processed orally within an organisation. The following are ways in which oral information can be received by, and sent from, an organisation:

- ▼ *receiving telephone calls* – an organisation will receive information from existing customers, prospective customers, suppliers and many other different organisations via the telephone
- ▼ *making telephone calls* – an organisation might make telephone calls in order to request information from existing and prospective customers, as well as suppliers and other organisations
- ▼ *face to face* – individuals who are representing the organisation may either pass on information or request it from representatives of other organisations using this means of communication. Face-to-face communication can take place in formal or informal situations, for example in visits to other organisations or the passing on of messages in person to other employees of the organisation

Figure 7.1.2 Telephone communication can be vital to an organisation.

▼ **the passing on of messages orally –** anybody who has a message to give to another member of staff verbally will be processing information orally for the organisation

▼ **giving instructions orally –** a supervisor or line manager who has to give instruction to his or her staff verbally will also be processing information on behalf of the organisation orally when this task is carried out

We look at the ways of processing information orally in more detail throughout this unit.

Visual information

Visual information is another way of passing information to an individual or distributing it to different sections of an organisation. Many individuals who give presentations to large numbers of people use visual aids to assist them in explaining a particular point, or use them to make very complicated or detailed information easier to understand. Visual information can take the following forms:

▼ **graphs –** these are often used when describing financial information or sales figures, and allow the individual giving the presentation to provide a paper copy of detailed information which can be referred to later

▼ **charts –** in much the same way as graphs, these are used to highlight the main points of a presentation and to make the information more interesting and easier to understand. Graphs and charts can both be produced to a very high standard and in different formats by using an appropriate computer program

▼ **signs –** when an individual visits an organisation it can sometimes be very difficult to find his or her way around. If an organisation provides signs which help with directions, then this will help the individual, as well as assisting the receptionist who has to give directions to the visitor

Electronic information

In Element 7.2 we give you detailed information about the different electronic methods of processing information. In this section we will list the ways in which an organisation can receive or request information electronically:

▼ **facsimile transmission –** messages can flow in to and out of an organisation using a fax machine. The documents being faxed can be quite complicated in nature and of any length

▼ **telex transmission –** messages can flow in to and out of an organisation using a telex machine, although the documents tend to be less complicated than those sent by fax as diagrams, charts and graphs cannot be sent by telex

▼ **electronic mail transmission –** if the organisation is linked via a modem to another organisation and to individuals within the organisation, information can flow in and out via E-mail. The types of information sent by this method are letters, memos, notes, messages and notices

Information for a business organisation

When we say 'information for an organisation' we are referring to information which will be sent from our organisation to another; in other words, outgoing information. The types of information an organisation sends out include the following:

▼ letters to customers or suppliers replying to a specific request for information or payment

▼ orders to suppliers for goods required

▼ invoices to customers for goods they have bought

▼ statements of accounts to customers requesting payment for goods for which they have been invoiced

▼ receipts to customers for payments they have made

▼ leaflets, brochures and price lists to customers and prospective customers,

informing them of the goods and services the organisation provides
▼ telephone calls, fax/telex messages and E-mail transmissions to customers and suppliers on various matters

Information within a business organisation

When we say 'information within an organisation' we mean the information which passes around the business but does not go outside it immediately. The information will have been received by the organisation and needs to be processed by individuals within the business. The types of information dealt with within a business organisation can include the following:

▼ *internal mail* – which can be copies of a document to be sent to several members of staff, accompanied by a covering memo
▼ *memos* – which are internal correspondence and may be written for a variety of reasons, including the passing on of information or instructions
▼ *internal telephone calls* – which are calls made from one office to another within the business
▼ *E-mail messages* – which can be sent from one computer to another within the organisation. This does not have to be within the same building, as computer-linked networks can be from one branch to another
▼ *face-to-face communication* – when different members of staff talk to each other in person in order to pass on messages or give information or instructions

Information from a business organisation

When we say 'information from an organisation' we mean information which will be sent to that organisation by another, in other words, incoming information. The information that an organisation will receive can include the following:

▼ *letters from customers* – these might include instructions from the customer regarding an order he or she has placed. The customer may also request information or complain about goods or services the organisation has provided
▼ *letters from suppliers* – these might include information about new goods the supplier may be offering. The supplier may also ask for information from the organisation about goods the organisation has requested from the supplier
▼ *order forms* – an organisation might receive orders from customers in the form of a pre-printed document
▼ *invoices* – an organisation might receive an invoice from a supplier in the form of a pre-printed document
▼ *statements of account* – an organisation might receive a statement of account from a supplier informing it of the amount it has to pay the supplier for goods it has purchased
▼ *receipts* – an organisation might receive a receipt from a supplier when it has made a payment owing
▼ *leaflets, price lists and brochures* – these will come from a supplier or prospective supplier for the organisation to file and use at a later date
▼ *telephone calls, fax/telex messages and E-mail transmissions* – an organisation might use these methods to contact customers and suppliers on various matters

Whatever the form the information received by the organisation takes, it is important that this information is processed, distributed and filed in an appropriate way. Obviously, it is very important that any information an organisation receives is dealt with accurately, but it is equally important that if the information is filed away for future use, it can be easily retrieved when required.

7.1.2 **Describe the main stages involved in processing information in a business organisation**

MAIN STAGES

In the previous performance criterion we looked at the ways information can flow in and out of an organisation. In this section we intend to deal with the ways that information is processed inside the organisation. We have already looked at the ways in which a business may receive information, but now we will see what happens to that information once it is received by the business. We do not intend, in this section, to go into great detail about the types of information involved, merely the stages involved in the processing of any information at all.

Receiving information

The processing of information refers to the way in which an organisation deals with the information it receives. We have already looked at the different ways an organisation can receive information in the previous performance criterion, and these include:

▼ in a written format, either received through the post or by means of a memo or notice, or electronically via fax, telex or E-mail
▼ in an oral format, either received via the telephone or face to face, by means of messages or instructions
▼ in a visual format, in the form of charts, diagrams, graphs or signs

Having received information, the business must ensure that it is collected, prepared, distributed and stored adequately. If this process is not carried out, the information will be of no use to the business in the future.

Collecting information

The collection of information might be the responsibility of one member of staff on a particular project or, alternatively, for one particular aspect of the organisational system. Only one person is normally responsible for 'managing' or 'bringing together' the information so that it does not go astray and for security reasons. The person carrying out this task must be able to locate the information easily and have a good knowledge of the other individuals working closely with him or her, as well as being able to identify immediately who else can assist or help with information.

Whoever is responsible for collecting information for a business, it is important that he or she remembers the following points:

▼ a record should be kept of what information has been received
▼ a record should be kept of the source of the information; in other words, where it came from
▼ a record should be kept of where that information has been stored

Preparing information

Having received and collected information which has been sent to an organisation, it then has to be prepared so that it is of use throughout all the systems in place within the business to deal with it. This preparation may include any of the following processes:

▼ it might need to be distributed (sent) to several different members of staff so that they can comment on the content
▼ it might need to be reproduced in a different format; maybe a written document will need to be presented in a visual form so that it is easier to understand

▼ it might need to be stored until it is required at a later date, in which case a record must be kept of where it has been filed

▼ it might need further action, for example a letter received from a customer may require an immediate reply

▼ it might need to be sent to a different department within the business, for example an order form will have to be sent to the sales department so that it can be dealt with, or a statement of account to the accounting department

so that it can keep a record of outstanding debts

Distributing information

The term **distributing information** relates to any of the sections of the information that have to be seen by several members of staff. The document or file might be distributed to several individuals so that they each have their own copy, it might have a circulation list attached to it so that each person reads it and passes it on to the next person on the list, or sections of the document or file will be copied and sent to the individual who deals with that section.

CIRCULATION SLIP

Please read and pass on in the order listed below:		
NAME	DEPARTMENT	INITIAL/DATE
Please return to: MISS C SHORTEN by: 24/5/199.		

Figure 7.1.3 A circulation slip.

Storing information

The storing of information relates to documents which are filed in a manual- or paper-based system and to information which is stored using a computer-based system. The person who is responsible for storing information in whatever form on behalf of the organisation needs to be efficient, well organised and have a good knowledge of the systems in use.

We look at the methods of filing information in detail in Unit 8.

7.1.3 **Identify and give examples of the most common methods of processing information in a business organisation**

This performance criterion is a practical one. For the purposes of meeting the requirements of this section, you need to focus on one particular business organisation. You may be able to use your work placement or part-time job for this, or your tutor might give you a case study to use for the information you require. You will find this section particularly useful when you complete the element assignment, as the information you gain during this performance criterion will be used to compile the report you are asked to complete in the assignment.

In the previous section we gave you the main stages in the processing of information. You now need to observe the way this theory is used in a practical situation. You must list the ways in which the business organisation of your choice carries out the following.

METHODS OF PROCESSING INFORMATION

Find out what methods your organisation uses to process information. Is it all done manually or is computer software used for processing? You should be looking at information such as:

▼ **customer details**
▼ **customer accounts**
▼ **sales information**
▼ **purchasing information**
▼ **organisational accounts**

Each organisation will have a different way of dealing with the information it uses. You need to be able to identify the most common ways and to give examples of at least two documents from each of the different methods used.

Oral methods

Again, using the organisation you have chosen, you must highlight the ways the organisation processes information orally. Look at things like telephone orders and find out what documentation is used to confirm such an order. Look at the ways in which the organisation deals with a customer request or complaint orally and find out how it ensures that such a situation is followed through adequately and efficiently.

Written documents and word-processed documents

Most organisations now use a word processor as their main method of producing written documents. Some do still use a typewriter, but those who use a word processor find that this method is much more efficient and reliable for producing letters and documents. The main reason for this is the fact that the document can be filed on the computer itself, rather than having large quantities of paper stored in a more traditional filing system.

You need to look at the way in which your

Figure 7.1.4 Oral communication at work (courtesy of Mercury Communications).

organisation deals with written information. Find out whether it uses word processors or typewriters and if it uses a paper-based method of filing as well as the computer-based one if it does use word processors.

Telecommunications

In recent years, organisations have found that they can operate much more efficiently and effectively by using telecommunication equipment. Although the fax machine and the use of E-mail are good examples of telecommunication, we felt it was also necessary to include the franking machine in this section, in relation to the receiving and distribution of internal and external mail.

You need to find out whether your organisation has a fax machine or an E-mail facility. Does it find these more efficient than sending letters by post? What types of documents does it send and receive using telecommunications?

7.1.4 *Identify and give examples of ways to track information during processing*

WAYS TO TRACK INFORMATION

If information is being received, prepared, distributed and stored, then it is important that the exact whereabouts of this information is known at all times. It would be a very poor system of tracking that did not manage to find a file or a document once it has been processed. In order to track the information that an organisation receives and distributes or, for that matter, sends out of the organisation, a suitable administrative system must be in place. Imagine what would happen if a customer had placed an order but never received the goods. How would the organisation be able to locate the original order if its tracking system was not efficient enough?

Figure 7.1.5 Digital telephone equipment improves communication efficiency (courtesy of Thorne Erickson Communication Ltd).

References

One method of tracking information used is to reference all the material that flows in and out of the organisation. If you look at letters you have received from an organisation you might find a reference number at the top. This reference number might relate to the person sending the letter and his or her typist, or the subject matter con-

tained in the letter.

In the same way, if you go to your local or centre library you will see that each of the different subjects is referenced under a unique number.

Referencing means that items of a like nature are clubbed together under a number so that all the information relating to that one subject is filed or kept together for future reference.

Filing

When documents are filed by an organisation, suspension folders held in filing cabinets are normally used. Each of these suspension folders will be labelled with either a letter of the alphabet, a number or the subject of the documents contained within. When a document has been dealt with it is not thrown away but filed away in case it is needed again. When filing, the person responsible for carrying out this duty will place the document in the appropriate suspension folder within the cabinet. We deal with filing in more detail in Element 8.3.

Keeping copies

As well as filing copies for future reference, copies are often made and sent to any members of staff who need to deal with the document. Each of these members of staff will have their own set of files where they can file the document once it has been dealt with. In this way, the organisation can track the different aspects of the document as it is being processed, rather than trying to make sure that everyone does their work on it before it moves onto the next person. Obviously, using this method of processing information relies very much on everyone being responsible and ensuring they are keeping their copies safely.

Keeping logs

One way in which an organisation can track both the documents being set out of the organisation and the money spent on postage is by completing a mail log daily. The person responsible for dealing with the outgoing mail will normally complete this log at the end of each day. In a similar way, an incoming mail log could also be kept to ensure that the organisation has a record of both the date the documents are received and also to whom they were passed for processing.

BUSINESS CONNECTION

PC 7.1

We have now looked at all the major ways of describing information processing. To test your memory and skill, complete the following business connection by turning visual information into notices. The last letter of each word or phrase is the first letter of the next word or phrase. To help you we have put in the first and last letter on each line, but you will have to do the rest.

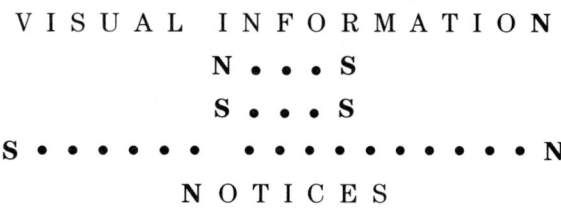

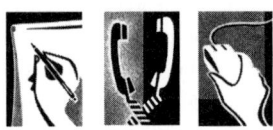

assignment

ELEMENT 7.1

PC 7.1.1–4
COM 1.1, 1.2, 1.4
IT 1.1, 1.2, 1.3

For the purposes of this element assignment you need to collect information which provides evidence of your knowledge of the different types of information which can flow in and out of a business organisation. It is possible to complete this assignment during a work placement, in a simulated (role play) situation or by links with business organisations you may be using for other assignments. Alternatively, your tutor may provide you with a case study to use.

task **1** PC 7.1.1

In the form of a report, you must identify the types of information which can be:

* *sent to an organisation*

* *distributed within an organisation*
* *sent from an organisation*

task **2** PC 7.1.2/3

The next part of your report should include a section which describes the main stages in processing information. This should also include the types of information normally found and the most common methods of processing each (give at least two examples of each here).

task **3** PC 7.1.1–4

The final part of your report should state the ways in which an organisation can track information during processing. Again, you should include at least two examples here.

element 7.2

PROCESS BUSINESS DOCUMENTS

Performance criteria

A student must:

1 Choose **methods** and **documents** to process different **types of business information**.

2 **Process** the information accurately.

3 Produce accurate **processed documents** using conventional business style and formats.

4 Check that **documents** are legible and accurate.

RANGE

Methods: oral, written, word processed, telecommunications

Documents: memo, letter, notice, telephone message, fax message, electronic mail message, order, instruction

Types of business information: enquiry, complaint; formal, informal; urgent, non-urgent; confidential, public

Process: prepare, copy, transmit, store, retrieve

Processed documents: handwritten, word processed; memo, letter, notice, telephone message, fax message, electronic mail message, order, instruction

7.2.1 *Choose methods and documents to process different types of business information*

In this performance criterion, you must process some business documents yourself. These documents can be provided as part of the rest of your course, or requested from your tutor. Whichever method is used for the processing of the documents, you must ensure that they contain legible and accurate information. We give you some help in this section and then, by completing the documents, you should have the evidence that you need for your portfolio. Because this is such a practical element, you will acquire the evidence as you go along and do not need to complete an element assignment. You will also be able to use a number of documents for Element 7.3.

METHODS

An administrative system needs to be in place in any organisation to track the following transactions which relate to the activities of the organisation:

▼ **purchases made**
▼ **sales made**
▼ **organisations and individuals with whom transactions have been made**
▼ **dates of transactions**
▼ **payments received and pending**
▼ **personnel records**
▼ **stock levels**
▼ **staff training and development**
▼ **accurate minutes of meetings**

Having established why an organisation needs to have administrative systems in place, you can now see that it is just as important for that information to be processed in an efficient and effective way. An organisation must ensure that its information processing staff are well trained and that they make the best use of their time and energy.

Oral methods

To be a good communicator takes practice and experience. It does not matter who you communicate with – it could be friends, parents, teachers or potential employers – they will all gain an insight into you, and how you conduct yourself, by what you say and how you say it. Here are some of the key things to remember when you are communicating:

▼ **always speak clearly**
▼ **do not speak too quickly or too slowly**
▼ **show confidence, both in yourself and in what you are saying**
▼ **think about what you say and try to make your responses logical and easy to follow**
▼ **use the right words for the situation; do not be too complicated or simplistic**
▼ **try to use the right tone for the situation; do not be too aggressive or passive or allow your feelings to confuse what it is you have to say. This can affect how the other person receives what you say: the same statement may be either acceptable or unacceptable, depending on your tone**
▼ **if you have a regional accent which is very strong or broad, you might have to talk slightly more slowly in certain situations**
▼ **if you think your voice is not pleasant to listen to, perhaps too high, try to lower the pitch a little. You can help counter this problem by controlling your excitement or speed of speech**
▼ **try to put the other person at ease**
▼ **do not interrupt someone who is speaking; wait until he or she has finished**
▼ **listen to what the other person is**

saying so that you can respond appropriately

When communicating orally in a face-to-face situation or on the telephone, we use a mixture of the two following skills.

Listening

During the course of a day, we might listen to a number of different people. It is a rare person who will remember everything that has been said to him or her, particularly if the way in which conversation is heard is unstructured and confused. In order to listen as effectively as possible, an individual must:

▼ **actually hear the message**
▼ **interpret the message**
▼ **evaluate the message**
▼ **act upon the message and make use of the information it contains**

In some situations it is a good idea to take notes during a conversation, or perhaps even to use a tape recorder.

Speaking

We have already discussed how to be a good communicator and much of this involves speech. In addition, the use of questioning techniques can be important in clarifying the exact nature of messages. To be an effective communicator the individual should:

▼ **clearly know his or her role in the conversation**
▼ **be aware of the receptiveness and interest of those listening**
▼ **have some knowledge of the listener's own knowledge of the subject of the conversation**

Being an effective communicator means making sure that the listener is always attentive and that any points raised within the conversation are not ambiguous.

Written methods

To be an effective writer an individual must take the following into account when presenting information:

▼ **that the information will be read by a variety of people in different situations**
▼ **that complex information needs to have sufficient background information in order to make it clear**
▼ **that the information should be capable of having a long life, in the sense that it may be referred to many times in the future**

As with other forms of communication, the written word can sometimes be ambiguous. Even the most informal of messages needs to be clear. Most organisations use standard formats for a variety of written communications, which have been designed to avoid ambiguity. Certain forms of written communication can be easier to understand than others, but the writer should ensure that the reader always has sufficient information in order to form an opinion if required. The presentation of data, for example, should be carefully considered since financial information, in particular, can often be misleading or unclear.

Word-processed methods

Keyboard skills are very useful for anybody who chooses a job in business. Using a keyboard does not necessarily mean typing, but also refers to the use of word processors and computers. Having keyboard skills can be of particular use to someone who regularly uses a computer. In fact, typewriters have now become things of the past in many organisations, although some smaller organisations have not yet been so affected by information technology and still use typewriters, even though most of these are now electronic.

Word-processing packages have gradually replaced typewriters as the preferred method for organisations to produce their printed documents. These have several advantages over typewriters:

▼ **the text can be read through easily**
▼ **mistakes can be easily altered**
▼ **changes can be made without having to retype the whole document**

▼ work can be stored for future reference

▼ work can be altered for different occasions or situations

These benefits are particularly useful when preparing long and complicated documents.

Most word-processing packages will have the following valuable features:

▼ the ability to edit text

▼ help screens which show you how to carry out functions available within the package

▼ a spell-checking facility. This is ideal for someone who is not good at spelling. It scans the text and compares your spelling with a built-in dictionary. If required, the correct spelling can replace the error. Additions can be made to the dictionary if required

▼ a thesaurus, which allows you to choose alternative words to those you have used

▼ a word counter to count the number of words in the document

▼ a print preview or the facility to view the document before it is printed

▼ mail merge or mail shot facilities, which allow for a standard letter to be merged with a number of names and addresses. This is very useful and time saving for an organisation that needs to distribute the same letter to several different organisations or customers

Telecommunications

A facsimile machine (fax) is capable of relaying documents and graphics via the telephone network to another location in just a few seconds.

The word **facsimile** actually means an exact and faithful reproduction of text, photographs or graphic images. These machines have become invaluable to most organisations, particularly if they have a number of sites within the group, or need to contact establishments abroad quickly. Fax machines are left switched on 24-hours a day, and do not have to be continually monitored throughout the night. This means that the time differences between countries is not a problem. We will explain how a fax message can be sent in the next part of this performance criterion when we look at documents.

Although the telex machine is not specifically mentioned in the range statement of this performance criterion, we felt it was necessary to include it here as so many small businesses still use this system of telecommunication.

The telex works along much the same principle as a fax machine, but is more limited in its use as it is not possible to transmit charts and diagrams via the telex. For this reason, the fax machine has really replaced the telex in most organisations. However, the same advantages apply regarding the transmission of messages to countries overseas. Telex messages can also be prepared and saved on electronic file and transmitted at a later time when they are dispatched automatically. The procedure for sending a telex message is as follows:

1 Prepare the text of the telex.
2 Find the telex number of the recipient, using the Telex Directory if necessary.
3 Make contact with the recipient by keying in the telex number.
4 Obtain confirmatory answerback code from the recipient.
5 Provide identification in the form of answerback code of the sender.
6 Dispatch the telex.

PC 7.2.1
COM 1.2, 1.3, 1.4
IT 1.1, 1.2, 1.3

00:20

*D*esign a form on computer for use by members of staff who wish to send a telex. This form will be used to write a draft of the message. It will be handed to the telex operator, who will then key the information in to the telex. Be sure to include all necessary information and details.

DOCUMENTS

Business documents are pieces of paper which are in regular use within an organisation. These can include the purchase, sales, payment and receipt documents, but also include documents such as memos, letters, notices, telephone messages, fax messages, electronic mail messages, orders and instructions. We intend to deal with these individually.

Memo

Internal memoranda are used for communication between different departments within the same organisation. These are often called memos for short. An example of a memo is given in Figure 7.2.1. It is normally shorter than a business letter and deals with one or more subjects. When more than one point is being made it is normal to number them. Memos are not signed in the same way

---

Smith & Nephew plc

Alum Rock Road
Birmingham B8 3DZ
Telephone: 021 327 4750
Telex: 338340
Telefax: 021 328 2740

Smith✛Nephew

Memorandum

To:

Date:

From:

Subject:

Figure 7.2.1 An example of headed memorandum paper used by Smith & Nephew plc.

as a business letter, but the person issuing the memo will often initial it at the end.

Letter

Business letters, unlike memos, are sent outside the organisation. It is important then that they are neat, accurate and well presented.

The headed paper used by an organisation for its business letters forms part of its **corporate image**. The example shown in Figure 7.2.2 gives the information an organisation wants its customers or clients to see regularly:

▼ **the name and address of the organisation**
▼ **the telephone number, fax number and/or telex number of the organisation**
▼ **the registered address of the organisation, as this may be different from its postal address**
▼ **the company registration number**
▼ **the names of the directors of the organisation**
▼ **any other companies the organisation may represent or be connected with**

The layout or format of a business letter will also usually be part of an organisation's corporate image, and different organisations have their own rules about the way in which a letter should be laid out. It is common now to use the fully-blocked method of display, which means that each part of the letter commences at the left-hand margin as in Figure 7.2.3 overleaf.

The following points show how a typical business letter is composed:

▼ **our reference – this can be made up of initials and/or numbers which the organisation sending the letter will use for filing purposes**
▼ **your reference – again, this is usually made up of initials and/or numbers which the organisation receiving the letter has used in previous correspondence**
▼ **the date – all letters must be dated**
▼ **the name and address of the person or organisation to which the letter is being sent**
▼ **the name of the town in capitals, and the postcode on a line of its own**
▼ **the opening greeting, such as 'Dear Sir/Madam/Mr/Ms/Mrs/Miss' etc.**
▼ **the heading – often, after the opening greeting, an organisation will give the letter a heading, which indicates what the letter is about. This is normally typed either in capitals or with initial capital letters only, and may be underlined or emboldened**
▼ **the body of the letter – this is typed, with each line of the paragraph beginning at the left-hand margin, and a line space being left between paragraphs**
▼ **the closing sentiment, such as 'Yours faithfully' or 'Yours sincerely'. When using 'Dear Sir/Madam', 'Yours faithfully' is used. When you know the name of the person you are writing to, 'Yours sincerely' is used**
▼ **after allowing space for a signature, the name of the person signing the letter is typed, as well as their title**
▼ **enclosure(s) – any enclosed additional information which is mentioned in the body of the letter is usually indicated at the foot of the letter, by typing 'Enc(s)'**

Notice

If an organisation wishes to pass a message on to a number of employees, it may place information on staff noticeboards.

These messages can be formal or informal, such as a change to normal organisational procedures or a social event being planned by the organisation's personnel department.

Notices allow the quick and easy sending of information to a large number of people. Noticeboards can also be used by individuals wishing to inform colleagues of items for sale or events planned.

WOOLWORTHS

Woolworths plc

Woolworth House
242/246 Marylebone Road, London NW1 6JL

telephone 071-262 1222
facsimile 071-706 5416
telex 24898

your ref

our ref

direct dialling telephone 071-706

Smith & Nephew plc

Alum Rock Road
Birmingham B8 3DZ
Telephone: 021 327 4750
Telex: 338340
Telefax: 021 328 2740

Smith✛Nephew

Telefax

To:

Date:

From:

Pages:

Fax No:

Subject:

Smith & Nephew plc

2 Temple Place, Victoria Embankment,
London WC2R 3BP
Telephone: 071-836 7922
Telex: 299494 SANACOM G
Telefax: 071-240 7088

Smith✛Nephew

ANNOUNCEMENT

Figure 7.2.2 Examples of headed paper.

14 Wellington Road
GREAT YARMOUTH
Norfolk
NR30 6BU

Tel No 0493 855677

Your Ref: BSD/223

Our Ref: CS.12

19 November 19..

Hightime Short Breaks
Princess Street
NORWICH
NR1 4TT

Dear Sir

HIGHTIME SHORT CAPITAL BREAKS

As I am unable to come to your offices to book a Short Capital
Break, I should be obliged if you could complete the booking form
on my behalf.

I wish to book an Hightime Capital Break to London, for 3 nights
commencing 15 June 19..

My first and second choice hotels are the Washington and the
Piccadilly Plaza respectively. I require a single room with
shower.

As detailed in your brochure, I would like to reserve a place on
the Special London Tour on 16 June 19.., and enclose the
completed form as suggested by you on the telephone.

I would like to pay by Access and my card number is 5224 0098
1768, the expiry date is 01/95.

I look forward to receiving a receipt and confirmation in due
course.

Thank you very much for your assistance in this matter.

Yours faithfully

MISS C SHORTEN

Enc

Figure 7.2.3 An example of a letter using a fully-blocked layout.

PC 7.2.1
COM 1.1, 1.2
IT 1.1, 1.2, 1.3

00:25

Prepare a notice to be placed on all staff noticeboards informing them of the date, time and venue of a social event of your choice. Tell the staff that the management would be pleased to see as many staff present as possible. Your notice should be word processed.

Telephone message

If you are responsible for taking telephone messages, it is essential that the information contained in these is correct and legible. All messages taken should be delivered to the person concerned as quickly as possible after the event.

Fax message

The procedure for sending a fax message is as follows:

1 Prepare the original document.
2 Prepare a covering sheet. This should include the name of the recipient, the name of the sender, the fax numbers of both and the number of pages being sent. It may also allow space for a short message.
3 Place the original document into the machine.
4 Key in the number of the recipient and follow the instructions given on the machine. Although these procedures may vary slightly from machine to machine, the principles for dispatching a message are the same. Regularly used fax numbers are often kept readily at hand, but if a number is not known it can be looked up in the Fax Directory, or found through Fax Enquiries.
5 If a connection is made, the original document will pass through the machine and you will be informed that transmission is taking place. If the recipient's line is engaged, the machine will automatically redial the number at intervals until a connection is made.
6 Once transmission has taken place, the machine will issue a transmission report. This will state the date, time and length of the call, the recipient's number, the sender's number, the number of pages sent and confirmation that transmission was acceptable. If there were any problems in transmission, the report will indicate this and retransmission may be necessary.

FACSIMILE MESSAGE

TO   ATTENTION OF ....

LOCATION/DEPARTMENT ....

FAX NO ....

FROM   ORIGINATOR ....

FAX NO ....

TEL NO ....

DATE ....

NO. OF PAGES (INCLUDING THIS ONE) ....

<u>IF TRANSMISSION IS NOT PROPERLY RECEIVED PLEASE CALL THE ABOVE NUMBER</u>.

Figure 7.2.4 An example of a front page, or covering sheet, for addition to a series of documents being sent by fax machine.

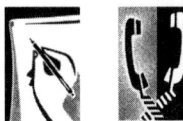 

FIGURE IT OUT

PC 7.2.1
COM 1.2, 1.3, 1.4

00:45

Using the example given in Figure 7.2.4 of a possible format for a front page used when sending a fax message, design your own front page. Remember to include all the necessary details.

Electronic mail message

Information is being increasingly transmitted electronically. The days of waiting for letters or documents have, for most organisations, long gone and the tendency to use electronic processes to transmit information is now more usual, particularly in larger organisations.

When considering computers and their effects on business, we must first be aware that there are, in fact, two main types of computer: mainframes and micros.

Mainframes

In varying forms, complexity, speed and ability, mainframe computers have been available since just after the Second World War. They are, in essence, machines with large memories and data-processing abilities which can be used to store a mass of information for immediate access and amendment. Mainframes normally operate 24-hours a day, 365 days of the year. The advantage with running these machines continuously is that routine data-processing work can be undertaken when demands on the machine are at their lowest, that is, at night. Mainframes are used as the work horses for networked computers, providing such services as word processing, database storage, spreadsheet calculations, graphics production, stock control, accounts and electronic mail.

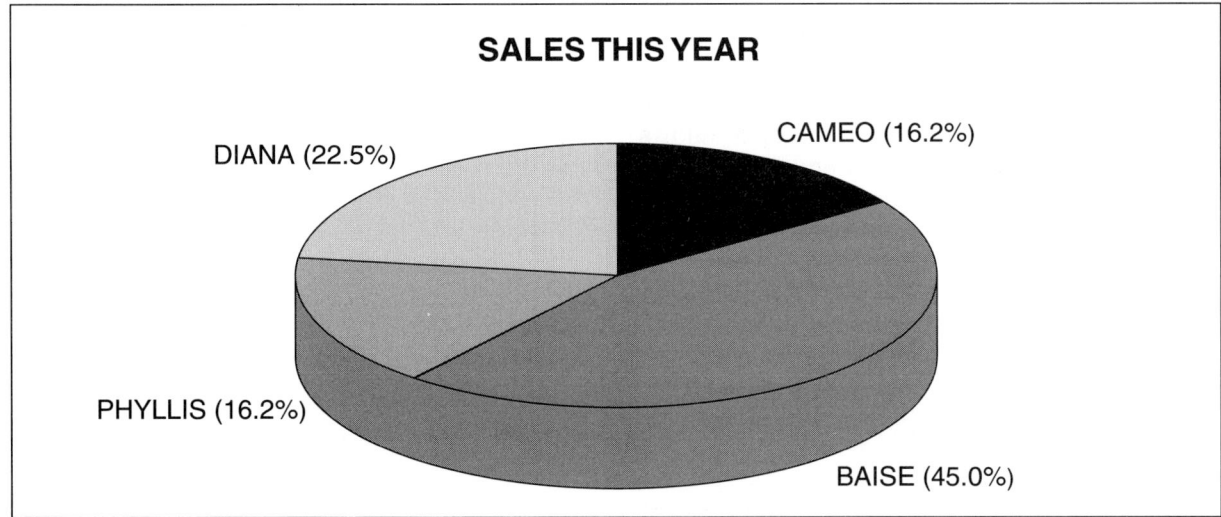

Figure 7.2.5 The use of computer software to present information.

Micros

Microcomputers have changed beyond all recognition since their initial development only 30 years ago. Modern microcomputers are now more powerful than mainframes ever were in the past. Technology is moving so fast that it is common for computers to become smaller, cheaper, faster, and more powerful each time they are updated. There are also new software packages being created continually. Recent developments have seen computers which can understand handwritten instructions on a touch-sensitive screen and machines which do not require a keyboard, but respond to voice activation.

Networking, or linking computer systems together, helps to improve the processing of information as well as communication within an organisation. Networks can be classified according to their location.

LAN (Local Area Network)

Most commonly, this is a network confined to one building with work areas containing microcomputers. These can be extended over an area of two or three miles.

WAN (Wide Area Network)

This is a computer network which is distributed nationally (or internationally) and makes use of telephone or satellite links.

By using LAN or WAN networks, an organisation has control over its own information processing, but also has access to the main database which may be held at head office. It also allows branches to communicate easily and quickly with each other and with head office.

The change from analogue signals, which were required to transmit at different frequencies, to a more flexible system called Digital, has made a lot of computer facilities available.

Digital signals are pulses which can be understood by computers. These are sent from one computer to another via a modem or similar device and may be accessed instantly.

Rather than rely on the traditional methods of sending information on hard copy through the post, electronic mail offers the opportunity to instantaneously transmit information to remote but linked computers. A further advantage of this system is the alarm device which informs recipients that the message is awaiting them.

Telex, Bureaufax and Intelpost are all different forms of electronic mail – where messages are sent over the telephone as electric signals which can be converted back into paper form at the other end. Privately-owned facsimile machines are also a form of electronic mail.

The most recent developments in electronic mail are computer-based systems. These allow people to send and receive messages and other information through their own 'electronic mailbox'.

The mailbox is a form of computer terminal linked to the telephone network, with a memory for storing messages and a means of putting messages into a system. A printer or typewriter is attached to allow messages to be printed as hard copy when required. Every user has a password to allow him or her to use the system. Word-processing facilities allow the message to be checked and corrected before it is sent.

When a message is sent, it can be to one mailbox or to a number of different mailboxes. This is handy when a memo or instruction has to be sent to all branches of a large organisation. On arrival at the recipient's mailbox, the message will be stored in an electronic memory until the mailbox is 'opened', that is, until the person checks to see the messages that have come in.

This service is particularly useful in a large organisation, where each office or department can have a mailbox and senior executives can have their own. This service will probably be extended so that almost everybody will be able to get in touch with everybody else through an electronic mailbox.

Telex and teletex provide an external electronic mail system that gives written messages with the security of 'answerback' codes which identify the sender and also the receiver.

Figure 7.2.6 A computer in use (courtesy of Mercury Communications).

finding out

PC 7.2.1.
COM 1.1
IT 1.3, 1.4

In groups of four, investigate the available computer technology within your school/college/centre.

Discuss the different uses to which the computers are put and whether there is a need to widen their availability.

Orders and instructions

Orders and instructions can take various forms. Amongst these are the documents that we have mentioned already, that is, memos, letters, fax messages etc., as well as receiving orders and instructions orally. Orally can refer to both face-to-face communications, and those over the telephone. We will be looking at the ways in which to deal with telephone calls in Element 8.2. You will also know how to deal with orders and instructions from your activities in Unit 4.

The basic difference between an order and an instruction is that an order tends to be a direct request to carry out a duty or activity. An instruction will probably involve more than this, such as some kind of description or background as well as the order.

TYPES OF BUSINESS INFORMATION

Broadly speaking, we must consider the types of business information in the following categories:

▼ internal business information between individuals or departments in the same organisation
▼ external business information between individuals or organisations
▼ basic enquiries or requests for information
▼ more complex enquiries involving a complaint or a problem
▼ formal or informal communication between individuals either within an organisation or outside the organisation
▼ matters which must be dealt with immediately and matters which are non-urgent
▼ matters involving a confidential subject matter or general information which is available to all

We will now look at the various types of business information which we have outlined above.

Enquiry

Enquiries, which may be either written or oral, usually involve an individual or organisation seeking information, advice or clarification about a certain matter. They may, for example, require information about a particular product or service which the organisation offers, or they may be asking about prices or availability. Depending on the approach made, the response to it will have to be either written or oral and, in some cases, both. Oral enquiries will need an immediate response as well as a follow-up letter to confirm what has been said on the telephone or in a face-to-face situation. Written enquiries can be dealt with by telephone but, again, will need a follow-up letter for confirmation.

Many organisations will have pre-prepared packs of information and standard word-processed letters so that their employees can quickly respond to typical enquiries without having to deal with them independently each time. Most enquirers will be seeking the same sort of information and a well-organised company will realise that it is better to invest in these information packs rather than waste valuable employee time preparing the same information time and time again.

Complaint

Again, with complaints the approach can be made either in person or via the telephone. In all cases, the organisation will expect its employees to deal promptly and courteously with the customer. If you refer to Element 9.1 you will find some suggestions about how to handle these situations.

Some customer complaints, particularly if the customer is there in person, should be dealt with immediately and efficiently. This may mean that only the necessary complaints documents are filled in at that time. Complaints can involve far more paperwork if the customer approaches the organisation by telephone or letter. Not only will the complaint have to be investigated and dealt with, but also the organisation will have to send out a written response, and contact the customer by telephone to assure them that the situation is being dealt with.

Formal business information

Business information which involves two organisations is usually of a formal nature. Letters requesting information or action will have to be responded to by telephone calls and formal business letters. Many individual customers will also approach an organisation formally, which might be by letter or personally. You should remember that dealing with a customer on any subject or problem is a formal situation, and should be treated accordingly. Customers will expect the organisation and its employees to behave in a professional manner, which will include addressing the customer correctly, making sure that all necessary paperwork is completed and that any promises made are fulfilled.

Informal business information

Generally speaking, informal business information is that which passes from individuals to others within the same organisation. It does not have to conform to the same kinds of rules that should be applied to business information involving external individuals. In this way, brief messages on notepads, handwritten memos and short messages on answerphones are all acceptable if you know the individual and you know that he or she does not expect you to respond in a formal manner. Although you may get to know customers quite well over a period of time, you should always adopt a more formal approach with them.

Urgent business information

No matter what kind of business information you are dealing with, the person involved will always expect you to give him or her priority; letters will often be marked as urgent; telephone messages will often say 'please phone back immediately'; and faxes may demand an immediate response. It would be very difficult for anyone to give equal priority to all of these demands. To some extent, you are the only person who will be able to judge whether you need to deal with something immediately or if it really is urgent. Obviously, if there is a problem that needs to be sorted out then this should be given priority and in this sense it is urgent. General enquiries need not be given immediate attention, but should not be put aside and forgotten about. It is very easy to get into the situation where you are dealing only with 'urgent' matters and as a consequence you fail to carry out all the other non-urgent things that need to be dealt with.

Non-urgent business information

Non-urgent matters or routine duties will make up the bulk of time and effort that you put into work. As we said earlier, it is easy to end up spending most of your time dealing with urgent matters and to forget the routine and non-urgent tasks that you should be paying some attention to. Whilst the urgent matters are probably more interesting and demanding, the non-urgent tasks make up the bulk of the job and, as such, need to be given time and effort in order to ensure they are carried out correctly and at the appropriate times. Remember that a non-urgent matter which has been pushed aside for a number of days will become an urgent matter as the deadline looms for its completion.

Confidential business information

There are two main types of confidential information which you are likely to encounter in the workplace:

▼ **confidential matters regarding the organisation itself, such as sales figures, complaints, customer records and internal problems**
▼ **confidential matters regarding customers or individuals who would prefer that this information is not made publicly known**

In both cases, it is often a question of who should be told and who should not be told. The general rule is that confidential matters regarding the organisation you work for should never be discussed or mentioned to anyone who is not an employee or directly involved with the organisation.

With regard to confidential matters relating to customers or other individuals, you will have to make a judgement about who else in your organisation needs to know this information. If a customer, for example, tells you that he or she is encountering money problems, then it is wise to inform the accounts department and the sales department so that they can make a judgement themselves about whether any action needs to be taken. Remember that the loyalty you have is to your organisation and not to the customer in this instance. You should not let personal friendships or the fact that you have been told something in confidence allow your organisation to suffer.

In some organisations you may be required to sign a non-disclosure or confidentiality agreement before commencing employment. If you work for the Civil Service or certain other government organisations, you may even have to sign the Official Secrets Act.

Public business information

As we mentioned earlier, many organisations have packs of information, order forms and price lists available for any individual or organisation on request. Any information which has appeared in booklets, newspapers, leaflets, documents or reports which are generally available to the public can be counted as being 'publicly available' and therefore not of a confidential nature. Individuals within an organisation will usually be told by their employers what information about the organisation is classified as publicly available.

7.2.2 *Process the information accurately*

PROCESS

In this performance criterion, you must process information accurately in the correct manner, using the right format and the right style. Remember that you should also pay attention to the fact that different documents are appropriate to different individual situations and purposes. If you are still unsure about which document you should use, it might be a good idea to read Element 7.2.1 again.

In order to cover this performance criterion, work through the activities under the following headings.

FIGURE IT OUT

PC 7.2.2
COM 1.1, 1.2, 1.3
IT 1.1, 1.2, 1.3

`00:30`

To cover the rest of this performance criterion, you will need to collect the names and addresses of all of the members of your group.

Prepare

Preparing information not only involves making sure that you have chosen the right format in which to present this information, but also that you have all the necessary details at hand in order to complete your preparation.

FIGURE IT OUT

**PC 7.2.2
COM 1.1, 1.2, 1.3
IT 1.1, 1.2, 1.3**

00:30

Using the information that you collected in the previous activity, prepare the following sets of lists:

- *the names and addresses in alphabetical order*
- *the names and addresses by postcode*
- *the names and addresses of those who live closest to your school/college/centre*
- *the names and addresses of those who live furthest away from your school/college/centre*

Copy

In many situations you will need to make sure that various individuals see particular business information. Your supervisor and colleagues may need to know the information that you have prepared and it is important that the copies that you create are identical to each other.

These days, copies of documents are usually made by using a photocopier, but however copies are made, you must be sure to include the correct information.

Copies of documents sent externally and internally will also be needed to file away for future reference.

FIGURE IT OUT

**PC 7.2.2
COM 1.1, 1.2, 1.3
IT 1.1, 1.2, 1.3**

00:30

Choose one of the lists that you prepared in the last activity to give to your tutor who needs to know who might be late in the mornings if there were to be a transport strike. In addition to the copy for your tutor, prepare further copies for each student who appears on the list.

Transmit

Transmitting information need not necessarily mean using electronic mail or a fax machine; we are using the word transmit in a much wider sense. If you pass on information by telephone or write it down and send it as a letter then you are still transmitting that information.

FIGURE IT OUT

PC 7.2.2
COM 1.1, 1.2, 1.3
IT 1.1, 1.2, 1.3

00:30

*B*efore you give the document to your tutor and the students involved, put the information on to a business document that you think is appropriate for this task.

Store

If you prepare business information on a computer then you will be able to save this as a file. If you have prepared information using a typewriter or it is handwritten then you will need to make sure that you can keep it safely and that you are able to find it again should it be required at a later date.

Storing information that has been prepared orally is somewhat more difficult. It is advisable to jot down some notes or reminders about what you have said and to whom you said it. In some organisations this problem is solved for you as all telephone conversations are routinely recorded on tape.

FIGURE IT OUT

PC 7.2.2
COM 1.1, 1.2, 1.3
IT 1.1, 1.2, 1.3

00:30

*I*f you have stored your information on computer, make a note of the file names and which drive these files have been saved on. If you have used a manual system, then make sure that you have filed the copies away in a safe place.

Retrieve

Retrieving information that has been stored on a computer is a simple matter provided that you can remember the file name and that you have saved it correctly. Handwritten or typed information that has been stored in more conventional filing cabinets or folders should be easy enough to find as long as you have filed them correctly.

FIGURE IT OUT

PC 7.2.2
COM 1.1, 1.2, 1.3
IT 1.1, 1.2, 1.3

`00:10`

Your tutor needs an extra copy of the document that you provided earlier to give to a colleague. Retrieve your file and produce a further copy.

7.2.3 Produce accurate processed documents using conventional business style and formats

7.2.4 Check that documents are legible and accurate

In order to fulfil these two performance criteria, you will have to produce four different business documents. They must be accurately processed; at least one must be produced using a computer; and at least one must make use of telecommunications.

Remember that the documents must use the correct business style and format and must be legible and accurate. You will have produced a number of business documents throughout this element and will have more than covered the requirements of these last two performance criteria, but you can use other business documents that you may have been asked to produce for other units. If you have a work placement, and provided the information is not of a confidential nature, then you will be able to use this as evidence for these performance criteria.

BUSINESS CONNECTION

PC 7.2

We have now looked at all the major ways of processing business documents. To test your memory and skill, complete the following business connection by turning complaint into enquiry. The last letter of each word or phrase is the first letter of the next word or phrase. To help you we have put in the first and last letter on each line, but you will have to do the rest.

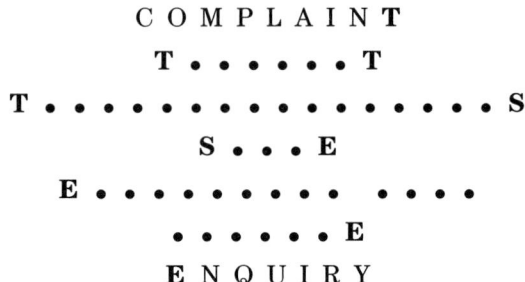

```
C O M P L A I N T
    T . . . . . . T
T . . . . . . . . . . . . . . . S
        S . . . E
    E . . . . . . . . . . . . .
        . . . . . . . E
    E N Q U I R Y
```

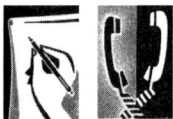

assignment

ELEMENT 7.2

PC 7.2.1–4
COM 1.4

For this assignment you will need to keep a file of any documents you have been responsible for processing either during the course of your studies, or whilst on a work placement. The documents must meet the following criteria:

- you should process at least four different business documents

- they must all be legible and contain accurate information
- one should be processed using a computer
- one should be processed using telecommunications
- you should use conventional business style and formats

element 7.3

PRESENT BUSINESS INFORMATION

Performance criteria

A student must:

1 Extract given types of **business information** from different sources.

2 **Record** the information accurately.

3 Produce and present a clear **summary** of the information.

4 Produce suitable, relevant **visual aids** to support the **summary**.

5 **Store** all documents so that they can be retrieved.

RANGE

Business information: enquiry, complaint; formal, informal; urgent, non-urgent; public, confidential

Record: written notes, key points, sources of information

Summary: information sources, list of key points, ideas for presentation

Visual aids: plan, chart, graph, memo, letter, notice, telephone message, fax message, electronic mail message, order, instruction

Store: alphabetical storage systems (by name, by subject), numerical storage systems (by file number, by date)

7.3.1 *Extract given types of business information from different sources*

7.3.2 *Record the information accurately*

BUSINESS INFORMATION

As you will remember, in Elements 7.1 and 7.2 we looked at various types of business information. For the purposes of this element, you should also consider information that can be gathered from the following sources:

▼ **visits to businesses**
▼ **interviews with business people**
▼ **existing files of information**
▼ **reference books**
▼ **leaflets and brochures**
▼ **other publicity material produced by businesses**

Since this element is essentially a practical one, we will be presenting you with a number of sources of information from which you are expected to extract, record, summarise, present and store various sorts of information. Each of the performance criteria addresses a particular aspect of this process.

For each of the range statements relating to the first performance criterion, we have simply provided you with an example of business information of that type. The second performance criterion, which asks you to record information accurately, will require you to extract and record information contained within each of these sources.

Enquiry

M & R COMPUTER SYSTEMS LTD
14 OLD CHURCH ROAD
NEWMARKET
SUFFOLK
TEL/FAX NO: 01403 777725

27 NOVEMBER 19..

Rodwell Stationers
Rodwell House
New Cut
GRAVESEND
Kent

Dear Sir/Madam

We are a recently established company in the computer services field. We require a reliable and responsive stationer who can provide us with a variety of different computer and non-computer related paper items.

We would be grateful to receive a full catalogue of your available products, your credit terms and delivery times and methods.

If possible, we would also like to be able to fax you a copy of our letterhead and logo, which we would like to have printed onto 2,000 sheets of 80 gsm cream bonded paper. Please inform us how quickly this order can be fulfilled and the approximate cost.

We look forward to hearing from you.

Yours faithfully

B Mercer (Mrs)
CHIEF BUYER

Figure 7.3.1 An enquiry from M & R Computer Systems, dated 27 November.

Complaint

M & R COMPUTER SYSTEMS LTD
14 OLD CHURCH ROAD
NEWMARKET
SUFFOLK
TEL/FAX NO: 01403 777725

25 MARCH 19..

Rodwell Stationers
Rodwell House
New Cut
GRAVESEND
Kent

Dear Sir/Madam

We are writing to you regarding our order number 2375, which was promptly delivered last Tuesday by the normal courier service.

Whilst the order was complete and intact, we must stress that the packaging was insufficient and poorly taped, and at some stage during transportation the parcel had split and was badly mended and re-sealed.

Upon opening the parcel we discovered that the majority of the computer stationery was soiled, torn or otherwise unusable. We would be grateful if you would supply us with another 5,000 sheets of continuous paper letterheads, as we feel unable to use what is left of the delivery.

We need this delivery to be made within the next 48 hours as we are running short of this stationery item. Could you please inform us whether you need the damaged delivery to be returned and how you intend to collect this. You may contact me on my normal extension number during office hours for confirmation of your actions.

Yours faithfully

B Mercer (Mrs)
CHIEF BUYER

Figure 7.3.2 A complaint from M & R Computer Systems, dated 25 March.

Formal business information

M & R COMPUTER SYSTEMS LTD
14 OLD CHURCH ROAD
NEWMARKET
SUFFOLK
TEL/FAX NO: 01403 777725

27 MARCH 19..

Rodwell Stationers
Rodwell House
New Cut
GRAVESEND
Kent

Dear Sir/Madam

Further to our letter of the 25 March, 19.., we have not received a response from you, despite several attempts to contact you by telephone. Since we could not obtain a replacement order from you within the required time, we have been forced to approach another printer to provide the urgent stationery.

Please cancel our order number 2375. We still await your instructions as to the collection of the damaged delivery. If we do not hear from you by return of post then we will assume that the damaged delivery items can be destroyed and we will be seeking the more permanent services of another printer.

Yours faithfully

B Mercer (Mrs)
CHIEF BUYER

Figure 7.3.3 An example of a formal business letter from M & R Computer Systems, dated 27 March.

Informal business information

RODWELL STATIONERS
RODWELL HOUSE
NEW CUT
GRAVESEND
KENT
KT21 9BR

29 March 19..

Mrs B Mercer
M & R Computer Systems Ltd
14 Old Church Road
NEWMARKET
Suffolk

Dear Brenda

Can I first say how sorry I am about the mess up regarding your last order. I am really sorry, but I have been away on holiday for the last ten days and nobody seems to have been doing my work.

I feel really bad about letting you down like this, and hope that you feel that you can trust us to give you a good service in the future. Please feel free to throw away the damaged order. I have today dispatched another 5,000 sheets of continuous paper letterheads, free of charge, in the hope that this can compensate you in some way. I have, of course, cancelled the order and I hope that we can put this problem behind us.

My best to you as always. I hope to hear from you soon.

Kind regards.

Doreen Rodwell
DIRECTOR

Figure 7.3.4 An example of an informal business letter from Rodwell Stationers, dated 29 March.

Urgent business information

M & R COMPUTER SYSTEMS LTD
14 OLD CHURCH ROAD
NEWMARKET
SUFFOLK
TEL/FAX NO: 01403 777725

FACSIMILE TRANSMISSION

TO: DOREEN RODWELL

FROM: BRENDA MERCER

DATE: 1 April 19..

No, of course, your response is not OK. - April Fool!

Sorry for the tone of my last letter, but we were running desperately short and needed to do something quickly. Hence this fax. As you will already know, we have recently landed a very big order with a chain of supermarkets to provide some computerised tills. I desperately need you to sort out some quotes for me for a whole range of new stationery and till rolls.

Please telephone immediately for details. You will need to have your price list to hand and details of how quickly you can turn these orders around, as we will need them by next Wednesday. This is very important and I am sure you will not let me down.

Brenda

Figure 7.3.5 An example of an urgent fax from M & R Computer Systems, dated 1 April.

Non-urgent business information

RODWELL STATIONERS
RODWELL HOUSE
NEW CUT
GRAVESEND
KENT
KT21 9BR

14 April 19..

Mrs B Mercer
M & R Computer Systems Ltd
14 Old Church Road
NEWMARKET
Suffolk

Dear Brenda

I hope everything went well with your supermarket chain deal and that our supplies all reached you on time and in good condition.

We were hoping that you were slightly less busy than you have been over the past three or four months and could join us in London for a meal on us. Evenings are OK, but perhaps you would like to pop down and spend a weekend at our expense as it would be nice to meet at last.

Perhaps you could get in touch when you have a little time and we can compare diaries to find a mutually convenient date.

Kind regards.

Doreen Rodwell
DIRECTOR

Figure 7.3.6 An example of a non-urgent letter from Rodwell Stationers, dated 14 April.

Public business information

M & R COMPUTER SYSTEMS LTD
14 OLD CHURCH ROAD
NEWMARKET
SUFFOLK
TEL/FAX NO: 01403 777725

P R E S S   R E L E A S E

EMBARGO DATE: 2 MAY 19..

M & R COMPUTER SYSTEMS LTD, a local business based in the
Newmarket area and jointly run by Brenda Mercer and Michael
Roberts, are proud to announce the confirmation and delivery of
revolutionary computerised tills to Halfways Superstores Plc.

This multi-million pound deal not only guarantees the long-term
prospects of the 73 employees at M & R COMPUTER SYSTEMS LTD, but
also means that the company can expand and is actively recruiting
for a further 22 new members of staff.

This will be a great boost to the local economy as it is the
company's policy to purchase the majority of its components and
materials from within the immediate area.

Brenda Mercer, co-director, is quoted as saying "After working
so hard for the past 12 years and really believing in what we do,
all our efforts have finally paid off. We would like to thank
our staff, our suppliers and our bank for their continued
support, even through the bad times."

For further information please contact Brenda Mercer on the above
telephone number.

Figure 7.3.7 An example of a press release issued by M & R Computer Systems.

Confidential business information

RODWELL STATIONERS
RODWELL HOUSE
NEW CUT
GRAVESEND
KENT
KT21 9BR

15 June 19..

STRICTLY CONFIDENTIAL

Mrs B Mercer
M & R Computer Systems Ltd
14 Old Church Road
NEWMARKET
Suffolk

Dear Brenda

Having been through the detailed accounts for the last year, some rather alarming information has come to light.

It appears that someone at your end has been adding items to the orders. I am not suggesting that this is necessarily someone acting dishonestly. These have been added by telephone after we have received your written order. I have investigated the situation and I can only tell you that the person ringing us is a woman. Obviously, we have assumed it was you.

This has apparently happened four times over the past six months, the total addition invoice value is £296.07. It really only came to my attention after the auditors provided me with a list of overdue accounts. I know that you pay promptly and I have checked the written orders and the items in question were added by us after verbal instructions.

I am unsure how to handle this, and would appreciate a call to see if we can tackle this together. I will not take any further action at our end until I have heard from you.

Kind regards.

Doreen Rodwell
DIRECTOR

Figure 7.3.8 An example of a confidential letter from Rodwell Stationers, dated 15 June.

Written notes

RECORD

Not only will you need to respond to different sorts of business information, but you may also need to transfer or record the information contained in the document in another place. Some documents are quite straightforward, such as orders or queries, and others are more complicated and require immediate action, such as complaints and urgent enquiries. In this part of the performance criterion you will need to re-read the various documents shown in this element and extract the main points included in them.

Written notes are usually made either for personal use or to be given to another member of staff. You should try to get into the habit of writing detailed notes to yourself even if you think, at the time, that you will understand a quickly written note when you have to deal with that information or task later. In a busy office you may forget to deal immediately with the contents of a note which, if looked at again later, might not make sense. Think about other people and how difficult it will be for them to understand a brief and garbled message. It does save time in the long run to write yourself or someone else a proper note so that there is no misunderstanding and it can be dealt with promptly and without having to refer back to the person who wrote the note in the first place.

We will now test your note-writing skills.

FIGURE IT OUT

PC 7.3.2
COM 1.2, 1.3, 1.4

00:15

Referring to the letter from M & R Computer Systems of the 27 November, put yourself in the position of Doreen Rodwell's assistant, to whom the letter has been sent. Read the letter and write a brief and clear note to Doreen, outlining the contents of the letter and what action she needs to take.

The key to writing a note is to make sure that not only is it clear, but also that it is as brief and to the point as possible. Even the most complicated problems can be reduced to a handful of words that give the reader clear information upon which to act.

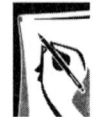  

FIGURE IT OUT

PC 7.3.2
COM 1.2, 1.3, 1.4

00:15

*A*gain, in the role of assistant to Mrs Rodwell, read the letter from M & R Computer Systems dated 25 March. Write notes to the following individuals who would have some involvement in, and responsibility for, processing and delivering Mrs Mercer's order:

- *Doreen Rodwell*
- *the dispatch manager*
- *the accounting department*
- *the sales department*
- *the courier representative*

Key points

Even in the shortest of communications, there will be a number of key points to be dealt with. These will need to be identified and passed on to the relevant individual(s). Key points are very similar to written notes, except that they are usually given to individuals in the form of a memorandum instead of a more informal note left on their desks.

FIGURE IT OUT

PC 7.3.2
COM 1.2, 1.3, 1.4

00:15

*A*gain, in the role of the assistant to Mrs Rodwell, read the letter dated 27 March and create a memorandum that should be circulated to all of the individuals mentioned in the previous activity. You should detail the main complaints that Mrs Mercer has outlined in both this letter and her previous letter of the 25 March. You may mark this memorandum 'for information', but if you feel that there are any particular lessons to be learned from this situation, you should also mention them in your memo.

Sometimes, individuals will need a list of key points before they respond to a letter or complaint. Someone who is aware of the particular situation will be asked to outline the main issues and suggest how they could best be dealt with.

PC 7.3.2
COM 1.2, 1.3, 1.4

00:15

*I*n the role of Doreen Rodwell's personal assistant, you have been asked to provide her with a list of key points regarding the problems with M & R Computer Systems. Assuming that her letter of 29 March has not yet been written, list the key points that she would need to know in order to respond in the way that she has chosen.

Sources of information

Sources of information that are relevant to any business organisation can be found in a variety of places. Under normal circumstances an organisation will be aware of developments in its area of activity, and routinely monitor the local and national press and any relevant magazines. For larger organisations this gathering of information can involve several people on a full-time basis. Indeed, some larger organisations have library facilities and members of staff who are wholly devoted to the collection, storage and distribution of relevant information.

PC 7.3.2
COM 1.2, 1.3, 1.4

00:15

*I*n the role of Doreen Rodwell's personal assistant, and referring to the fax from M & R Computer Systems dated 1 April, prepare a memorandum to inform all relevant members of staff about the news included in that fax. It obviously contains important news that is relevant to a number of individuals and departments.

7.3.3 *Produce and present a clear summary of the information*

SUMMARY

Information gathered from various sources can often be presented in a format which is difficult to understand, or simply too long-winded for many people to take in, and so there is a definite need for someone to read and understand the information and reduce it to its barest points. In this performance criterion we will look at how to translate information from a longer and more complicated original version to a form that can be easily understood by any relevant individual.

Here are some guidelines to help you prepare a summary:

1 Read through the whole document first. Do not worry if you do not understand everything that is being said in the document; just try to get the general meaning.

2 Re-read the document more thoroughly, highlighting anything you think to be particularly important. You can also cross out any information that you do not feel to be of importance.

3 Make a list of the items that you feel are important to include.

4 Compare your list with the original document to make sure that you have not missed anything out.

5 Write a draft summary and ask your boss to have a look at it to see if you are on the right track.

6 If you and your boss are happy with your draft, then you can write your final summary.

7 Finally, show the summary to someone who has not seen the original document that you worked from. If they understand your summary then it is a good one.

Information sources

It is expected that you will accurately state the information source from which you have prepared your summary. If it is from a magazine article, for example, you should state the writer's name, the original title of the article, the name of the magazine and the date that it was published. In the case of a book, you should quote the author, the title, the publisher, the publication date and the pages which you have summarised. If you are using a report, press release or other form of information source, you should always attempt to identify who has written the original and when it was published or released. If relevant, you should also quote the title that was given to the original piece.

In some cases you may be summarising from a number of different sources. You should mention all of the original material that was used in the preparation of the summary. It is normal practice for these sources of information to be mentioned at the end of the summary in alphabetical order according to the writer's surname.

List of key points

For some purposes and sources of information, a list of key points might be provided in addition to a summary. Key points are quite useful as they can outline the most important aspects of the original source of information without really needing to create whole sentences, paragraphs and conclusions. Key points are also useful for inclusion in memoranda, as they can put across important information in an easy-to-read form.

In cases when even a summary is too long, key points mean that the readers need not go through the summary unless they want or have to.

Ideas for presentation

Many integrated software packages now allow you to choose a variety of formats and styles of presentation. Under normal circumstances, a series of bullet points would be ideal for a list of key points. For a summary, a more traditional approach is normally expected and will consist of a series of short paragraphs. You may, of course, be asked to present summarised information or key points in other ways, for example as overhead projection sheets which can then be used for larger presentations to a number of different people.

As we will see in the next performance criterion of this element, there are many other ways of presenting information. We have already mentioned memoranda and summaries, but there are a number of different ways to present, in particular, numerical data in a more acceptable and understandable format. These, of course, include charts, tables, graphs and diagrams and can, again, be produced to a high standard with appropriate computer software.

So far, we have been assuming that you will have to summarise or identify the key points of a written source of information, but you might have to present information that has been obtained from other sources, such as telephone calls. This information is normally presented in the form of a telephone message and we will look at this in the next performance criterion.

Finally, as technology has improved, new ways of presenting information have become available to businesses. Electronic mail, for example, allows you to send text, charts, tables and other styles of presentation to any number of other terminals. Fax messages are perhaps a little less flexible and merely send a copy of the sheets which you have prepared in whatever format you thought was appropriate.

7.3.4 *Produce suitable, relevant visual aids to support the summary*

VISUAL AIDS

Whenever you need to display, explain or pass on information, particularly in the form of a summary, it is a good idea to try to use as many visual aids as possible. Not only is this a quick way of getting information across, but it is also an easy way of putting figures, in particular, into a simple format. In this performance criterion we will be looking at the types of visual aids which can help you present visual information to an audience or colleague in a work situation.

Plan

There are two ways of using plans as visual aids. The first involves creating a list of actions and procedures that need to be undertaken in relation to the business information, or as a result of it. Most business information is passed on with a request to do something; it is all very well to present people with information in whatever format you decide upon, but they need to know clearly what is expected of them once they have read and understood the information. It is, therefore, a good idea to offer a series of suggestions as to how they can best carry out the request.

The other way of using plans as visual aids is to present information in the form of maps and plans of buildings showing the location of machinery, equipment, staff and office furniture. Holiday brochures, for example, often include floor plans of the rooms, chalets, flats or apartments and will indicate clearly where certain furniture or facilities are located. This is a quick and easy way of describing something that is purely visual. Not only does it take up less space but it also makes the information easier to picture in your mind.

Chart

Charts are used to make complicated information easier for the reader to understand. If you had to explain in words the organisational structure of a business, this would not only take a very long time, but would also be very confusing and hard to follow. An organisation chart simply and clearly shows names, job titles, departments and who is responsible for different sections.

Although it may be difficult to get the hang of computer software that allows you to create charts, it is well worth trying to learn this. In the meantime, handdrawn charts are acceptable but you should always make sure that any lines are drawn with a ruler. Remember that, as with any visual aid such as a chart, people are more inclined to look at this and understand it than page after page of text.

Graph

This is another way of displaying information. There are a great many software packages that can quickly and efficiently do this job for you. All you need do is put the information on to a spreadsheet and then select the type of graph that you prefer. In this way, you can create line graphs, bar charts, pie charts and three-dimensional graphs and charts. Again, people will take in this information far more easily than if it were explained in words.

Memo

Memoranda are used for internal communications, usually between different departments or individuals within the same organisation. They are normally much shorter than business letters and tend to deal with a single subject. If your memorandum needs to contain a number of different points then it is acceptable to number them. Memos are usually signed rather than initialled. For an example of the format of a memorandum, refer back to Element 7.1.

Letter

In Element 7.1 we saw how a letter should be laid out. If you are unsure about this, then you should look at the sample letters that were included at the beginning of this element. If you are writing to a business you will be expected to use the correct format and to include any necessary information, such as the name, address, telephone number, fax number of your organisation and references. It is a good idea to adopt the correct style of business letter for all your correspondence from now on as it is a very useful skill to acquire.

Notice

Another form of internal communication is the notice. This is an ideal way of getting messages across to members of staff without going to the trouble of distributing memoranda or letters to each and every one of them. Most organisations will have a noticeboard and employers will use this to relay a number of urgent and non-urgent messages to the workforce. It is important to remember that noticeboards need to be maintained and any old or out-of-date notices removed, otherwise they may clutter the noticeboard and make it difficult for people to see new messages. Notices should be kept short and to the point and should use a large font or pitch if they are word processed. You should also make sure that a notice is error-free as this not only confuses the message, but could be very embarrassing for the person who wrote it.

Telephone message

If you work in an office you will probably be expected to take messages for people who are not available from time to time. If this is the case, you should follow the organisation's procedures for greeting the caller and listen carefully, extract and record the information that is being passed on to you appropriately. Many calls will simply require you to write down on a telephone message pad the caller's name, company, telephone number and the message or actions required. Using telephone message pads is a far more efficient way of recording this information than simply scribbling a note on a piece of paper. Provided that messages have been written with care and an appreciation of the needs of the caller, however, then they are both capable of passing on the necessary information to the person concerned. If you refer to Element 8.2 you will see an example of a telephone message form.

Fax message

Fax messages can take several forms. They might be fully blocked and correctly formatted business letters that have simply been sent by fax instead of post, or brief and informal notes. Just like telephone calls, fax messages can also be put into urgent and non-urgent categories. The major advantage that you have with a fax is that the information contained within it does not have to be translated on to another form or document. This is, of course, assuming that you are not expected to do a summary of the content of a fax.

Fax messages provide the person receiving them with a true and accurate copy of the original document prepared by the sender, and so there can be no real chance of mis-interpreting the content of a fax as the person it was intended for will receive the full version.

Electronic mail message

Many organisations enjoy the benefits of an internal electronic mail system. With this system, they are able to relay written and visual messages to any other computer terminal in the organisation. The technology behind this simply consists of a series of computers linked together via a cable (and perhaps a modem) to a central computer system which then relays the electronic mail message onto the intended destination (which is another computer terminal). Each of the terminals will have an identity known to the software system and it will be able to identify exactly where the message is intended to go.

Electronic mail messages can also provide a copy of the original document which can be printed out via the receiving individual's computer. Alternatively, the message can simply be read from the screen and then deleted from the system if a record of the message does not need to be kept.

Order and instruction

There are two aspects to consider with regard to orders and instructions:

▼ **the way in which the order or instruction has been formatted by the sender for ease of understanding and prompt action**
▼ **the way in which the order or instruction is translated by the receiver and turned into a format that can be acted upon**

The main thing to consider is that the order or instruction needs to be translated in such a way that the meaning or requirements of the order or instruction are not lost.

7.3.5 *Store all documents so that they can be retrieved*

STORE

For this performance criterion, you must prove that you are competent at storing documents so that they can be easily retrieved at a later date. In order to do this you should make sure that your portfolio of evidence is suitably labelled and indexed so that each document you save in it is actually filed away. The use of divider cards and plastic pockets will make the portfolio look more attractive and will also make you more efficient when filing pieces of work away in alphabetical or numerical order.

Another way to gain evidence for this performance criterion is to keep a record of all the filing that you are asked to do on your work placement, in your part-time job or in a simulated situation within your study centre.

We have covered the different methods and ways of filing documents for ease of retrieval in some detail in Unit 8. If you are studying Unit 8 as part of your course you will not need much assistance with the alphabetical and numerical methods of filing. If, on the other hand, Unit 8 is not one of your options, then the following two headings will be of some assistance to you. Remember that computerised filing systems allow you to file documents both alphabetically and numerically. Obviously, if either alphabetical or numerical filing is used, then it is important that the person responsible for the storage of documents is fully aware of the system so that any errors or mistakes are avoided. If a document is filed incorrectly then a great deal of time could be lost looking for it.

Alphabetical storage systems (by name, by subject)

Alphabetical storage systems are the most common method of filing documents in industry. Alphabetical filing simply means that the documents contained in each file are placed in strict alphabetical order, using the first letter of the surname. In addition, each of the files in the filing cabinet is also filed in strict alphabetical order, with A at the front or beginning and Z at the end.

Each of the files will have a label placed along the top edge of the suspension folder and this will show the letter of the alphabet under which the files are housed.

When filing alphabetically by name, the first letter of the surname determines where the file should be placed; for example **A**bbey will come before **B**ond. When the first letters of the surname are identical, then the second and subsequent letters will determine where the file goes; for example, B**l**ack will come before B**r**own and Ca**l**dwell will come before Ca**n**well.

When filing alphabetically by subject, the first letter of the title of the subject or topic contained in the file will also determine where the file should be housed. In the same way as for the filing of names in alphabetical order, if the first letter of the subject is the same, then the second and subsequent letters will determine where they

are placed; for example science would come before sociology and history would come before humanities.

Numerical storage systems (by file number, by date)

Numerical storage systems are also used regularly in industry, although they are a little more complex than alphabetical filing systems, mainly because a card index is needed as well.

When storing files by number a label is also used, but this time it will state the number(s) of the files contained within that section. The files will be in number order, with the lowest number at the front and the highest number at the back. The card index will also be in numerical order and each card will state the details of the file contained within the system under a particular number. Sometimes files can be stored under a combination of alphabetical and numerical systems and this is known as alpha-numerical filing.

When files are housed in date order, for example at a travel agents where the information relates to departure and arrival dates, then each month will have a section in the filing cabinet. The files contained under each month will be in numerical order and the labels will state both the month and the day of the month. This method of filing by date order is known as chronological filing.

BUSINESS CONNECTION

PC 7.3

We have now looked at all the major ways of presenting business documents. To test your memory and skill, complete the following business connection by turning visual aids into letter. The last letter of each word or phrase is the first letter of the next word or phrase. To help you we have put in the first and last letter on each line, but you will have to do the rest.

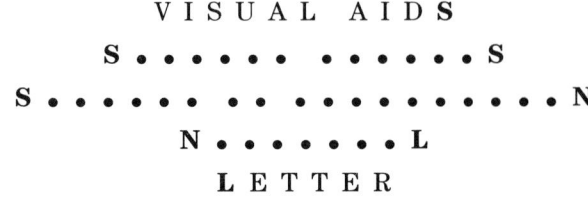

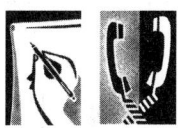

assignment

ELEMENT 7.3

PC 7.3.1–5
COM 1.1, 1.3, 1.4

This element assignment can be linked to the one that you completed in Element 7.2 if you wish. For the purposes of completing this assignment you should choose two different types of business information. You can gather your information from any visits you have made, any interviews you have undertaken, from files, reference books, leaflets and publicity materials you have collected.

Once you have collected your information you will have to give a presentation to the remainder of your group and teaching team. This presentation will explain two different types of business information. Your talk should concentrate on the following:

- the two different types of business information you have chosen
- whether the information is confidential or public information, and the difference between the two

You should include some visual aids in your presentation. Make sure that you keep copies of these for your portfolio, as well as a copy of your written notes and the documentation you are presenting.

WORDSEARCH

How many of the words listed below can you find? They run backwards and forwards across and up and down the grid.

```
K  L  O  V  R  E  T  U  I  V  M  O  D  E  M  O  F  P
L  W  R  I  T  T  E  N  I  N  F  O  R  M  A  T  A  L
E  V  A  S  O  O  P  K  L  M  X  C  Y  K  O  P  X  D
C  O  L  U  E  J  E  V  S  T  I  P  R  J  M  E  M  O
A  B  J  A  K  I  M  X  C  W  R  O  I  P  L  X  E  S
F  I  J  L  O  P  R  B  C  D  E  F  U  I  L  M  S  O
O  U  T  S  O  U  R  G  E  N  T  P  Q  I  J  K  S  M
T  T  I  P  L  C  O  P  Y  X  M  L  N  Q  R  P  A  E
E  X  M  O  L  K  N  O  N  U  R  G  E  N  T  I  G  L
C  O  S  M  I  J  T  P  J  M  C  V  B  I  X  L  E  M
A  B  N  O  T  I  C  E  X  Y  Z  M  I  L  L  P  E  D
F  O  A  M  M  T  X  C  B  M  O  T  T  G  I  P  I  G
W  O  R  D  P  R  O  C  E  S  S  E  D  N  I  J  K  L
O  R  T  M  C  A  G  H  L  M  O  Q  R  I  P  P  G  G
I  D  M  G  F  H  R  R  S  M  P  O  S  L  B  B  D  D
O  E  P  H  X  C  O  S  G  O  L  G  N  I  P  E  E  K
E  R  X  C  Z  Y  T  R  M  P  W  R  T  F  K  E  E  P
J  X  C  I  L  I  A  M  C  I  N  O  R  T  C  E  L  E
```

CHART	FORMAT	ORDER
COPY	KEEPING LOGS	TRANSMIT
ELECTRONIC MAIL	MEMO	URGENT
ENQUIRY	MODEM	VISUAL
FACE TO FACE	NON URGENT	WORD PROCESSED
FAX MESSAGE	NOTICE	WRITTEN
FILING	ORAL	

element 8.1

HANDLE MAIL

Performance criteria

A student must:

1 Identify and give examples of **procedures for handling incoming** and **outgoing mail**.

2 Open **incoming mail** without damaging its contents.

3 Distribute **incoming mail** promptly to the correct people following identified procedures.

4 Ensure that **outgoing mail** is securely **fastened/sealed**.

5 Ensure that addresses on **outgoing mail** are legible and correct.

6 Complete **mail records** clearly and accurately.

7 Report any problems or mistakes to the correct person immediately.

RANGE

Procedures for handling incoming mail: receiving mail, opening mail; dealing with enclosures, dealing with remittances, dealing with items marked urgent or confidential; distributing mail, recording mail movement, dealing with problems or mistakes

Procedures for handling outgoing mail: fastening and sealing mail, addressing mail, identifying postage rate (first class, second class, airmail)

Incoming mail: letters, parcels; to the organisation, to an individual

Outgoing mail: letters, parcels; to destinations outside the organisation, to individuals within the organisation

Fastened/sealed: manual seal, self-seal, protective wrapping

Mail records: of incoming mail, of outgoing mail

8.1.1 Identify and give examples of procedures for handling incoming and outgoing mail

As the whole of this element is very practical, we have not included an element assignment. For the purposes of providing evidence of your competence to deal with both incoming and outgoing mail, you need to keep logs of your mail-handling duties on a regular basis throughout the programme of study. These logs can be completed whilst on a work placement or by simulation at the centre in which you are studying this course. You should include in your evidence logs of both incoming and outgoing mail, as well as items with enclosures and items marked urgent or confidential. You should also include notes in your evidence on how you have dealt with any problems you may have encountered in the handling of the mail.

PROCEDURES FOR HANDLING INCOMING MAIL

Every organisation, whatever its size or type of activity, will have procedures which it will expect its employees to abide by. Some of these procedures will relate to day-to-day tasks that staff members carry out. Others, on the other hand, will be procedures which have been put into place in order to deal with any unexpected events or, indeed, cases of emergency.

Whoever is responsible for dealing with the organisation's post each day must be aware of the guidelines regarding both incoming and outgoing mail.

The term **incoming mail** refers to the post which is delivered to the organisation at the beginning of each day. This may include the following documents:

▼ **letters for specific members of staff**
▼ **general letters**
▼ **invoices**
▼ **quotations**
▼ **estimates**
▼ **job applications**
▼ **orders**
▼ **statements**
▼ **advertising material**

Receiving and opening mail

It is important that all mail is opened and distributed as quickly and efficiently as possible so that the office staff can begin their work immediately. One member of the mailroom staff might have the responsibility of distributing the mail, and this is often a junior member of staff. The job involves a good knowledge of the layout of the organisation, particularly if this is large and spread over an extensive area.

An organised routine is important if the mail is to be opened, sorted and distributed quickly. The following are guidelines:

1. Sort the mail first, taking out any envelopes marked 'private' or 'personal' as these will not be opened but delivered to the individual still sealed.
2. Open the mail using a letter knife along the edge of the envelopes. This will ensure that the contents are not damaged in any way. Sometimes electrically operated letter openers, which remove a tiny strip of paper from the edge of the envelope, are used.
3. Date stamp the documents. Sometimes the time will also appear on the stamp. Care should be taken not to mask any typed or written information. Personal or private mail should be date stamped on the envelope.

Dealing with enclosures

Always check the mail for enclosures. An enclosure is an item which has been sent with the letter and could be a cheque, leaflet, photograph or catalogue. Any paperclips should be removed and the enclosures stapled to the accompanying documents. This will ensure that the items are not parted during the distribution of the mail.

Dealing with remittances

Some organisations record the receipt of cheque payments at this stage in a remittances book. This lists the date the remittance (amount of money) was received, from whom, the amount received and a signature by the person opening the mail. In the same way, it is also the policy of some smaller organisations to keep a register of incoming mail.

Dealing with items marked urgent or confidential

In a similar way to the way in which you would deal with private or personal mail, you will also have to deal with mail which is marked urgent or confidential. Urgent mail should have an 'urgent' sticker attached to it and be taken to the person to whom it is addressed immediately. Confidential mail should have a 'confidential' sticker attached to it and should be left unopened. If the mail is urgent or confidential, then it should be handed to the person concerned rather than leaving it on his or her desk.

Distributing mail

The exact destination of the mail can be located by items such as the FOR THE ATTENTION OF line, the subject heading on the letter, or a reference given at the top of the letter.

If none of these items appears, the person sorting the mail needs to read through the letter quickly to determine who should receive it within the organisation. In some instances, more than one person might need to see a letter, so it will need to be photocopied and sent to the relevant people, or a circulation slip or routing slip attached to the document. The most common use for one of these slips is for books or magazines which are expensive to copy for several people. The slip lists the names of the people to see the document, their department and a column for them to initial once they have read the literature. It also states the name and department of the person to whom the document should be returned.

In a small organisation, the person responsible for distributing the mail may have to walk only from one room to another with the post. Distribution is, however, much more involved the larger the organisation becomes. Distributing mail in a very large organisation can be a full-time job for several employees. They will be involved in taking vast amounts of mail to several floors of a large establishment. They may use trolleys, sectioned into the names of individuals, much like filing cabinets, to do this.

Often the person delivering the incoming mail to each department or section within the organisation will also collect the outgoing mail at the same time. This will be taken back to the mail room for sorting.

Some mail, for example RECORDED or REGISTERED MAIL must be signed for when it is delivered. This procedure is carried out so that there is proof that the item has been delivered and received.

165

Recording mail movement

Some smaller organisations still keep a record of outgoing mail in the same way that they would the incoming mail. This record allows them to keep a check on the amount of money spent on postage and gives a form of clarification as to when mail was actually dispatched from the office. This method of recording postage is normally the responsibility of one individual and allows the monitoring of cost to be ongoing.

Dealing with problems or mistakes

If you are confronted with a parcel or package which has been delivered to your organisation in a damaged state, you should refuse to sign for it or to accept delivery. Alternatively, you may think that a parcel that has been sent to your organisation is suspicious in some way. If your organisation deals with confidential material and is likely to be targeted for a letter bomb, vigilance is of the utmost importance. Do not handle the item. Clear the area of personnel immediately and call the police.

PROCEDURES FOR HANDLING OUTGOING MAIL

Unless an organisation is very small, it is usual for a franking machine to be used instead of stamps. If an organisation does still use stamps, a record will normally be kept of the stamps used, including the details of the correspondence sent.

A franking machine prints the value of postage in red. The value can be changed very easily, in much the same way as a date stamp is changed. In addition, it allows space for a printed advertisement for the organisation, as well as the time and date of posting. This avoids the somewhat tedious task of licking and sticking stamps, and recording their use. Regular envelopes can be franked directly, but more bulky items require an adhesive label, which is franked before being stuck onto the mail.

Franking machines can be hired or purchased from the manufacturers, although a licence has to be obtained from the Post Office before the machine can be used. Although there is no charge for this licence, the Post Office will set the meter on the machine to keep a record of units bought, used and still in credit to the organisation on its machine.

The person dealing with the outgoing mail will use the following guidelines:

1 Sort the mail into first and second class.
2 Change the date on the franking machine.
3 Check the value of the postage on the franking machine.
4 Check the quality of the printer on the franking machine.
5 Check the credit left in the franking machine – once this reaches a certain pre-determined level, the machine will have to be re-credited by contacting the Post Office. This can be

done via the telephone on the more up-to-date machines which are fitted with a mini-modem, linked to the franking machine via the telephone. With these newer machines it is no longer necessary for the organisation to take the machine into the Post Office itself. Those machines which are not linked directly to the Post Office will do the same job, although it is more time consuming to have to take them to the Post Office to be credited. It is also necessary for these machines to be accompanied by a book which the Post Office clerk will complete each time the machine is credited with units.

6 Add any necessary adhesive stickers to the mail, such as 'urgent', 'airmail', 'recorded delivery'.

Once the mail has been franked it can by-pass the Post Office sorting office and be handed over the counter at a Post Office. It is either tied in bundles or placed in a special Post Office bag designed for this use.

Fastening and sealing mail

Another duty of the mailroom assistant is to weigh any parcels which have been prepared ready for dispatch from the organisation. This is done within the department and the parcels are taken to the Post Office with the rest of the mail at the end of each day. Manual or electronic scales are used to weigh items and calculate the postage due on each. As we will see in Element 8.1.4, there are particular ways of ensuring that outgoing mail is securely fastened and sealed.

Addressing mail

Stick-on labels are usually used for parcels. The name and address of the sender should also be displayed clearly on the parcel so that it can be returned should there be a problem with delivery. A further precaution is to include the name and address of both the sender and the recipient inside the parcel.

Identifying postage rate (first class, second class, airmail)

Obviously certain items will need to be sent more quickly than others, and one of the duties of anybody dealing regularly with the outgoing mail is to identify whether the letter needs to travel to its destination by first or second class post or, indeed, airmail. Naturally there is a cost implication here, and it may be company policy for everything to be sent by second class mail, unless a senior member of staff authorises that it is sent first class. Normally first class mail will arrive at the destination the following day, whilst this cannot be guaranteed with second class mail.

FIGURE IT OUT

PC 8.1.1
COM 1.2

`00:20`

Y̲ou are going to be away on holiday for two weeks and you need to leave a detailed list of instructions for the temporary member of staff who will be dealing with the outgoing mail. Ensure that you include details regarding the preparation of parcels in your guidelines.

8.1.2 Open incoming mail without damaging its contents

8.1.3 Distribute incoming mail promptly to the correct people following identified procedures

We have put these two performance criteria together as they are both very practical in nature and require you to prove your competence in carrying out these duties.

INCOMING MAIL

In order to provide evidence that you are able to open and distribute incoming mail correctly, you will need to keep a log of the times when you have carried out this task. You might be able to compile this log from a work placement or part-time job. Alternatively, if you are responsible for this duty at the centre in which you are studying this programme, your tutor will need to observe you opening the mail and will sign the log to reinforce the fact that you have carried out the task accurately and efficiently.

You will find very concise details about how to deal with incoming mail and ensure that it reaches the correct member of staff in the previous sections of this unit. Before you ask your tutor to observe you doing this, you may find it useful to read the sections again.

Letters and parcels to the organisation or individuals

All organisations have procedures for dealing with incoming mail and staff will be expected to follow these.

Letters or parcels arriving at an organisation might be addressed to a specific individual, but sometimes they will not include a name or department. In these cases, the mail will have to be opened, read briefly to work out which member of staff needs to see the correspondence and then passed to the appropriate person.

Some documents are delivered by the company's messengers and are inter-departmental (they do not go out of the organisation at all). These are internal mail and are often in the form of memoranda (see Figure 8.1.2). The documents are placed in large envelopes which have space on the front for the name of each recipient to be listed. After the document has been opened the name is crossed off and the envelope is ready to be used again (see Figure 8.1.1).

Larger organisations will have a department which deals with the internal and external (both incoming and outgoing) mail on a regular basis, but smaller ones will probably give the responsibility of dealing with the post to one or two individuals as part of their regular duties.

The person distributing the incoming mail may also collect some items for the outgoing mail during the course of their deliveries. However, the busiest time is obviously in the afternoon when the day's post is being prepared for posting. The mailroom probably stipulates a deadline or final collection time, after which no mail will be accepted. This may be necessary to ensure that the staff process the mail in time for final posting times at the Post Office.

It has become common in recent years for the mailroom to deal with all aspects of the outgoing mail. The secretary or clerk sending out the letter, quotation or invoice simply prepares the envelope and leaves it sealed in the 'outgoing mail tray'. The junior or messenger from the mailroom collects this and places it in the batch of mail for either first or second class posting.

FOR INTERNAL USE ONLY
(CANCEL PREVIOUS ADDRESS)

NAME	NAME
DEPT	DEPT
LOCATION	LOCATION

NAME	NAME
DEPT	DEPT
LOCATION	LOCATION

NAME	NAME
DEPT	DEPT
LOCATION	LOCATION

NAME	NAME
DEPT	DEPT
LOCATION	LOCATION

NAME	NAME
DEPT	DEPT
LOCATION	LOCATION

NAME	NAME
DEPT	DEPT
LOCATION	LOCATION

NAME	NAME
DEPT	DEPT
LOCATION	LOCATION

PLEASE USE REVERSE

Figure 8.1.1 An internal envelope.

B·A·A

Date

from

to

Figure 8.1.2 An example of memorandum paper used by industry for internal communication.

8.1.4 **Ensure that outgoing mail is securely fastened/sealed**

FASTENED/ SEALED (MANUAL-SEAL, SELF-SEAL, PROTECTIVE WRAPPING)

When wrapping parcels, take care to ensure that they are secure and not likely to be damaged during transit. The Post Office deals with hundreds of parcels each day, and although it takes every possible care, it is inevitable that they will meet with some knocks and bumps on their way. Any damage to parcels can cause delay or loss and expense to your organisation.

Parcels should be packed as follows.

Inner packing

If items are fragile it is important to use plenty of suitable soft cushioning to absorb any knocks the parcel might receive. Items such as crushed newspaper, kitchen paper, tissue paper or corrugated paper can be used as inner packaging, as well as plastic or polystyrene chips and air-bubble polythene. The box should be filled with the inner packaging so that the contents do not move around. If the items are not fragile but are awkward shapes, make sure that no part of the item projects through the packaging.

Even non-fragile items like sheets and clothing can still be damaged in transit, and care must also be taken when preparing parcels of these. Corrugated paper could also be used before the application of a layer of strong brown paper, sealed with self-adhesive tape and tied with string.

Outer packaging

It is advisable to use a strong box, such as one that is used to carry groceries from a supermarket, or one that is supplied by the Royal Mail. The sizes of these vary and they can be bought at most Post Offices. In addition to special boxes, padded envelopes, known as 'Jiffy' bags, can also be purchased. Where these are not necessary, it is still advisable to use a layer of corrugated paper before wrapping in strong brown paper.

Sealing

If a box is being used it should be firmly sealed along each of the edges with self-adhesive tape.

When just corrugated paper and strong brown paper are being used, the parcel should be sealed with tape and then tied with string, knotting the string tightly where it crosses.

8.1.5 *Ensure that addresses on outgoing mail are legible and correct*

We have dealt with the different ways of fastening and sealing both parcels and letters in this unit. For the purposes of proving your competence in this, and the previous, performance criteria, you have to be responsible for dispatching the outgoing mail. This may be achieved through role-play exercises or you may be able to prove your competence in this from a work placement or part-time job. Again your tutor will have to observe you carrying out the duty and sign to say that you have met all the criteria.

OUTGOING MAIL

Letters

Letters should always be addressed clearly. The Post Office requests that the address on an envelope be in the bottom half only so that none of the name and address is obscured by the postmark. Always try to use the correct postcode, and the preferred way to include this is on a line of its own. The name of the town is often typed in capitals, and if the letter is for a particular individual within the organisation, then a 'for the attention of' line can be included on the envelope.

Remember to mark the envelope 'private', 'personal' or 'confidential' if this is necessary.

Parcels

Care should always be taken to ensure that parcels are securely fastened and sealed. In addition, you should make sure that the address the parcel is being sent to is clearly marked on the parcel, as well as your own address. By showing both the sender's and the recipient's addresses, this will help the Royal Mail to make sure that the parcel does not get lost if it cannot be delivered.

The procedure for sending out parcels is as follows:

1 *Weigh the parcel* using manual or electronic scales. The electronic scales automatically calculate the postage due. If using manual scales then the operator will need to refer to the Postal Rates Guide issued by the Post Office.
2 *Frank the label* with the necessary amount of postage and stick it to the parcel.
3 *Stamp the parcel* with any necessary stickers, e.g. 'fragile', 'urgent' or 'handle with care'.

The parcel is now ready to be taken to the Post Office for handing over to the counter clerk.

All parcels and packages that are being sent overseas need a declaration label which describes the contents. This includes airmail and surface mail. The reason for this is to inform the Customs Officers in the country to which the parcel is being sent of its contents. Some articles have to have a tax paid on them by the recipient. This is called a **duty**. Duty is put on some goods to discourage people from sending them. Gifts may be allowed in duty free in certain countries if described on the label as 'gifts'.

To destinations outside the organisation

If a letter or parcel is to be sent out of an organisation, then it will have to travel by Royal Mail or by a courier service. The fact that you yourself will not be responsible for the delivery of the post will make it even more important that you are accurate and thorough in the way you prepare the post for dispatch.

To individuals within the organisation

If the letter or parcel is for someone who works within the same organisation as yourself, then it will travel through the internal mail system. This does not mean, however, that less care can be taken in the way the letter or parcel is prepared. The rules regarding the confidentiality of the letter or parcel stipulated by the company for which you work should also be taken into account, as should the speed with which the post is delivered to the person concerned.

8.1.6 Complete mail records clearly and correctly

8.1.7 Report any problems or mistakes to the correct person immediately

MAIL RECORDS

In order to complete these two performance criteria you must keep a record of the incoming and outgoing mail that you have been responsible for during your course of study. Mail can be recorded by using a variety of forms: while you are on your work placement, the organisation you are working for might provide you with their own forms or your tutor will provide you with some to use.

Mail records of incoming mail

You may be asked to list the mail which the organisation receives through the external post each day. This incoming mail log will itemise the different types of mail being received and will allow you to state whether or not any remittance (payment) was attached or whether any other enclosures were included in the envelope. An incoming mail log will also allow you to state how you dealt with the different items of mail by showing how you distributed it or circulated it, and to whom you sent it for attention.

Mail records of outgoing mail

The records you will have to keep may be simple postage books, which are used to record the mail being sent out of an organisation each day. In addition, a postage book is a good way of recording how much is being spent on postage by the organisation on a regular basis.

If the organisation has a franking machine, then obviously it will not be necessary to record the amount of postage being spent, but a log may still be kept of the outgoing mail so that there is a record of when it was sent should evidence be required at a later date.

B U S I N E S S   C O N N E C T I O N

PC 8.1

We have now looked at all the major ways of handling mail. To test your memory and skill, complete the following business connection by turning receiving mail into second class. The last letter of each word or phrase is the first letter of the next word or phrase. To help you we have put in the first and last letter on each line, but you will have to do the rest.

```
R E C E I V I N G   M A I L
      L . . . . R
      R . . . . D
D . . . . . . . . . . S
S E C O N D   C L A S S
```

element 8.2

PROCESS TELEPHONE CALLS

Performance criteria

A student must:

1 Identify and give examples of **procedures for dealing with incoming** and **outgoing** telephone **calls**.
2 Identify and give examples of **procedures for dealing with and acting on emergency calls**.
3 Identify and give examples of **possible problems** and actions to be taken in the event of problems and emergencies.
4 Follow **procedures for dealing with incoming calls**.
5 Follow **procedures for dealing with outgoing calls**.
6 Communicate clearly, politely and tactfully whilst dealing with **incoming** and outgoing calls.

RANGE

Procedures for dealing with incoming calls: use of house style, speed of response, identification of callers, identification of the purpose of calls, transferring calls, taking and passing on messages, closing calls

Incoming calls: to the organisation, to an individual

Procedures for dealing with outgoing calls: looking up telephone numbers, correct dialling, establishing contact, stating purpose of calls, closing calls, follow-up action

Procedures for dealing with and acting on emergency calls: making calls for 999 emergency services, connecting calls, giving details of the emergency; taking and passing messages

Possible problems: recipient of urgent call unavailable, interrupted calls, difficulty in obtaining numbers, incorrect messages

8.2.1 *Identify and give examples of procedures for dealing with incoming and outgoing telephone calls*

PROCEDURES FOR DEALING WITH INCOMING CALLS

The manner in which a customer or, indeed, anybody who telephones an organisation is dealt with can reflect strongly on the impression that person receives of the organisation as a whole. Most organisations have guidelines for dealing with incoming calls, which they expect their staff to follow. There are, however, some general points to remember when communication is via the telephone:

▼ **pick up the telephone as quickly as possible**
▼ **have a pen and paper handy to take a message**
▼ **be polite and helpful**
▼ **if callers need information that is not readily available, then offer to phone them back**
▼ **if you have promised to call back, then do not forget to do so**
▼ **remember that unless the call is put on 'hold', callers will be able to hear what you are saying**
▼ **do not give out confidential information without checking with a supervisor first**
▼ **if the call is interrupted and the caller is cut off, then it is normally the person who made the call who rings back**
▼ **it is acceptable to ask callers to repeat a message in order to make sure that facts or figures are correct or a complicated name is spelt correctly. If there is still uncertainty, repeat the message back to them**
▼ **if asked for details or information, make sure that all the necessary information is to hand before calling back**
▼ **quote figures in pairs as they are easier to understand and remember**
▼ **complete the call by saying 'thank you'**

Use of house style

House style refers to the manner in which all individuals within an organisation are instructed to answer the telephone. This may simply mean that they always state the name of the organisation or their own name, or that they answer with a phrase such as 'good morning/afternoon', the name of the organisation, their own name and 'how may I help you?' The use of a consistent house style will give anybody calling the organisation the impression of an organised and efficient business.

Speed and style of response

Have you ever been greeted by a receptionist in an unwelcoming way? How did that make you feel? We are sure you did not feel pleased about it!

All organisations require their reception staff to greet visitors politely, promptly and courteously, and the same applies to dealing with telephone callers. Some organisations have a policy of answering the telephone after only three rings and guaranteeing customers that their request will be dealt with in a certain amount of time. Organisations have realised that a prompt response may well be one of the criteria that a customer uses when deciding whether to purchase something from them. It is also likely that efficiency in this area will then be related to friends, relatives and business contacts.

Identification of callers and purpose of call

Once callers have been greeted in a courteous and helpful manner, it is then necessary to identify who they are and how you can be of assistance to them. The caller might know exactly what he or she requires and who can help her or him and, in this case, it is a very simple matter to transfer the call to the appropriate person or department. On the other hand, callers might be new to your organisation and might not know who they need to speak to in order to get the information they require.

In this instance, you must identify the purpose of the call. By asking what information or help callers require, you will be able to ascertain which member of staff will be the most useful to them. Before transferring the call it is wise to ask for the caller's name so that you can inform the member of staff concerned who it is he or she will be speaking to before you put the caller through.

Transferring calls

When you have established the reason for the call and the best person to deal with it, you can transfer the call:

1   Keep the caller informed of what you are doing at all times, so tell him or her that you are transferring the call and that the person who can help will be able to do so shortly. Tell the caller who will be dealing with him or her.

2   Contact the member of staff concerned via his or her extension number and state the name of the caller and the purpose of the call. When doing this make sure that the caller is put on 'hold' so that he or she is unable to hear your conversation with the member of staff.

3   Go back to the caller and tell him or her that the member of staff is available and that you are putting the call through to the extension number.

Taking and passing on messages

If a caller wants someone who is unavailable, use the following procedure:

1   Once you have established that the person

the caller wants to speak to is unavailable, ask if you or someone else can help.

2 If there is no one who can help, either ask the caller to ring back, or promise that the person he or she wanted to speak to will call back.

3 If necessary, take a message and ensure that it gets to the right person.

Closing calls

Your role, when answering the telephone, is to bring the request to a satisfactory conclusion. This may mean that you have to spend more time than you would like in dealing with one particular call or making several other calls as a result of one call from a customer.

Before you can say the call has been dealt with satisfactorily, you must be sure that the caller has received all the information or advice that he or she requires. The caller should be the one to end the call; after all, he or she is the one who rang and is paying for the call. It is always polite to thank callers for phoning the organisation and to assure them that if they do require any further information or help, then they should not hesitate to call again.

PRIDE

TELEPHONE TECHNIQUES

Telephone contact is often the first "view" a customer has of your dealership. Those of your staff who spend a large part of their time speaking to customers over the "phone" fulfil a particularly vital role. They can instantly create the "right" or "wrong" image and therefore need to be aware of the importance of telephone handling skills in every department within the dealership.

Objectives:

* To show the importance of the job of the telephone user.

* To provide the confidence and ability to deal with every caller and their needs. ·

* To show how colleagues can be helped to improve the service they give to customers.

CONTENT

PREPARATION	What the customer expects
	Attitudes
	Knowledge required
	The work area
RESPONSE	Answering the "phone"
	Use of names
	Qualifying the call
	Listening and taking control
INTEREST	Representing the Company
	Commitment
	Showing Empathy
	Calling back
DECISION MAKING	How to say "no"
	Offering alternatives
	Keeping promises
	Following up other staff
EXIT	Transferring calls
	How to say goodbye
	Making a record of it
	Follow up
	14.

DURATION: One day

ATTENDED BY: Key telephone users within the dealership and held after the launch event. Dates and locations to be advised.

Figure 8.2.1 Peugeot Talbot is very aware of the importance of customer awareness. Its training for staff includes lengthy sessions on providing good service, particularly when on the telephone.

INCOMING CALLS TO THE ORGANISATION AND TO AN INDIVIDUAL

A great many requests from customers will be by telephone. If the request is to be dealt with in a manner which the customer feels is satisfactory, then the members of staff concerned should make sure that they have all the information which is likely to be required by customers readily available and that they are conversant with the products and services the organisation offers.

Remember that telephone calls are different from face-to-face conversations in three ways:

▼ **all explanations must be given in words; you cannot use non-verbal communication to help make a point clear**

▼ **your attitude cannot be indicated by your face, it must be conveyed in your voice**

177

▼ voices sound different over the telephone

The following are guidelines for receptionists in how to deal with callers by telephone:

▼ **do not let the telephone ring longer than necessary. If the person who normally answers the telephone is busy, you should answer it**
▼ **if the call is external (from outside) answer in the organisation's house style**
▼ **if the call is internal (from inside) answer with 'reception' followed by your own name**
▼ **pick up the receiver with the hand you do not write with. This leaves your writing hand free to write down any messages**
▼ **have a pen and pad by the telephone. If possible use a special telephone message form (see Figure 8.2.2). The headings on the form will help remind you of questions you may need to ask. In addition, the recipient will be able to locate this special form on a desk which may be full of plain paper**
▼ **if the caller requires information which will take some time to collect, make a note of the details, take the caller's name and number and offer to ring him or her back in a short time – but make sure you do!**
▼ **if the call is not for you and the person required is not available, ask if you can take a message**
▼ **when you have written down the message, read it back to the caller to ensure that you have all the details correct**
▼ **take all messages to the person concerned immediately or leave in a prominent place**
▼ **if the caller does not wish to leave a message, offer to ask the person he or she wants to speak to to call back later**
▼ **take a note of the name, address and telephone number of the caller**
▼ **do not use slang expressions on the telephone – this leaves a sloppy impression and sounds too familiar and impolite**

PROCEDURES FOR DEALING WITH OUTGOING CALLS

The key to making efficient telephone calls lies in having all the necessary information to hand. Obviously, it would not give a good impression of your organisation if you made a call to a customer or supplier and then had to leave them waiting while you went off to find additional facts or figures. Before making any call make sure that you have all you need beside you and that you know exactly what you want to say.

Looking up telephone numbers

If you have to call a number of people on a regular basis, then you will probably have a record of relevant telephone numbers in an index card box or in a diary or telephone book. This record will contain the dialling code, the telephone number of the organisation and any appropriate extension numbers.

If, however, you have to look up the telephone number before you can make the call, then you should remember the following points:

▼ **the telephone directory and the *Yellow Pages* directory are printed in alphabetical order**
▼ **there may be several surnames which are identical and you should make sure that you know the initials of the individual concerned or the exact name of the organisation**
▼ **make sure the number shown in the**

TELEPHONE MESSAGE FORM

TO .... DEPARTMENT ....

FROM ....

NAME OF COMPANY ....

DEPARTMENT ....

TELEPHONE NUMBER .... EXTENSION ....

FAX NUMBER .... TELEX NUMBER ....

<u>MESSAGE</u>

<u>ANY ACTION TAKEN</u>

MESSAGE TAKEN BY ....

DATE .... TIME ....

Figure 8.2.2 A telephone message form.

telephone directory is the correct one for the person or organisation you wish to contact

▼ write down the telephone number for yourself and look up the STD code (if applicable)

Correct dialling, establishing contact and stating purpose of calls

Once you have found the telephone number you require, make sure that you are careful to dial the correct number. Remember that all calls cost money and any wrong numbers will also be charged to your organisation's telephone bill.

Once the organisation or person you have dialled answers the telephone, listen carefully to make sure that you have reached the right place. Tell the person who answers the telephone exactly what you require or who you wish to speak to and then give him or her a chance to pass on any necessary information to you. Be thorough if you need to explain what your particular problem or request is; you cannot be transferred to the correct extension if you have not given all the facts.

FIGURE IT OUT

PC 8.2.1
COM 1.2, 1.3

00:10

*U*sing the blank telephone message form in Figure 8.2.2, draw and complete one for the following message which was left on the answerphone today. Remember to leave out any unnecessary pieces of information, but be sure to include the important ones.

Hello, my name is Susan Yallop. I would like to leave a message for Mr David Suffield please. I should have phoned earlier, but I have been a bit busy doing my shopping and picking the children up from school, and when I got in the car to drive home I found I had a flat battery, so it took me a lot longer than I expected. Would you please tell Mr Suffield that Jon has telephoned, and that his cold is a lot better now. He phoned to say that he will be able to make the deadline by Friday of next week (I can't remember the date, perhaps you would be good enough to find that out for me). He knows this means it will be later than originally planned. The whole manuscript will be bigger than previously stated because there are several bits and pieces which he didn't think would have to be included at first but now he really does think it would be best to put them in. Will you also tell him that we still haven't had any money for the last lot of stuff we sent. Thanks ever so much, I had better go now and get some dinner on, otherwise the children won't get fed. How is everything with you? Hope you are all well. Bye for now.

finding out

PC 8.2.1
COM 1.2, 1.3
IT 1.1, 1.2, 1.3

Using your local *Yellow Pages* directory, find the following. Make a list of their telephone numbers and word process the list before giving it to your tutor:

- a florist
- a unisex hairdresser
- the local football stadium
- a pet shop
- a dentist
- a medical centre
- the local hospital
- the local police station
- a veterinary surgeon
- a local leisure centre

Closing calls

Once you have completed the call to the person or organisation then it will be up to you to close the call as you made the call and are paying for it. Make sure that all the details you have written down are covered and that you will not have to make another call to get more information that you may have forgotten. Thank the person you have spoken to for his or her assistance and say goodbye.

Follow-up action

Once you have closed the call, it is important that you record the details or information gained by making it. Write down any details you have been given immediately. By doing this straightaway you will not have to rely on your memory later when you might forget some of the information if your train of thought is disturbed.

If you have made the call on behalf of someone else, then you should make sure that you pass on all the relevant information to him or her immediately. The date and time of the call should be noted in case you have to provide evidence in the future of when the call was made.

8.2.2 *Identify and give examples of procedures for dealing with and acting on emergency calls*

PROCEDURES FOR DEALING WITH AND ACTING ON EMERGENCY CALLS

Making calls for 999 emergency services, connecting calls and giving details of the emergency

You might, one day, have to deal with an emergency situation and this could be at work, home or anywhere. You might be the only person who is able or available to deal with the emergency and the seeking of professional help will therefore be up to you. At work, the following situations might arise:

▼ **an accident at your workplace which requires an ambulance to be summoned**
▼ **a security threat or incident which requires the police to be called**
▼ **a fire or the threat of fire at your workplace which requires the fire brigade to be summoned**

The obvious way to summon help from any of the emergency services is to dial 999. This number is a direct link with these services and your call will be received by trained personnel.

Once your call has been connected, you will be asked a series of questions, which may include the following:

▼ **where is the emergency?**
▼ **what is the nature of the emergency?**
▼ **what telephone number are you calling from?**

Having received this information the switchboard personnel will put the dispatch of the relevant service into action.

You must remember that, as in all calls, the person receiving the call will require you to be as calm as possible and to give the information in a clear voice which is easy to understand. Take care to give all the information you have and do not be tempted to over-dramatise the situation; only the facts are needed.

A 999 call should never be made unless an emergency situation has arisen. Whilst the services are dealing with an unnecessary call they may be unable to attend a real emergency.

Taking and passing messages

As a result of making the call to the emergency services, you might be given instructions or messages to pass on to someone else, such as details of the estimated arrival time of the ambulance which you will have to pass on to the first aider in temporary control of the situation. If you are given such information, write it down. Do not rely on your memory. Such situations can sometimes cause confusion and panic. If you write down any information you receive, there will be less chance that you pass on incorrect information.

As well as taking messages and passing them on at the time of the incident, you might have to contact people to inform them of what has happened. You may have to speak to relatives of the injured or sick person to tell them the details of the hospital that the injured person has been taken to. Try to put yourself in the position of the person at the other end of the telephone. Do not over-dramatise here either, just give the facts. Try to be understanding, patient and tactful and assure the person that you are still available for assistance should he or she require it from you or from the organisation.

FIGURE IT OUT

PC 8.2.2
COM 1.1, 1.2

00:15

*I*n pairs, think about and write down the action that you think a receptionist would need to take if somebody who was visiting the organisation was suddenly taken ill in the reception area. Remember that they would not just dial 999 immediately. Compare your thoughts with those of the rest of your group.

8.2.3 Identify and give examples of possible problems and actions to be taken in the event of problems and emergencies

POSSIBLE PROBLEMS

We all know that things do not always go as planned. When making telephone calls difficulties might be encountered which make the simple task much more complicated than originally expected. In this section we look at possible problems and how we would deal with them if we were to encounter them.

Recipient of urgent call unavailable

Earlier, we discussed how it was preferable for all calls to be taken to a satisfactory conclusion. However, this does not always happen; sometimes we have to settle for the next best alternative.

If you received a telephone call which was described as urgent and the caller wished to speak to one individual in particular, then you would ask for the caller's name and try to connect him or her. You may then find that the person is not available and that you have to think about the alternatives available to you. The same would apply to you if you were trying to make an urgent phone call to someone who was unavailable.

In such circumstances, as a caller, we would have to settle for second best and, when taking a message, we would have to offer the caller the next best alternative. The following actions could be taken if the person you are calling is unavailable:

▼ **leave a message with someone to pass on to them**
▼ **stress that it is very urgent and that**

you need to speak to him or her as soon as possible
▼ if it is possible, give an outline of what the call is about so that the person taking the message is aware of the situation
▼ make sure you leave your name, telephone number and extension number with the person taking the call so that there is no problem in passing this information on

The following actions could be taken if the person your caller wishes to speak to urgently is not available when he or she phones your organisation:

▼ offer to take the message yourself
▼ offer to find someone else who might be able to help
▼ assure the caller that you will deal with the situation and that you will get the specified person to contact him or her as soon as possible
▼ write everything down
▼ be sure to get the message to the specified person at the earliest possible moment

Interrupted calls

If you find yourself in the situation where you are taking a telephone call and someone enters the office wishing to speak to you, then you should be sure to deal with it in the correct way. Interrupted calls cost callers money and they would not be pleased if you were to leave them holding on for any length of time whilst you spoke to someone who was standing beside you. When this situation occurs you should remember the following:

▼ the caller is paying for the call
▼ the person who is in the same room as you may have to wait
▼ you can indicate to the person in the room with you that you will only be a few minutes. If it is an emergency, then you will be able to tell by his or her manner that you have to close the call

because your attention is needed urgently
▼ if it is unavoidable that you have to keep the caller waiting, then you should apologise and offer to call them back

Some telephone systems have the facility to inform you whilst you are speaking on the telephone that another call is waiting. This can sometimes be regarded as an interruption as the line is disturbed intermittently by a beeping noise. The caller may wonder what this noise is and you should explain that you have another call waiting and offer to call them back.

Difficulty in obtaining numbers

Difficulty in obtaining numbers can occur for the following reasons:

▼ the organisation or person may have a fault on the line
▼ the organisation or person may have changed the number
▼ the organisation or person may be constantly engaged, either because of pressure of work, or because a telephone has been left off the hook by mistake
▼ you may be dialling incorrectly or have copied down a number or the dialling code wrongly from the telephone book

If you find you are unable to contact a particular telephone number for any length of time, then first of all you should double-check that you have dialled the correct number. If this proves to be the problem, then you should amend any records you keep which include this number.

If, on the other hand, it is not an error on your part but a fault or problem with the telephone of the organisation or person concerned, then you should telephone 151 to report the fault and try to contact the individual or business by another means.

Incorrect messages

We have already covered the need to ensure that all details taken on a telephone message form are correct, legible and accurately noted. Much time and effort, not to mention the reputation of the organisation, can be lost if information is incorrectly passed from one person to another. Be sure to double-check all information before passing it on. This includes dates, names, addresses, telephone and extension numbers as well as facts and figures.

8.2.4 **Follow procedures for dealing with incoming calls**

8.2.5 **Follow procedures for dealing with outgoing calls**

8.2.6 **Communicate clearly, politely and tactfully whilst dealing with incoming and outgoing calls**

These performance criteria are practical in nature. You must prove that you are competent in dealing with the procedures involved in carrying out these tasks by means of records you have kept of the outgoing calls you have made and the incoming calls you have dealt with. In addition, you must show that you can communicate clearly, politely and tactfully whilst dealing with these calls. You can obtain this evidence by keeping a log of the calls you have dealt with either at your workplace, in a part-time job, or in a simulated situation within your study centre. The logs should be authenticated by the person who is supervising you at the time. You will also need to be observed by your tutor carrying out this task and he or she will complete a check list which lists the qualities you must prove in order to claim competence.

Because this whole element is so practical, you will not have to complete an element assignment in order to provide evidence. This evidence can be collected on an on-going basis throughout the duration of your course of study. You should, however, make sure that you provide some notes in your portfolio which prove that you are aware of the procedures for dealing with incoming, outgoing and emergency calls. The notes should give an example of each of these types of calls, as well as solutions to any problems that might be encountered.

BUSINESS CONNECTION

PC 8.2

We have now looked at all the major ways of processing telephone calls. To test your memory and skill, complete the following business connection by turning outgoing calls into dialling. The last letter of each word or phrase is the first letter of the next word or phrase. To help you we have put in the first and last letter on each line, but you will have to do the rest.

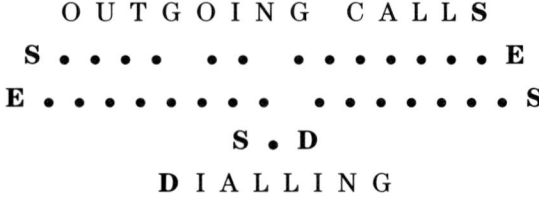

OUTGOING CALLS

S . . . . E

E . . . . S

S . D

DIALLING

element 8.3

FILE AND RETRIEVE DOCUMENTS

Performance criteria

A student must:

1 Identify and give examples of **procedures for filing documents**.

2 File documents in the correct place and sequence **as instructed**.

3 Retrieve documents **as instructed**.

4 Record **document movements** correctly.

RANGE

Procedures for filing documents: paper based, computer based; alphabetical order, numerical order, date order, for safe and neat storage, for rapid retrieval

As instructed: orally, in writing; by manager, by colleague

Document movements: into file, from file; to manager(s), to others; document absent card, file absent card

8.3.1 *Identify and give examples of procedures for filing documents*

PROCEDURES FOR FILING DOCUMENTS

Paper-based filing

The safe and secure storage of information and the easy access or retrieval of that information is imperative if an organisation is to function successfully and efficiently.

'Filing' or 'indexing' is the basis of record-keeping and entails the processing, arranging and storing of documents in an efficient system which will allow the easy retrieval of that information when required. The documents are placed in consecutive order and preserved in that system until they are required for reference. This is carried out in many different forms – a telephone directory is an index of alphabetical names and addresses and your own address book is also a method of indexing in alphabetical order.

So, what are the basic techniques required to ensure that the storage and retrieval of information and documents is efficient? The procedure for filing paper copies is as follows:

1 Ensure that the papers which have been passed for filing have been marked in some way to indicate that they are ready for storing.
2 Remove any paperclips and staple documents together – this will ensure that they do not get separated during the filing process.
3 Sort the papers into order so that they are grouped appropriately for the system being used (see pages 190–3).

Staff who undertake filing should also:

▼ organise each individual file in date order, with the most recent documents at the top or front
▼ be neat with the documents – curled edges can easily become torn
▼ file daily if possible – this makes it less of a chore and also ensures that the files are up to date
▼ follow organisational procedure regarding file 'out' or 'absent' cards (we look at these in the final performance criterion of this element)
▼ chase up all overdue files regularly, i.e. when they have been borrowed by another member of staff or department, by using a bring forward or follow-up system (see Figure 8.3.1)
▼ use a cross-reference system whenever a file is known by more than one name
▼ 'thin out' files when necessary. There will be an organisational policy regarding the length of time documents are held in the system. When they become obsolete or out of date they may be transferred to the 'archives' – an additional storage area where files are stored in boxes in case they are required for reference
▼ be aware of health and safety regarding filing cabinets. Always close drawers after you have used them and lock drawers and cabinets before leaving the office at night
▼ always ask for help if you are unsure where something should be filed, and do not be afraid to offer ideas if you think the system could be more efficient with some improvements

Computer-based filing

A database is a computer-based filing system. It is a common 'pool' of information organised in such a way that it can be accessed by a great number of users, possibly for many different uses. Therefore, instead of each department within an organisation keeping and maintaining its own set

FOLLOW UP FORM

		DATE
NAME		TELEPHONE NUMBER
ADDRESS		LETTER DATE
SUBJECT		
REMARKS		
RETURN TO	ON	
	ON	
	ON	

Figure 8.3.1 A follow-up system form.

of files, they are grouped together to form a database.

Such databases have advantages over traditional filing systems:

▼ **there is no unnecessary duplication of information, which is more economical, and is also more effective in keeping information up to date**
▼ **there is less chance of inconsistency of information**
▼ **comprehensive information is more readily available**
▼ **any enquiries can be dealt with 'on demand' rather than by going through the normally tedious process of obtaining files**

Electronic databases are normally defined under two main systems.

Centralised systems

In a centralised system, all processing of information is carried out by one central computer, even though it may be linked to terminals. This means that each of the offices or departments may have its own terminals, but the information is stored and retrieved by the central computer.

Distributing systems

This system allows for some processing of information to be carried out by the terminals. These terminals have their own storage and retrieval programs so information can be input and manipulated on them, rather than just on the central computer.

Microfilm is another type of computer-based filing system. It is a method of using film not only to condense the space occupied by documents, but also to preserve old or valuable documents by ensuring they are not handled too much. The original documents are photographed and processed on to the computer which is used to access the information required, by 'scrolling' through the film. The specific page of a document can then be viewed on the screen of the computer and, if necessary, printed. Libraries tend to use this method as they store such huge amounts of information, as well as some business organisations, such as banks which use them for storing customers' statements of accounts.

Any information stored on computer must be protected against loss or damage. Organisations which use this method of storage and retrieval must ensure that:

▼ **back up copies of disks are made and safely stored**
▼ **passwords are used by staff with access to the computer, and that these are changed regularly**
▼ **if necessary and as an addition to passwords, user codes are used. These codes are known only to those who are authorised to access the information and/or specific files or documents stored on the computer**

Alphabetical order

This method refers to the filing of documents according to the first letter of the surname and tends to be the most common form of filing adopted in business organisations. This is normally the first letter of the surname of the correspondent, although in a personnel department files could be arranged in alphabetical order, determined by the first letter of the surname of the member of staff.

Advantages:

▼ **it is a convenient and easy-to-understand system**
▼ **it requires no indexing, unlike numerical filing (see pages 191–2)**
▼ **it is useful for incorporating miscellaneous documents**

Disadvantages:

▼ **it can become very large and cumbersome**
▼ **confusion can occur when names are the same or similar**
▼ **cross referencing is necessary as there is a possibility that files may be requested under different names**

Some rules for alphabetical filing include the following:

▼ **take the first letter of the surname and then each letter after that, e.g.:**
  Bronson, Brian
  Brown, John
  Browne, Margaret
▼ **if the surname is the same, place the first name or initial in alphabetical order, e.g.:**
  Jones, David
  Jones, John
  Jones, William
▼ **if the surname and the first name are the same, file by second name or initial, e.g.:**
  Smith, Brian A
  Smith, Brian D
  Smith, Brian P
▼ **treat surname prefixes as part of the name and all names beginning with M', Mc or Mac as if they were spelt with Mac, e.g.:**
  McConnell, Maud
  McGreig, Walter
  MacMasters, Philip
▼ **file all 'St' surnames as if they were spelt Saint, e.g.:**
  St John, Ian
  St Luke's Church
  St Mary's Hospital
▼ **ignore titles, e.g.:**
  Brown, Sir Michael
  Green, Lady Jessica
  Simms, Major Duncan
▼ **ignore words like 'The' and 'A' in the name of an organisation, e.g.:**
  Card Shop, The
  Office Equipment Centre, The
  Tea Shoppe, The
▼ **numbers should be filed as if spelt in full, e.g.:**
  55 Club, The
  99 Boutique, The
  22 Association, The

FIGURE IT OUT

PC 8.3.1
COM 1.2

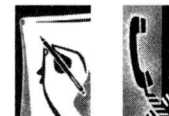

00:30

*P*lace *the following list of names in alphabetical order:*

Henderson, Paul
Cooke, Michael
Hunter, Anne
Hunter, Tony
Woodfield, Angela
Jones, Richard
Simpson, Jake
St Clair, Alice
Hywell, Ryan
Connell, Steven
Compton, Peter
McDonald, Sally
Harvey, Brian
Anderson, John
Seargeant, Mary
Sergeant, Desmond
Watling, Shaun
Gower, Roger
Little, Michael

A quick way of putting a list into alphabetical order is to put it into numerical order first, by writing the number of the position the entry will be in an alphabetical list next to the relevant entry, and then writing the list out again in numerical order.

Numerical order

This method is linked by means of index cards to the alphabetical method. Each document or folder is given a number and is filed in numerical order. The information contained within the files is sorted into alphabetical order.

Advantages:

▼ **the numbered files are more easily found**
▼ **the numbered files are less likely to be returned to the wrong place**
▼ **the number reference can be added to any correspondence**

▼ **the numbered files can be easily increased, thereby expanding the system**

Disadvantages:

▼ **a card index has to be used with this method of filing**

FIGURE IT OUT

PC 8.3.1
COM 1.2
AON 1.1, 1.2

00:30

*P*lace *the following list of numbers in numerical order:*

744
176
19
275
119
332
264
88
346
218
189
66
28
231

Date order

Documents stored according to the date are filed in a chronological filing system, again with the most recent date being at the front or top of the file. Travel agents are likely to use this method, filing travel documents for clients in date order, either of departure, or of payment date.

Advantages:

▼ **for some organisations a date is the most significant information available**

Disadvantages:

▼ **there are no major disadvantages, as it is unlikely that any organisation other than one particularly needing this method would consider using it**

FIGURE IT OUT

PC 8.3.1
COM 1.2, 1.3
AON 1.1, 1.2

00:30

*P*lace *the following list of dates in chronological order, putting the most recent at the top:*

> *30 January 1989*
> *19 September 1978*
> *4 August 1991*
> *27 June 1993*
> *19 June 1985*
> *14 November 1990*
> *9 May 1995*
> *27 June 1991*
> *25 November 1995*
> *10 November 1994*
> *11 September 1992*
> *17 June 1990*
> *28 August 1979*
> *31 December 1991*

For safe and neat storage and rapid retrieval

The main purpose of any filing system is to store documents safely and neatly in such a way that they can be quickly found again when they are required at a later date. Obviously, if an organisation is to operate efficiently and effectively, then it needs to have access to the different types of business information which it receives and transmits daily.

Whenever a filing system is designed or purchased, whether it is paper based or computer based, it is important to remember that the amount of storage space will have to be increased eventually and this consideration should be taken into account when setting up a new system.

8.3.2 *File documents in the correct place and sequence as instructed*

8.3.3 *Retrieve documents as instructed*

These two performance criteria are both practical in that they require you to physically file and retrieve documents accurately and by following instructions. You will be able to record the filing and retrieving which you do on a regular basis at your work placement if this is possible, but you may need to carry out this duty in the centre in which you are studying this course. Wherever you carry out these duties, it is important that you are observed carrying out instructions regarding the filing and retrieving of documents and that you are competent in the tasks you are set. As the gathering of this evidence is ongoing, we have not included an element assignment here.

FILE AND RETRIEVE DOCUMENTS AS INSTRUCTED

As with the handling of internal and external mail and, indeed, any administrative task being carried out in a business, it is important to follow all instructions given. These instructions may be in the form of either verbal or written instructions from a superior, or may be the operating instructions supplied with a machine that the business uses to carry out its administrative duties.

All businesses have their own procedures for carrying out tasks. When people join an organisation these procedures will be explained to them so that they have a clear idea of what to do in certain situations and who they should contact if they need help or assistance. Any instructions you receive regarding filing should be confirmed before you waste any time in carrying out this task incorrectly.

Orally

You might be given instructions to file and retrieve documents orally. These may even be passed on to you very quickly and in a somewhat garbled fashion. It is important to remember here that your manager or colleague would much rather you asked him or her to repeat the instruction if you are unsure of what is required of you, than go away and end up not doing the job properly.

Whenever people ask you to do something for them at work it is essential that you listen very carefully. Filing a piece of paper in the wrong place could mean hours of work and frustration for yourself or someone else at a later date when it needs to be retrieved. The waste of time would also cost the organisation money. When the instructions have been given you should go over them again, so that you are sure you have properly understood either where to file the document, or which file is being required for retrieval.

In writing

Sometimes it is company policy for the name of the file into which the document has to be placed to be written on the top of the front sheet of the document. Sometimes the manager or manageress will do this him or herself and it will be up to the person responsible for filing to simply place it in the correct file. On the other hand, the request for filing may be a scribbled note left on your desk which says something like 'please put the Jones file on my desk by 4.00'. It is possible that there are several files which could be known as the 'Jones' files, for example it could be the surname of several of your customers. If you are given vague requests for files in writing, then it is

```
               CROSS REFERENCE SHEET



FOR INFORMATION  ON: ...............................


PLEASE REFER TO: .................................




SIGNED: ...................... DATE: ..................
```

Figure 8.3.2 A cross-reference slip.

important that you do not attempt to 'struggle on' yourself, but seek help. Maybe you could even help the organisation by suggesting a way in which this problem could be dealt with?

It is possible that one file could be known by more than one name and therefore be difficult to trace. If a file has been updated, for example if an organisation has changed its name, or if a personnel file changes name because the member of staff marries, some people may still refer to the file, or look for it, under the old name. For this reason a system has to be in place which enables the clerk, or anyone else seeking the file, to find it without too much difficulty.

Such a system is known as **cross reference**. A cross-reference slip is placed either in the old or in the new file, directing the person seeking the file to the correct place.

By manager and colleague

When you join an organisation, one of your first duties will probably be to file and retrieve documents. This is a very routine duty, but it does mean that you are in a position to become more familiar with the types of information the business handles, as well as the roles of the different managers and other individuals within the organisation.

If this is the case, you will be asked by both your manager(s) and your work associates to file or retrieve documents from a file so that they can make use of the information contained within

them. You might have to complete a file or document out or absent card when retrieving the documents (we look at these two items in more detail in the next section). You may also have to use a cross-reference system because the file has been requested under the wrong name. Remember that although these are sometimes quite laborious jobs, they are still very important to the people who have asked you to do them.

Your manager or colleague may require the information he or she has requested urgently if someone is waiting on the telephone or if he or she has promised to call back immediately. Always carry out such instructions quickly and efficiently.

8.3.4 *Record document movements correctly*

Again, this very practical performance criterion requires you to keep a record of all the times you have dealt with paperwork which has moved both in and out of files. You can provide this evidence by keeping a log of the filing you have completed whilst either on your work placement or in a simulated situation at the centre in which you are studying this course.

DOCUMENT MOVEMENTS

Document movements are simply the tracking of where the document is at any given time. Some of the information contained in the document may have to be seen by more than one member of staff either within the organisation or at various branches of the organisation. We already know that such items are distributed within the mail system (we dealt with this in Element 8.1) and that a circulation slip would be attached to the document(s). Obviously, it would be of no use if this document went missing and there was no copy available. In order to ensure that mistakes such as this are avoided, the recording of the whereabouts of the document should be of prime importance. It is always advisable to take an extra copy 'for file' in case it does go missing – it is better to end up with too many copies than not to have any left in the end.

Into file

Whenever a letter is sent out of the organisation a copy should be placed in the relevant file. This will ensure that a record is kept of the date the document was sent, as well as the person to whom it was dispatched.

If you are responsible for the filing within the organisation, then you may find that it is company policy to date stamp everything before it goes into the filing cabinet. By doing this it is easy to identify when it was last dealt with. Obviously, if it is required at a later date, then a file absent or out card would show the date(s) the file was borrowed and the name of the person who borrowed it.

From file – to manager(s) and others

It would not be sensible to operate a filing system from which anybody could take documents or files without the knowledge of the person responsible for this duty. Filing cabinets should always be locked and should have restricted access.

We look at the document out or absent card system of tracking the movements of a file or document a little later, but even if this system is not in operation, then some form of 'logging out' of files and information should be in place to help make sure that security and confidentiality of information is upheld.

The movements of documents must be recorded in some way or whole files could go missing and staff might end up spending a great deal of time trying to track them down – they might be anywhere within the organisation and may end up buried on someone's desk.

Document absent card/file absent card

An efficient organisation needs to keep track of the whereabouts of all files housed within its filing system (see Figure 8.3.3). In order to do this a file 'out' or 'absent' card is inserted each time a file is borrowed. In this way, the clerk always knows the exact location of a particular file, when it was borrowed and by whom. Individual pieces of paper or documents should never be removed from a file. To ensure that nothing is lost or misplaced, the whole file should be taken from the drawer.

BUSINESS CONNECTION

PC 8.3

We have now looked at all the major ways of filing and retrieving documents. To test your memory and skill, complete the following business connection by turning numerical order into rapid retrieval. The last letter of each word or phrase is the first letter of the next word or phrase. To help you we have put in the first and last letter on each line, but you will have to do the rest.

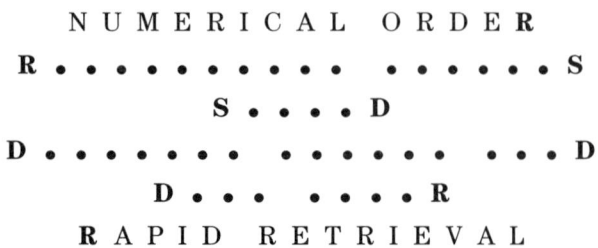

FILE 'OUT' CARD

FILE NAME	BORROWED BY	DEPARTMENT	DATE BORROWED	DATE RETURNED

Figure 8.3.3 A file 'out' or 'absent' card.

WORDSEARCH

How many of the words listed below can you find? They run forwards and backwards across and up and down the grid.

```
M  N  D  W  P  L  A  C  I  T  E  B  A  H  P  L  A  M
O  M  I  S  D  I  R  E  C  T  E  D  O  L  M  C  J  K
G  H  A  H  D  Y  R  O  T  C  E  R  I  D  L  O  X  D
S  E  L  F  S  E  A  L  A  S  D  G  H  M  I  N  P  P
B  V  L  S  S  L  E  C  R  A  P  Q  R  S  T  N  P  E
O  O  I  Q  R  L  M  N  Q  F  G  H  K  L  D  E  A  G
O  P  N  S  T  O  R  A  G  E  B  N  V  C  X  C  P  A
Q  E  G  L  P  W  P  O  S  T  A  G  E  R  A  T  E  S
M  B  N  Q  L  P  K  U  E  T  T  M  M  O  B  I  R  S
A  B  S  E  N  A  O  T  A  C  T  F  U  L  S  N  B  E
I  M  M  O  L  G  P  G  A  L  K  S  S  E  E  G  A  M
R  L  I  J  K  E  P  O  A  S  D  R  E  E  N  O  S  P
M  K  O  P  I  S  W  I  W  L  K  I  E  Q  T  I  E  L
A  M  N  C  V  E  R  N  B  B  I  E  K  S  T  L  D  T
I  N  C  O  M  I  N  G  N  I  L  I  F  G  H  O  L  L
L  M  E  I  T  I  O  R  L  K  J  S  P  P  D  K  I  S
J  O  S  R  E  B  M  U  N  E  N  O  H  P  E  L  E  T
C  L  O  S  I  N  G  C  A  L  L  S  P  I  M  N  T  O
```

ABSENT
AIRMAIL
ALPHABETICAL
CLOSING CALLS
CONNECTING
DIALLING
DIRECTORY

FILING
INCOMING
MESSAGE
MISDIRECTED
OUTGOING
PAPER BASED
PARCELS

POSTAGE RATE
SELF SEAL
STORAGE
TACTFUL
TELEPHONE NUMBERS
YELLOW PAGES

element 9.1

INVESTIGATE QUALITIES OF BUSINESS EMPLOYEES

Performance criteria

A student must:

1 Describe the **corporate image** of a business organisation.

2 Identify the **effects** of a business organisation's image on employees.

3 Identify and give examples of the **main qualities** a business employer is looking for in an employee.

4 Identify the **importance** of the **main** employee **qualities**.

5 Identify the **legal responsibilities** of an employee.

6 Identify **behaviour** that will lead to **disciplinary action** being taken against an employee.

RANGE

Corporate image: advertisements, logos, packaging; service to customers; appearance of employees

Effects: suitability of potential employee for recruitment, suitability of new employee to remain employed by the business organisation

Main qualities: dress and appearance, manner of speaking, social skills, punctuality, attendance, following instructions

Importance: company image, customer relations, working relations with colleagues, reliability, health and safety

Legal responsibilities: health and safety, compliance with terms of employment contract

Behaviour: non-compliance with health and safety rules, non-compliance with contract

Disciplinary action: warning, additional training, dismissal

PC 9.1.1
COM 1.3

00:20

*I*n groups of three, try to remember and roughly draw the logos of the following organisations:

- *Shell UK Ltd*
- *Birds Eye Wall's*
- *Lloyds Bank plc*
- *Halifax Building Society*

9.1.1 Describe the corporate image of a business organisation

CORPORATE IMAGE

A corporate image is the impression that a business wishes to make on customers, other businesses, the general public and employees. As we will see, it includes advertisements, any logos or slogans used and the training and appearance of its employees. Given the fact that many organisations spend considerable sums of money attempting to create a corporate image, they are often at pains to ensure that this corporate image remains consistent throughout all their operations and activities.

Advertisements

For many people the first impression they will get of an organisation will be through the advertise-ments that the organisation places in newspapers or magazines or on the television. Advertisements cannot say everything there is to say about an organisation; they can only give a very brief and uncomplicated view of it and hope that the potential customer finds something appealing or familiar in the corporate image.

We have come to recognise a number of corporate images which do not necessarily need any explanation to understand what it is that the organisation is trying to convey. It runs even deeper than this. In many cases the mere fact that we recognise a corporate image means that we will be prepared to buy things from that company. A Coca-Cola can, for example, not only tells us what is inside the can, but also guarantees to us that what we find in the can is of the same quality and standard as the last can we opened. Some organisations, despite their best efforts, do not have a terribly good corporate image, for example Skoda, the car manufacturer. As a result, it found another way of appealing to the general public, through its association with Volkswagen. Volkswagen has a very good reputation in the car market and in associating with Skoda part of Volkswagen's corporate image 'rubs off' on Skoda.

As we have said, most advertisements are uncomplicated (and these are often the ones

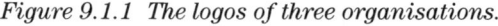

Figure 9.1.1 The logos of three organisations.

Logos

which are most successful) and do not have a great many words in them. It is therefore vital that the organisation's corporate image can carry the message and the necessary information to the customer.

Logos are just as important as getting advertisements right. An organisation can pay hundreds of thousands of pounds for the right logo which matches its corporate image and appeals to its customers. A poorly designed logo can prove dis-

astrous to an organisation wishing to make an immediate impact on the customer. If there were only one rule about logos then it would be that they should not be messy, confusing or too elaborate. Simple logos which work just like a shorthand version of the organisation's name are often the best sort of logo to use. Good examples of these would be BP for British Petroleum, BT for British Telecom and 'the black horse' for Lloyds Bank. In all these cases, we can picture in our minds the style, colours and shapes used in the logo, which we then associate with the company it stands for.

FIGURE IT OUT

PC 9.1.1

*L*ook at the logos given in Figure 9.1.1 and try to identify the organisations concerned.

Packaging

A company's corporate image is always carried over into the packaging of the organisation's products. Not only will each of the products display the organisation's logo, but it will also have a similar style and use of colours and design to further remind customers of the corporate image of the organisation. The idea is to make customers automatically recognise a particular sort of packaging as being from a particular organisation. This means that when they are faced with a wide variety of different products, their eyes will be drawn to something familiar that they can remember from advertising or logos or even leaflets and other publicity material.

Service to customers

It is no longer enough to simply produce the best product at the best price. It is not even enough to produce a product which is more attractive and more reliable than that of any other company. Even further, it is not enough to be able to offer a good level of support to customers after they have bought the product. Most organisations have realised that in order to keep customers happy and ensure that they always think about their organisation first, they must offer a full service before, during and after the purchase of a product.

To this end, organisations spend large sums of money training their employees to respond to exactly what their customers ask for. This may be advice and guidance, assurances of continued help and support or even a guarantee that any problem in the future will be dealt with promptly, professionally and without question. The differences between products offered by different organisations are so minimal that they are of no real importance. Indeed, prices may be too similar to give any particular concern to the customer. The real deciding factor is the level of service and the way in which that service is offered. This is why many organisations set up customer service centres or helplines to make sure that they are one step ahead of their competitors.

Appearance of employees

For organisations that have direct contact with their customers, it is obviously important that employees look presentable. We expect supermarkets and superstores to supply recognisable uniforms to all their employees. Other organisations which do not provide a uniform as such have various dress codes, such as insisting that male members of staff wear a tie and jacket. They may even insist that female members of staff always wear skirts. Even in organisations that in the past had only a simple 'smart appearance' dress code have now moved over to the use of uniforms. A good example of this is the various building societies who actually provide shirts or blouses to be worn with their employees' own clothing.

Being able to recognise a particular person in a shop or office as definitely being a member of staff is obviously a big advantage to the customer. Instead of standing around hoping to catch the eye of someone who may be an employee, greater efficiency and level of service is achieved if it is obvious that a particular person is a member of staff.

Some organisations carry the 'appearance' of their employees beyond that of uniforms, and may insist that hair is short for their male employees or that their female employees wear shoes of a particular colour. After all, a scruffy employee does not convey a good message to the customer.

9.1.2 Identify the effects of a business organisation's image on employees

EFFECTS

Once an organisation has established a particular corporate image, it will have a picture of an ideal potential employee in its mind. To some extent this employee will need not only the

Figure 9.1.2 Although most petrol stations are owned and operated by independent dealers, these businesses contract with an oil company to sell its products for up to five years. In many cases the oil company agrees to refurbish the site in its own livery (courtesy of Mobil Oil Ltd).

particular qualities it will be looking for to fill a post, but also the general appearance or suitability that fits the organisation's corporate image.

Suitability of potential employee for recruitment

As we will see in the next element when we consider interviews, the initial appearance of poten-tial employees can affect the way in which potential employers feel about them and whether they consider them suitable for recruitment. Obviously there are some organisations, such as the police force or fire brigade, that require a particular height, build or level of fitness. You would think that for most jobs these things do not necessarily matter, but unfortunately they do. Given the fact that employers in this day and age can pick and

Figure 9.1.3 As well as an attractive and convenient station design, good lighting and a readily recognised livery, the most important consideration is a friendly and attentive service (courtesy of Mobil Oil Ltd).

choose from any number of potential employees, they will be looking for an individual who most closely fits the 'kind of person' they are looking for. As we have said, this goes way beyond that person's ability to do the job. That person has to look right, behave in the right manner and have the potential to fit into the organisation with the minimum of fuss and training. It is still the case that a potential employee who is well groomed and smartly dressed will be taken far more seriously than someone who has turned up for an interview with unbrushed hair and wearing a favourite pair of jeans.

FIGURE IT OUT

PC 9.1.2
COM 1.1

In the role of manager of a shop, make a list of the qualities you would be looking for in a Saturday shop assistant. What kind of things would put you off a potential applicant? Jot down your own thoughts and then discuss this as a group.

Suitability of a new employee to remain employed by the business organisation

Only the most unreasonable and demanding of employers will expect you to be able to fit in without any problems immediately. There is always a period of time in which the employer allows you to 'get the hang of' the job and fully appreciate exactly what is expected of you. In a great many organisations there is nothing written down about the dress code or preferred length of hair; this is something that a new employee will have to pick up from existing members of staff. A new employee will have to rapidly adopt not only the procedures and policies of the organisation, but also decide whether he or she will need to make a great deal of effort to fit in or adapt. Fitting in is never easy, particularly if there are not only complicated rules and procedures to consider but also a strict dress code. These dress codes are not written down by the management of the organisation because employers simply rely on the fact that since every other employee dresses and behaves in a particular way, the new employee will conform to these standards without actually having to be told.

FIGURE IT OUT

PC 9.1.2
COM 1.1

`00:10`

*H*ow long should a new employee be given to 'settle in'? At what stage should the new employee's supervisor or manager begin to think about his or her suitability for continued employment? Discuss this as a group.

9.1.3 Identify and give examples of the main qualities a business employer is looking for in an employee

MAIN QUALITIES

Since most employers will have to make some kind of choice about the candidates they are going to see before they have actually seen them, the CV, letter of application and any references taken up prior to the interview are all important. As we will see in the next element, going through an interview process can be difficult enough. So how do employers decide how to short list without having seen the candidates? All we need to concern ourselves with at this stage is that by some means they manage it. In this element we look at how first impressions of a potential employee are extremely important.

Dress and appearance

Phrases like 'looks aren't everything' and 'appearance doesn't matter' will not help us in interview situations. Although potential employers may be sympathetic to an individual who has never worked before, they will expect that candidate to have made an effort with his or her appearance for the interview. Many employers will make a snap decision about candidates based on the way they look before they have even opened their mouths.

As we have said previously, some jobs require a candidate of particular height, age or physical ability, but for the most part, the way in which you dress yourself and, for that matter, groom yourself prior to a meeting, will drastically affect your chances of being taken seriously.

FIGURE IT OUT

PC 9.1.3
COM 1.1, 1.2

00:30

*A*gainst the following list of jobs, write down the clothing the person holding this job would be expected to wear by the employer. Work in pairs on this.

- *a male working in a shop*
- *a female working in a restaurant*
- *a female working in an office*
- *a male working in a post office*
- *a male working in a garage*
- *a female working in a hairdressers*

Manner of speaking

Although you can hear any number of different accents on TV or radio, many employers still prefer accentless voices. A slight accent is often quite acceptable, but a broad accent that would prove to be difficult to understand unless you were familiar with it, could be a disadvantage to the employer if you had to talk to customers. One way around this if you do have a broad accent is to try to speak more slowly and to think about the way in which you pronounce certain words. Unfortunately, this way of handling it might make you appear to be rather slow. If you want to soften your accent, the only way to really do this is to try to change the way you speak completely, and not just when you are talking to customers. If you speak in one way to customers, which is different to the normal way in which you speak, you may find yourself slipping into your normal pattern of speech before you realise it has happened.

The other main consideration with speech is the way in which you use particular words. In business, the use of overcomplicated words or jargon and shortened ways of saying things can often be off-putting to the customer. Bear in mind that the customer, in speaking to you as an employee of an organisation that he or she wishes to buy something from, is looking to you for understandable advice and information.

You may have to simplify some things for customers. Do not assume that they know as much about the product or service as you do; if they did, then they would not need to talk to you, they could simply ask for what they wanted. Many customers need guidance and, above all, clear guidance. This should be your main goal (and not trying to lose your own accent).

Finally, you should *never* use bad language which includes swear words and slang, and try to avoid sloppy English, such as 'yeah'.

Do not be tempted to use bad language to get a point across to a customer. Also, avoid using words such as 'don't' or 'isn't' in writing or speech. Neither of these are attractive or business-like.

FIGURE IT OUT

PC 9.1.3
COM 1.1, 1.2

00:15

*W*ithout using bad language, write a list of the kind of words and phrases that would be unacceptable in the workplace, particularly when dealing with customers. Spend 10 minutes making your list and then put your suggestions to the rest of the group.

Social skills

Perhaps one of the most important social skills that an individual can have is the ability to talk and relate to a variety of different people. Working for an organisation will often involve having to deal with very different sorts of customer, as well as members of staff. Being able to appear friendly, approachable and helpful are all key social skills that need to be developed.

Remember that you will not only have to interact with customers, but you will also have to cope with a variety of different people who work for the same organisation. They will be looking for a number of social skills which include:

▼ **the ability to explain things clearly**
▼ **the ability to listen without interrupting**
▼ **the ability to work as a member of a team**
▼ **the willingness to be told about something or instructed to do something without appearing bored or unwilling**
▼ **the ability to adapt to different situations**
▼ **the ability to inform others if you feel that you need assistance with something**

Punctuality

No matter what the size or nature of the organisation in which you work, the ability to arrive on time is important. Not only do you have to arrive on time, but you should also be prepared to begin work immediately. Most employers will understand and accept occasional lateness, but persistent lateness may lead to an employer wishing to take action against you which may result (in extreme circumstances) in dismissal.

Punctuality is also important within the workplace. If you can effectively manage your workload, you will be able to ensure that any project which you have been asked to complete by a particular time is finished. If it does not look like you are going to be able to finish the project on time, then it is a good idea to tell someone that you are having difficulties and when you expect the work to be finished. For employees who have to attend regular meetings, lateness to these can be embarrassing, not least because this might leave a lingering feeling in other people's minds that they do not place as much importance on the meeting as they should, or that they are simply poor timekeepers. If you have arranged a meeting and you are going to be late, it is common courtesy to ring up and try to set a new time.

Attendance

Employers, up to a point, will accept the fact that you will be occasionally ill. What they will be unprepared to accept is unexplained absences. It is worth getting into the habit of ringing up if you are not intending to be at work or college on a particular day. Not only is this common courtesy, but it also covers you to some extent as people will know that you are away for a particular reason. Schools and colleges, in line with the requirements of employers, will expect you to attend more often than you are away. This figure should not fall below an 80–85% attendance rate. Remember that it is easy for an employer to look at and analyse your pattern of absences. If, for example, you are required to work on Saturday and, over a period of time, your level of absence on Saturdays was high, an employer could quite easily match these against the fact that the local football team played at home on those Saturdays. Also, regular non-attendance on a Friday could show that you had rather too much of a good time when you went out on Thursday night. If an employer recognises unexplained patterns of absence he or she could take disciplinary action against you. In extreme circumstances you could even lose your job.

Following instructions

Even the most senior employees have to show that they are able to follow instructions from their superiors. It does not really matter how vague or unclear these instructions are, as if they were not understood then you should have asked what was really required at the time. Not following an unclear instruction is as bad as ignoring a clear one. Remember that people who give you instructions will assume that you understand what is required of you if you do not ask them

exactly what they mean. Employers are not looking for people who just follow instructions without question. They are looking for people who can understand, adapt and act upon instructions no matter what they are or how unclear they may be.

9.1.4 **Identify the importance of the main employee qualities**

IMPORTANCE OF QUALITIES

Since, in most cases, the employee represents 'the face of the organisation' to customers, choosing the right person for the job and then making sure that he or she is adequately trained on a regular basis is of utmost importance to the organisation. As we will see, even if the organisation has spent considerable sums of money in developing its corporate image and putting various training programmes into operation, a bad employee on an even worse day can destroy many months of time, money and effort.

Company image

Employers will expect their employees to adopt the corporate image of the organisation as much as possible. Bearing in mind that this corporate image has been created as a result of trying to follow the corporate aims and objectives of the organisation, the only way that the employer can realistically expect employees to follow the corporate aims is to tell them what they are. This will obviously involve staff development and training but, as you will no doubt discover when you are in work, any amount of staff development and training is not enough; the organisation has to constantly remind its employees about the standards and procedures which are expected of them. The organisation does not have to spend a lot of money in doing this. Indeed, it does not have to retrain or refresh its employees' memories by holding expensive training events; regular staff newsletters or other forms of communication can be enough to jog the memories of those who have attended the training programmes. This is not a foolproof way of making sure that the corporate image is followed, but it is one of the best ways.

The other major problem is that the corporate image in the minds of decision-makers in the organisation is constantly changing. What they must not assume is that employees are mind readers and that they can automatically adopt new ways of doing things without being told about them. Not only does this mean that employees can get confused about what they are supposed to do in certain circumstances, but also that they are not considered when employers 'change their minds about something'.

Customer relations

Just making sure that employees are well presented and well groomed is not enough to ensure that customers are treated correctly when they visit the organisation. Customer relations is a rather broad term which covers all of the ways in which employees deal with customers, whether this is face to face, on the telephone or in writing.

If you have studied or are going to study Unit 8, then you will have looked at the ways to handle mail and process telephone calls. In this element we will concentrate on handling customers in face-to-face situations.

Broadly speaking, there are two different sets of situations that you may be faced with. In an office environment customers or visitors to the organisation will have to be greeted and dealt with at reception. In a retail environment customers will have to be dealt with at a variety of different places, such as on the shop floor, at the cash till or at a customer information desk. Let us look at these different situations in a little more detail.

The office environment

Reception areas should be welcoming and comfortable and staff friendly and helpful. Remember that this is the first impression that most visitors will get of an organisation. Visitors will approach reception areas for any number of reasons. We could not possibly cover every one of these here, but the following list will give you a general guide to reception areas and how to greet visitors when they arrive:

▼ the reception area should be as close to the entrance of the building as possible

▼ if the reception is not near the entrance, then it should be clearly signposted

▼ the name of the receptionist should be displayed at the reception desk

▼ there should be a waiting area for the customers to sit and read while they are waiting to be dealt with

▼ the receptionist should ask customers or callers their names and ask them who they are visiting

▼ the receptionist should attempt to contact the person the visitor is there to see as soon as possible and inform him or her that the visitor is waiting

▼ visitors should be asked to fill in the visitors book which will have space for name, company, the person being visited and the time of arrival

▼ if the visitor has not arranged an appointment to see someone, then if the person being visited does not wish to see the visitor, he or she should be told that the person is not available or out of the building

▼ if the visitor has a complaint then the receptionist should always try to remain calm and pleasant and attempt to get someone to deal with the problem as soon as possible

▼ a receptionist's main role is to deal with all callers either personally or by making sure that they receive attention from someone who can help them

VISITORS LOG

DAY AND DATE			
TIME	DETAILS	SEEN BY	ACTION TAKEN
	Name Firm Address		
	Name Firm Address		
	Name Firm Address		
	Name Firm Address		
	Name Firm Address		

Figure 9.1.4 A visitors book.

The retail environment

Assuming that the customer or caller can recognise that a particular person works in the shop, then normally it is the visitor that will approach the employee. In many cases visitors will not necessarily realise who works for the shop and, in this case, it is the employee who will have to approach the visitor.

Once customers have confirmed that the person they are speaking to actually works in the shop, they will then explain what they need. The easiest and most straightforward situation to deal with is that of a customer simply wishing to pay for something. The cashier should be polite, make sure that items have been entered correctly on the cash register and then state the total amount due. Since different retail shops have different policies about methods and ways of payment, the simplest thing that we can say here is that cashiers should check that the correct amount has been given to them and that any change, along with a receipt, is handed directly to the customer or the receipt placed in the bag along with the goods purchased. A simple 'thank you' or 'goodbye' will complete this task.

At the customer service desk the employee is likely to come across a great many different problems. Some may be fairly simple, such as an enquiry regarding the location of something within the shop, and others will be more compli-cated, such as dealing with faulty or returned goods. Much of the time spent at a customer service desk is taken up by having to deal with complaints regarding faulty or damaged goods. Again, each organisation has its own policy regarding returns, although certain general points can be made:

▼ **always listen to what the customer is saying first before making any comments**
▼ **once the complaint has been stated, calmly tell him or her about the organisation's policy regarding the complaint**
▼ **if the response to the complaint falls within company policy, then you can deal with it immediately**
▼ **if the response to the complaint is not covered by company policy, then you may have to ask for a more senior member of staff to assist you**
▼ **above all, regardless of the attitude of the customer, you should remain calm and not lose your temper**

On the shop floor employees may have to deal with anything from a customer wishing to pay, in which case he or she can be directed or taken to the cashier, to a customer wishing to make a complaint about something. In the first instance a simple direction may be the only thing required, and in the second a complaint may be dealt with on the spot, or at the customer service desk if the shop has one.

Many of the approaches which a customer makes to an employee will require information or advice to be given. Simple directions to find a particular product may make up the majority of an employee's contact with customers. If the shop sells more complicated products then the employee may have to explain or demonstrate how the products work. Although this may be somewhat frightening for employees to begin with, after only a few days they will become quite confident in explaining and demonstrating almost anything in the shop.

When an employee has to approach a customer, such as if he or she appears lost or confused, or if making a direct approach to a customer is the organisation's policy, the employee should be careful not to appear too pushy. Simply ask the customer whether you can help and then wait for the reply and respond to it in exactly the same way as you would have done if he or she had approached you. In some cases a customer may simply reply 'no, I am simply looking', in which case the employee should walk away and leave the customer to browse.

If employees follow a consistent approach to customers and this fits in with the organisation's idea of dealing with customers, a good standard of customer relations can be guaranteed.

---

finding out

PC 9.1.4
COM 1.1, 1.3

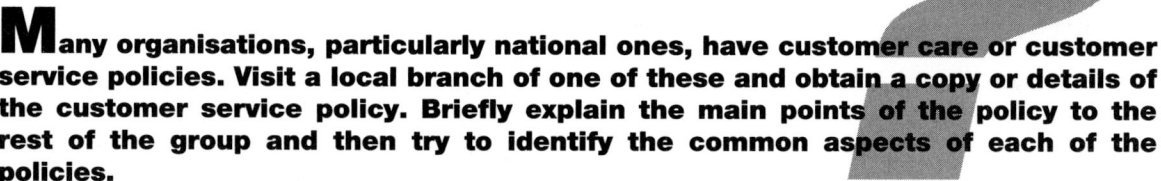

Many organisations, particularly national ones, have customer care or customer service policies. Visit a local branch of one of these and obtain a copy or details of the customer service policy. Briefly explain the main points of the policy to the rest of the group and then try to identify the common aspects of each of the policies.

Working relations with colleagues

Maintaining a good working relationship with your colleagues is probably as important, if not more so, than being able to deal with customers in the right way. Bearing in mind that you will spend a considerable amount of time working with them and that you may in fact spend some of your leisure time with them, it is a good idea to make your working relationships as pleasant as possible. Here are some key points to think about when establishing and maintaining good working relations with colleagues:

▼ always be punctual and reliable, since someone else will have to cover for you if you are not

▼ try to be pleasant at all times, even if provoked

▼ try to keep a good sense of humour at all times

▼ always listen carefully when you are given instructions so that you do not have to be told again and again how to do something

▼ never bring your personal problems to work with you

- ▼ **do not gossip about other members of staff**
- ▼ **do not discuss company business outside work**
- ▼ **make sure that you carry out all your routine tasks on a regular basis and do not let paperwork or filing build up**
- ▼ **keep your desk and work area clean and tidy**
- ▼ **do not bring lots of personal belongings into the workplace**

- ▼ **try to work quietly, without interfering with other people**
- ▼ **take care with your appearance and personal hygiene**
- ▼ **always ask if you are not sure about something, as this is better than getting it wrong**
- ▼ **do not be tempted to make personal telephone calls using company time and money**

FIGURE IT OUT

PC 9.1.4
COM 1.1

00:10

*Y*ou will have, by now, undertaken a number of group assignments and activities. Re-form the last group that you worked with. Try to identify how you worked together as a team and whether there were things about the way you worked together that were good or bad.

Reliability

As we have already mentioned in this element, punctuality, attendance and following company rules and procedures, as well as having a good working relationship with your colleagues, are all part of being a reliable employee. The employer will always be looking for members of staff who are reliable so that they can be left to do their jobs while the employer concentrates on other things.

Health and safety

If you have covered Unit 5 you will have looked at health and safety in detail. Being aware of potential health and safety problems is the first main step in ensuring that the workplace is a safe place in which to operate. Remember that you should always take reasonable care in what you

do in the workplace and not put anyone else at risk as a result of your actions. You should also never interfere with anything that could cause an accident or create a potential hazard. If you ever see anything that could cause a health and safety problem you should always report it as soon as possible. Here are some key things to look out for in the workplace:

- ▼ **make sure that gangways between desks or aisles are not blocked**
- ▼ **make sure that fire exits are not blocked**
- ▼ **make sure that fire doors are not propped open**
- ▼ **make sure that electrical appliances are turned off at the end of every day**
- ▼ **make sure that electrical cables or leads are not trailing across areas that people walk through**

▼ make sure that any faulty electrical equipment is reported and repaired
▼ report any loose, torn or frayed carpets or floor coverings to your supervisor or manager
▼ make sure that first-aid boxes are accessible and well stocked

▼ make sure that you know how to use fire extinguishers and other fire appliances, as well as knowing what the fire drill is
▼ make sure that doors and windows are locked before leaving the building

---

finding out

PC 9.1.4
COM 1.1

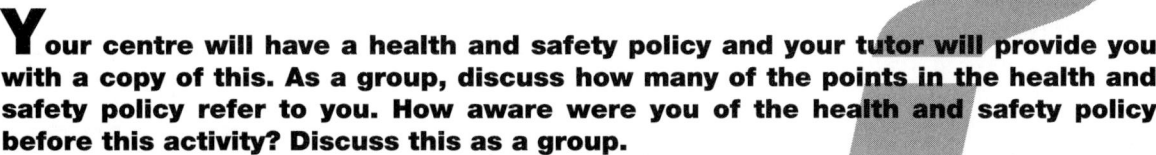

Your centre will have a health and safety policy and your tutor will provide you with a copy of this. As a group, discuss how many of the points in the health and safety policy refer to you. How aware were you of the health and safety policy before this activity? Discuss this as a group.

9.1.5 Identify the legal responsibilities of an employee

LEGAL RESPONSIBILITIES

The relationship between employers and employees is not left solely for the two parties to agree upon. There are a range of laws which control the relationship and make sure that an employee is protected from a unreasonable employer. In this performance criterion we will focus on the two main legal responsibilities which relate to health and safety and the contract of employment.

Health and safety

An employee can quite rightly expect to work in conditions that are neither hazardous to life nor health. If you have already covered Unit 5 you will already be familiar with the Health and Safety at Work Act. This piece of legislation sets out that the employee must work in an environment that is healthy and safe and that the employer must consider the welfare of the employees. Employers are responsible for any hazards or accidents which may be caused by not following the legislation. The employer will have to pay very heavy fines if found guilty of ignoring potential dangers. Examples of ways in which the employer could maintain a healthy and safe environment are:

▼ **fitting protective guards to machines**
▼ **taking care that any hazardous or toxic chemicals are housed in safe and leak-proof containers**
▼ **ensuring that the quality of air is good**

▼ **not instructing employees to undertake duties which are dangerous and could result in injury**
▼ **providing protective clothing for employees**

For a fuller list of protective measures refer to Unit 5.

Compliance with terms of employment contract

As we will see in a moment, just as the employer will be expected to fulfil any obligations as set out in the contract of employment, so too will the employee. Employees will be expected to comply with all the aspects of the contract and accept responsibility for their actions at work.

Employees have a responsibility to be loyal, hard-working and honest. They must also accept any reasonable directions from supervisors or managers. The contract of employment is a legal document and, as we will see, the employer can take action against the employee if the contract is broken. See Figure 9.1.5.

Normally, a contract of employment includes the following:

▼ **a description of the job role**
▼ **the job title**
▼ **wage or salary details, including how it is paid and how often**
▼ **how additional payments are made**
▼ **rules about overtime**
▼ **rules about bonuses and commission**
▼ **starting times and finishing times of work**
▼ **total number of hours to be worked per week**
▼ **number of paid holidays**
▼ **rules about sick leave**
▼ **rules about maternity leave**
▼ **pension scheme details**
▼ **disciplinary procedures**
▼ **grievance procedures**
▼ **period of notice to be worked or given**
▼ **resignation details**

In addition, the employer may also include the following:

▼ **the company rules and regulations**
▼ **codes of behaviour**
▼ **an organisational chart**
▼ **details about social activities and events**

9.1.6 *Identify behaviour that would lead to disciplinary action being taken against an employee*

BEHAVIOUR

We already know that an employer is expected to provide a safe working environment for the employee and to expect members of staff not to do anything which could put them in a dangerous situation. The employer is also looking for a certain level of behaviour which is acceptable in all circumstances. In particular we will look at health and safety rules and then the rules within the contract of employment.

An employee will be well aware of the behaviour expected of him or her by reading the contract of employment.

Non-compliance with health and safety rules

Just as the employer must take heed of the requirements of health and safety legislation, so must the employee. Employees may, however, suffer harm or injuries which are not necessarily the fault of the employer. If employees are negligent (which means they have not taken care in what they do) and cause injury to themselves or others, then the employer will be in a difficult position. The employee may claim that it was not

---

STATEMENT OF MAIN PARTICULARS OF TERMS OF EMPLOYMENT

We are required under current employment legislation to issue you with a statement setting out certain terms and particulars relating to your employment. The attached statement has been issued for this purpose.

It would assist us to bring our Personnel Records up to date if you would answer the questions below and return this form to your Supervisor/Manager.

---

1. **New Employees Only**

Enclosed with this form is my P.45 (delete if not applicable) and any S.S.P. Leavers Statements issued to me by my previous employer(s).

My P.45 is not enclosed because:

....

....

My National Insurance Number is: ....

---

2. **All Employees**

My name is: ....

My address is: ....

....

My telephone number is: ....

My next of kin is: ....

My next of kin can be contacted by telephone at: ....

I have read the Employee Information Binder including:-

Absence Record Form
Rules
Disciplinary Procedure
Appeals Procedure
Grievance Procedure
Holiday Entitlement and Conditions
Working Arrangements

I have been shown all of the following:-

Toilets
Fire Appliances
Fire Alarms
Fire Exits
First Aid Provisions
The Company's Health & Safety Policy Statement

I understand that the Employee Information Binder is kept in the ....
and that it is my responsibility to familiarise myself with its contents.

I accept that the attached Statement of Employment in conjunction with the Rules and Disciplinary Procedure and Working Arrangements contained in the Employee Information Binder and which I have read and understand, form part of my Contract of Employment.

Signed: ....

Dated: ....

Figure 9.1.5 This statement, which is signed by the employee, confirms that the employee has read and understood all aspects of the contract, as well as disciplinary procedures and health and safety policy.

really his or her fault, but as long as employers provide safe working conditions and practices, then apart from accidents caused by negligence, they have done everything that they can to make sure that the workplace is a safe place. As we will see shortly, not only can disciplinary action be taken against employees, but they may be dismissed.

Non-compliance with contract

If an employee fails to follow the rules as laid down in the contract of employment, then the employer may take action against him or her. As we will see in the last part of this element, non-compliance with the contract can result in disciplinary action being taken against an employee.

215

For it to be considered that an employee has failed to comply with the contract of employment, one or more of the following may have happened with regard to his or her behaviour at work:

▼ **the employee might have been away from work too often**

▼ **the employee might constantly turn up late for work**

▼ **the employee might refuse to carry out instructions**

▼ **the employee might be unable to do the job properly**

▼ **the employee might have deliberately endangered his or her life or the lives of others**

▼ **the employee might have behaved in an unacceptable manner**

▼ **the employee might have stolen property from the employer**

▼ **the employee might have sexually or racially harassed other employees or customers**

▼ **the employee might have been sleeping at work**

▼ **the employee might have been under the influence of alcohol or drugs at work**

▼ **the employee might have been fighting at work**

DISCIPLINARY ACTION

Regardless of the reason for the disciplinary action in the first place, there is a recommended procedure that should be followed:

▼ **all stages of the procedure should be written down as a record of events**

▼ **copies of the procedure should be available to all employees**

▼ **employees should know who operates the procedure within the organisation**

▼ **employees should know who is likely to get involved during the procedures**

▼ **the employer should make it clear what kind of disciplinary action will be taken in certain circumstances**

▼ **employees should be made aware of the fact that they can appeal**

▼ **employees should know that unless the 'offence' was very serious, they will not be dismissed the first time**

▼ **employees should be sure that the procedure is fair**

▼ **employees should be sure that they will not be discriminated against**

As we will now see, dismissal is not the automatic result of non-compliance with health and safety or the contract of employment. There are stages in the disciplinary actions.

Warning

Warnings are given by employers to employees whose behaviour is unacceptable. The giving of warnings follows a strict procedure and can, in the extreme, lead to suspension. The procedure is as follows:

1   Verbal warning – if an employee's conduct, behaviour or performance does not meet an acceptable standard he or she will be given a formal verbal warning. If the employee behaves correctly after this warning then the matter will be dropped. If not, the disciplinary action will move onto the next stage.

2   Written warning – if the employee carries on with the same behaviour or if the offence was serious enough, a written warning will be issued. This written warning will detail the complaint against the employee and state what he or she has to do to sort the situation out. The employee will also be told how much time is given to improve before further action is taken.

3   Final written warning – if the employee is still failing to improve his or her behaviour or performance a final written warning will be issued. Again, in serious cases the employee may be issued a final written warning straight away. The final warning again details the complaint and tells the employee that dismissal is just around the corner if improvement is not made.

4   Suspension – in some cases the next stage after the final written warning is to suspend

the employee from work without pay. Normally this lasts for about a week and gives both the employee and the employer time to 'cool off'. Hopefully, when the employee returns to work the situation can be sorted out and no further action needs to be taken. However, if further action is needed then the employer has no choice but to move onto the last stage of the disciplinary procedure (dismissal).

The employee can choose to appeal at any stage in the disciplinary procedure. The employee needs to inform his or her superior within two working days and then the appeal will be set in motion. The manager's decision is final but the employee can always seek legal advice or take the matter to court.

Additional training

If the reason for the disciplinary action is based on an employee's fitness or ability to do a job, in other words, if he or she does not have the necessary skill, health, physical or mental ability, then the employer can insist that additional training is undertaken. This, in effect, gives the employee the chance to 'brush up on' and improve his or

her overall abilities so that their duties can be carried out in the correct manner. If, however, the training is unsuccessful and the employee is still unable to do the job it is likely that the employer will have to begin disciplinary action.

Dismissal

Dismissal is the termination or cancellation of an employee's contract of employment by the employer. As we have seen, this usually relates to unacceptable behaviour in the past. The employer will have given the employee notice of the intention to terminate the contract, although in some extreme circumstances dismissal can be instant. The employer needs a valid reason for dismissing an employee and at all times the employer's conduct must be fair towards the employee. Basically, there are four main reasons why someone might be dismissed:

▼ *capability and qualifications* – **in which the employee has shown him or herself to be unable to do the job even though training and retraining has been given on a number of occasions**
▼ *redundancy* – **this occurs when the employer closes down the business or**

part of the business and certain jobs are no longer required

▼ *misconduct* – as we mentioned in the previous section when we looked at behaviour, this relates to non-compliance with the contract of employment

▼ *statutory contraventions* – this means that the employee has broken the law at work, or has broken the law and it will affect his or her work. For example, if a male lorry driver loses his driving licence he can no longer do his job and this is a reason for dismissal

BUSINESS CONNECTION

PC 9.1

We have now looked at all the major ways of investigating the qualities of an employee. To test your memory and skill, complete the following business connection by turning corporate image into disciplinary action. The last letter of each word or phrase is the first letter of the next word or phrase. To help you we have put in the first and last letter on each line, but you will have to do the rest.

C O R P O R A T E   I M A G E
E • • • • • • E
E • • • • • • R
R • • • • • • • T
T • • • • • D
D I S C I P L I N A R Y   A C T I O N

assignment

ELEMENT 9.1

PC 9.1.1–6
COM 1.1, 1.2
IT 1.1, 1.2, 1.3

You may be asked to carry out this assignment along with Elements 9.2 and 9.3 which will include researching a business organisation, having an interview there and looking at the employment induction package. To cover the performance criteria of this element on its own, however, you will have to carry out the following tasks.

| task | **1** | PC 9.1.1–4 |

Give a summary of the corporate image of a chosen business and highlight the importance of employees' qualities in maintaining that image. By looking at the range statements of this element you will be able to make a check list of the kind of things to look for.

| **task** | **2** | PC 9.1.5–6 | | **notes** | |

You should also include in your summary employees' legal responsibilities and behaviour that might lead to disciplinary action. You will probably find this information in the company handbook or in a blank pro-forma copy of the contract of employment.

Your summary and check list should be word processed.

element 9.2

TAKE PART IN INTERVIEWS

Performance criteria

A student must:

1 **Prepare** for an interview.

2 Take part in an interview for a job in a business organisation.

3 **Assess** the effectiveness of his or her performance at an interview.

RANGE

Prepare: travel places (including timings), address of interview, location within an organisation, time, person to meet, personal appearance, attitude, information (about the job, about the organisation), answers to anticipated questions, own questions

Assess: effective preparation, right place, right time, personal appearance, answering questions, asking questions, clear communication, self-confidence, demonstrating understanding (of the job, of the organisation), reviewing outcome of the interview

9.2.1 *Prepare for an interview*

PREPARATION

If you have been asked to attend an interview, then this is something of an achievement in itself. You will have received a letter which tells you the time and place of the interview. You must first confirm that you will be attending and then begin to prepare yourself for the interview itself.

Travel places (including timings)

Unless you are lucky enough to be attending an interview within walking distance, it is a good idea to find the quickest and most reliable way of getting to the venue of the interview before you make the actual journey. This may involve looking at bus or train timetables to check times and to see how frequent the service is. If you are going to do a 'test run' of the route, make sure that you do it at the same time as you will have to travel to get to the interview; if you travel at the weekend when the time of the interview actually means you will have to travel during the rush hour, then you will not be aware of the impact of the rush hour on the speed of the transport you are using.

When you decide on the route you will take, do not assume that all buses or trains will actually be running on time or at all. You should consider taking an earlier bus or train just in case there is a problem; it is better to arrive at your destination early than sit on a train or bus which has been delayed and worry.

---

finding out

PC 9.2.1
COM 1.2

Individually, work out the quickest and most reliable route to the following:

- **your local town or city hall**
- **your local job centre**
- **your nearest airport**
- **your nearest railway station**

Address of interview

By the time you get to the interview stage you will, of course, know the address of the organisation that you are visiting. You should consider the following in relation to the address you will be visiting:

▼ **you may not know exactly where it is – you may know where the street or road is, but not at which end the building is situated**

▼ **the organisation which you are visiting may only occupy part of the building in which it is situated. If this is the case, you will need to know how to get to the exact venue of the interview once you have entered the building. We discuss this in the next range statement**

▼ the place at which the interview is taking place may not necessarily be the same as the business address of the organisation. Some interviews take place in hotels or even in local job centres and employment agencies. Be aware of this and make sure you do not go to the wrong address

Location within an organisation

Assuming that you have found the right building and got to the right part of that building, you must now find the room in which the interview is going to take place. A room number might be stated on the letter that was sent to you by the organisation and there will probably be a reception area where you can ask for directions. If this is not the case, you can only hope that the building is well sign-posted to enable you to find the right room.

Time

It is important that you arrive for the interview 5–10 minutes before you are expected. This extra time may prove useful if you get delayed for any reason or cannot find the right room in the build-ing. The danger of being late and the worry that this might cause will mean that you are not prop-erly prepared for the interview and this should be avoided at all costs. Also, it does not look good if you arrive late for an interview. This is the first impression that the organisation will get of you and does not put you in a very good position.

Organisations do not mind if you arrive early but you should not arrive more than about half an hour early as you will have to sit around and wait for your appointment time.

Person to meet

Make sure that you know exactly who you need to see. If the letters that you have received from the organisation simply ask you to come and see the personnel manager, for example, make sure that you ask at reception who this person actually

Figure 9.2.1 Making sure that you take careful note of all the details given to you over the telephone is essential preparation for an interview (courtesy of Mercury Communications).

is so that you know his or her name before the interview. If the person you are seeing has written to you directly, there will be a signature at the bottom of the letter with the name printed underneath. Finding out the exact name of the person is also important if the name is not clear at the bottom of the letter or the name simply gives the initials and not the first name of the person involved.

Personal appearance

We are not all fortunate enough to have a selection of smart clothing to suit any set of circumstances. It is, however, normal practice to dress as smartly and tidily as possible when attending an interview. The following are some general points to consider:

▼ **men should wear a collar and tie in most situations and women should wear a skirt**

▼ **it is also a good idea to think about having your hair cut or tidied prior to the interview since untidy hair can often give the wrong impression**

▼ **men should make sure that they have shaved if they need to**

▼ **women should make sure that they do not wear too much make-up, and that what is being worn is applied carefully**

Attitude

Knowing exactly what the interviewer is looking for is not easy. He or she will be looking for someone who does have a certain amount of confidence but who is not *too* confident. Whilst you should try to get your point of view across during the interview and appear to be interested at all times, do not simply sit there and expect the interviewer to do all the hard work. You will be expected to contribute to the conversation and respond to questions, as we will see later. You will not be expected to know everything about the organisation or the job, but the interviewer will assume that you have done some homework before coming to the interview. Simply shrugging

your shoulders and saying you do not know will not give a very good impression.

Information (about the job and organisation)

As we have said, doing some homework before the interview is a good idea. To have got this far you will have filled in an application form, read the job description and any other leaflets, booklets or information that were sent by the organisation to you. Not having read these does not put you in a very good position. It is a good idea, particularly if you have to travel some distance to the interview, to take all the information you have about the organisation and the job with you; you can then read and review this *en route* to the interview. This will refresh your memory and put you in a much better position to answer questions. Whilst you are reading all of this it is always a good idea, again as we will see later, to think about what you will be asked and whether you have any questions yourself.

Answers to anticipated questions

The best starting point is to look at the list of skills or qualities that the organisation is asking for in a potential employee. Phrases such as 'ability to work on your own', 'organised' or 'good communication skills' are all potential starting points for questions about your own abilities and skills to do the job. You may be asked even more general questions, like 'why do you think you would be good at this job?' and 'if we offered you this job, would you accept it?' Although the answer to this may be obvious to you, as you would not be at the interview if you did not want the job, you are in fact being asked why you want the job. Simply saying that you are unemployed or you want to earn some money is not enough. Depending on the type of job and organisation, you can answer by saying things like 'it is a good career start', 'I have always been interested in this type of work' or 'it is what I have been trained for'.

Own questions

Most interviewers will not expect you to simply sit there and answer questions all the time. To put across a good impression you should have thought about the kinds of things you would like to ask. Although you will have considered this before the interview, be aware that the question that you were going to ask may have already been answered before you ask it, and that you would look foolish to ask again. Sometimes questions spring into your mind during the interview; think about these and then decide whether you are going to ask them when you are given the opportunity. Above all, listen to the answer and appear to be interested in the response; there is no point in just asking the question and thinking that is all that you need to do.

9.2.2 Take part in an interview for a job in a business organisation

This performance criterion is a practical one and forms the central part of the element assignment. It is probably a good idea to practise your interview performance at your centre, particularly if you are going to go for a real interview or have an interview with someone outside your centre. Not only will this give you a chance to try out different sorts of questions, but it will also give you some idea as to how confident you may or may not feel when the real interview takes place. Nobody is expecting you to perform perfectly the first time, although you will be expected to improve with practice.

In order to give you some basic practice at interviews, try the following activity with one of your group members.

FIGURE IT OUT

PC 9.2.2
COM 1.1

In pairs, take the roles of interviewee and interviewer alternatively. Ask your partner the following questions and see how he or she responds to them:

- *can you tell me a little bit about your GNVQ course?*
- *what kind of leisure or social activities do you enjoy?*
- *why do you think good organisation skills are important in almost any job?*
- *what is your career intention?*
- *would you be prepared to undertake any further training and education and, if so, what would you like it to be?*

9.2.3 **A**ssess the effectiveness of his or her performance at an interview

ASSESSMENT

Assessment involves reviewing the good and bad aspects of your interview. There will be times when you feel that you could have done better than you did, or others when you feel that you gave exactly the right answer at exactly the right time. This last performance criterion asks you to keep an accurate log of your performance and for you to note anything relevant about your performance so that you can review it at a later date. By keeping a log you will also be able to create a check list of good and bad practice.

Effective preparation

No matter how much or how little preparation you have undertaken before the interview, you will only know if you have done enough when the interview actually begins. An interviewer will nearly always ask you about something you have not even thought about; you may be asked something particularly awkward just to see how you react, or asked a question to which you are not expected to know the answer, just to see how you cope with the situation. There are very few people who can walk into an interview perfectly prepared and give a faultless interview performance without a single problem. Do not be surprised if your performance is not exactly perfect.

Obviously, the more preparation you do, then the more chance you have of getting things right. However, although no preparation is foolish, over-preparation can cause confusion as you will have too many things to remember. Undertake your preparation logically and systematically, tackling only what needs to be done immediately before you move onto the next stage of the inter-

view preparation. There are many things you cannot prepare for until other things have been completed.

Right place

As we discussed earlier, knowing the exact location of the interview and how to reach it is very important and you should prepare for this in advance. One thing you cannot prepare for, however, is if the location is changed to perhaps a different site of the same organisation or a different room within the same building without your knowledge. If this does happen, you will probably be redirected when you arrive at the original location.

Do not make any particular assumptions about the type of room in which you are interviewed. It may be a standard office with the interviewer behind a desk or it may be slightly more frightening with a row of people throwing questions at you. However, the interview may not necessarily be this formal; it may simply be a conversation in comfortable surroundings where you are encouraged to discuss the position.

In terms of assessing your performance to be in the right place, you should consider the ease with which you found the interview location and your ability to follow any directions that were given to you about where the building was or where the interview room was located.

Right time

As we said earlier, you should attempt to get to the interview location before the interview time. Remember that you are probably not the only person being interviewed for the job and that the interviewer has a busy schedule of interviews. If you are late you not only run the risk of giving the wrong impression, but you may also even lose your chance to have the interview at all. Arriving late means unnecessary panic and may not give you the opportunity to collect your thoughts or make sure that you look your best.

In assessment terms, when you consider getting to the interview at the right time, you should think about how early you arrived at the location and whether your pre-planned route worked. Was it a good idea to allow some extra time for travel, or did you arrive at the location far too early and were forced to wait around outside the building before entering it?

Personal appearance

It is possible that you may be surprised by the appearance of the interviewer. If you have made an effort to look as smart and tidy as possible and the interviewer is scruffy and unkempt then you may think that you made the wrong choice about your own appearance. This may not necessarily be the case. People in a working environment have to adapt to whatever the normal dress codes are and may not have to wear smart clothes at all times. This is particularly true if you are being interviewed for a job which involves some form of manual work. It is always best to assume that you will be expected to look smart and well presented for the interview.

In terms of assessing yourself, did you make the right choice of clothing? Did you feel comfortable in what you were wearing and did you wear clothes that were suitable for the weather? Were

your shoes sensible if you had to walk a long way? Did you feel out of place and that everyone else in the building, particularly other interviewees, looked different or better than you?

Answering questions

Assuming that you did do some preparation before the interview, then you will have known something about the organisation that you were visiting. A good interviewer will not ask you questions that are designed to trip you up; the questions will be aimed at trying to find out how much you know about the organisation and how much you know about yourself. The interviewer will have a copy of your application form in front of him or her, and will also have a job description and a check list of the sorts of skills and qualities that are required. Hopefully your application form or CV will show that your skills match the requirements as closely as possible. If they do not, then this will be a probable area of questioning, as the interviewer will try to establish whether or not you are suitable for the job.

In any job interview expect to be asked about

Figure 9.2.2 Formal dress for both men and women is still very much expected for an interview (courtesy of Mercury Communications).

your own career intentions. The interviewer will want to know whether you intend to stay with the company for any length of time or whether you just see this job as a stepping stone to a better position. No employer will necessarily expect you to stay for life, but will be looking for a certain amount of commitment, for at least a couple of years or so.

In terms of assessment consider how easy and how fully you answered any questions put to you. Hopefully, you did not dry up or feel that you were unable to understand or answer a question. Equally, you should not have talked for ages in response to a simple question. It is inevitable that once you have left the interview room you will think about something that you should have said in response to a question that did not occur to you at the time. Do not worry about this as it is perfectly normal, but it is worth noting down in your assessment as you will be aware of this the next time.

Asking questions

Preparing and asking your own questions is a good idea, assuming that the interviewer has not already covered this ground with you. Do not feel that you necessarily have to ask a question if nothing occurs to you naturally. It is better not to ask a question than to ask something that is pointless and makes you appear foolish. The other thing to remember when asking questions is not to try to be too clever. Putting the interviewer 'on the spot' and making him or her feel uncomfortable if unable to answer the question you have asked is not in your best interests. If you can, try to ask something that you know is of interest. This will give the impression that you are interested in this too and may be of great value when the interviewer reviews the performance of all of the interviewees. If he or she can remember you in more detail than someone else, then you will have a better chance of success.

In terms of assessment, think about the way in which you phrased your questions and how easily the interviewer responded. Remember that you are not restricted to just asking one question, but that you should not ask too many as the interviewer may be on a tight schedule and another

interviewee may be waiting. This will make the interviewer uncomfortable and he or she may become irritated by too many questions from you.

Clear communication

As an essential part of answering and asking questions, your speech should be clear and easy to understand. It is extremely important not to mumble or talk into your hand or your chest. This can show a lack of confidence, as well as making it very difficult for the interviewer to understand what you are saying. The interviewer will not expect you to be brimming with confidence, as even the most experienced people suffer from nerves during interviews. The main point about clear communication is to ensure that what you need to say to the interviewer is said in the clearest, most concise and pleasant manner.

Self-confidence

As we said earlier, showing a degree of confidence, even if you may not feel confident inside, is an important part of playing the interview game. Bearing in mind that the interviewer will have seen or will be seeing a number of potential candidates, he or she will be looking for some very basic ways of reducing the number of candidates that need serious consideration. If you show a high level of nervousness or uncertainty at the interview, then regardless of your ability to do the job or the amount of relevant skills you may have, the interviewer will probably eliminate you as being unsuitable.

Gaining self-confidence is something that can only be done with practice. Being a good interviewee means taking on a role. That role may not truly reflect your personality or your normal behaviour. You will have to quickly assess what you believe the interviewer is looking for. Again, this comes with practice and it is worthwhile looking at advertisements for jobs in your local newspapers and trying to figure out the kind of qualities that an interviewer would be looking for in candidates for these positions.

Demonstrating understanding (of the job and the organisation)

As already mentioned earlier in this element, it is essential that you do some background reading on the organisation and its activities. From the time you decide that you would like to be interviewed for a particular job you should begin to collect information to assist you. Most employers who respond to applicants by post will include an information pack in either the letter containing the application form or the letter informing the applicant of the interview date. This collection of material will include many things that do not appear to be very useful. Indeed, much of the information may not be relevant at interview. However, it is better to have read at the very least the information sent to you by the organisation. If the interviewer has not provided you with all the basic information, then you must take it upon yourself to research the organisation and find out as much as you can about it.

Reviewing the outcome of the interview

In a real interview situation the ultimate way of reviewing the outcome would be whether you

Figure 9.2.3 As part of the interview process, some employers may expect you to show practical understanding of the job (courtesy of the Employment Department Group).

were offered the job or not. In a simulated interview you will be assessed on your performance and, in your tutor's opinion, whether you would have got the job had it been a real interview. Here are some questions which you may like to ask yourself in order to help you review the outcome of your interview:

▼ **what happened? Try not to make judgements or conclusions; just simply describe what happened**
▼ **what were your reactions and feelings during the interview?**
▼ **was it a good or bad experience?**

▼ **what sense can you make out of the situation?**
▼ **what conclusions can you draw from your experience?**
▼ **what are you going to do differently in this type of situation next time?**
▼ **what steps are you going to take on the basis of what you have learnt?**

Your tutor may be able to help you bring out the main points regarding your performance, behaviour and attitude during the interview. Remember that it is always important, even during a simulated activity, to take the situation as seriously as you would if it had been the real thing.

BUSINESS CONNECTION

PC 9.3

We have now looked at all the major ways of taking part in interviews. To test your memory and skill, complete the following business connection by turning preparation into success. The last letter of each word or phrase is the first letter of the next word or phrase. To help you we have put in the first and last letter on each line, but you will have to do the rest.

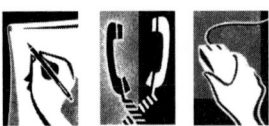

assignment

ELEMENT **9.2**

PC 9.2.1–3
COM 1.1, 1.2, 1.4
IT 1.1, 1.2, 1.3

In order to cover the performance criteria of this element you will need to actually prepare, take part in and then assess your personal performance at interview. You will be asked to do this as part of your work experience, when applying for an actual job or in a role-play situation with your tutor at the centre.

task 1 PC 9.2.1

Obtain all the necessary information regarding the time, place and person involved in your interview. You will have to include a letter confirming that you will attend at the appointed time. You should also obtain timetables and routes to the interview location. As a final piece of preparation you should also think about the kind of questions that you may be asked.

task 2 PC 9.2.2

This task is based around the actual interview itself. Remember that you will be assessed on your performance but you should also be assessing yourself. In this respect a good assessment of a bad interview is more useful than a bad assessment of a good one.

task 3 PC 9.2.3

In the final part of this assignment you should assess your performance before, during and after the interview. Using the range statements at the beginning of this element, you must word process a series of comments on all of the aspects under assessment.

notes

It is a good idea to keep a log as an accurate record of your performance completed by yourself. Your tutor or assessor will then be able to verify the log as an accurate record of what actually happened. Bear in mind that for evidence purposes your tutor or assessor may wish to video or tape record your interview. This could prove to be very valuable when you have to assess your performance in Task 3.

INVESTIGATE PAYMENT FOR WORK

Performance criteria

A student must:

1 Identify and give examples of the main **types** and **forms of payment**.

2 Identify and give examples of **common fringe benefits**.

3 Identify and give examples of **common deductions** shown on pay slips.

4 **Calculate** take-home pay accurately using given data.

RANGE

Types of payment: hourly wage, salary; gross, net; piece rate, hourly, weekly, monthly; bonuses, overtime

Forms of payment: cash, cheque, credit transfer to bank

Common fringe benefits: subsidised meals and drinks, travel, discount on purchases, loans, health insurance, pensions, sports and social clubs, clothing

Common deductions: tax, national insurance, union subscription, pension

Calculate: percentages, addition, subtraction, totals, gross pay, net pay

9.3.1 *Identify and give examples of the main types and forms of payment*

TYPES OF PAYMENT

Depending on the type of job you are doing, you will be paid either a wage or a salary. Wages tend to be based on the number of hours which you have worked in a particular week. Salaries, on the other hand, are one twelfth of your annual pay. In both cases payment is nearly always made 'in arrears', which means that you work for several days or even a few weeks before you get paid. As we will see, wages tend to be paid on a weekly (or sometimes fortnightly) basis and salaries tend to be paid on a monthly basis, or every four weeks.

Hourly wage

If your employer quotes you an hourly wage, then it is relatively easy to work out how much you will be paid per week. All you need to do is to multiply the hourly payment by the number of hours you have worked. You should also remember that employers do not count lunch breaks as a working hour, but may count morning or afternoon tea breaks into the total amount they will pay. In the past, workers paid hourly tended to be manual employees who did not undertake office work. However, many employers now use the hourly rate to pay many of their workers, including office staff. As we will see later, employees paid by the hour are either paid at the end of the week they have worked, or paid at the end of the second week they have worked so that they are paid one whole week in arrears.

Salary

A salary is calculated per annum or pa (yearly) and then paid monthly in 12 equal amounts to employees. This method of payment means that employees know exactly how much they can expect to receive (before any overtime payments or deductions other than national insurance and income tax, which everyone must pay). Salaried staff tend to be paid towards the end of the month and may have had to work as much as five weeks before they are paid. Normally the employer will pay the monthly salary on the same day of each month, but bear in mind that since some months are longer than others, there can be longer gaps between payment. For example, if

---

FIGURE IT OUT

PC 9.3.1
COM 1.1, 1.2

00:10

Without using any of the examples we have given, in pairs, make one list of jobs which you think would be carried out by 'wage' earners and another of jobs carried out by 'salaried' personnel. Discuss your findings with those of the rest of the group.

someone is paid on the last Friday of the month, this payment will be relatively early if the month has only 28 days, but may be much later if the month has 31 days.

Gross pay

Whenever you are quoted a wage or salary you must always remember that this is the amount that will be paid before tax, national insurance or any other deductions have been made. This is known as your gross wage or salary. Only self-employed people will be paid the full gross amount since they have to work out and pay their own tax and national insurance. The majority of people will receive net pay.

Net pay

Net pay is what is left of your wages or salary after deductions have been made. We will look at the more common deductions a little later in this element. With tax, national insurance, pension schemes and other deductions, you could be left with as little as half of your gross pay and this is worth bearing in mind when looking at the wages or salaries offered by employers; you should really be thinking about what you will actually take home rather than the gross pay they are quoting.

Piece rate

Piece rate is quite common in factories and in home working which involves some form of assembly or manufacture by hand. For example, those working at home making lampshades, stitching clothing and addressing envelopes will all be paid on the piece-rate method. This means that every item they have completed (subject to some very close quality checks) will entitle them to a small payment. For piece-rate workers to earn a good level of pay they not only have to be fast but they also have to be accurate and produce high quality work.

Piece-rate workers tend to be paid on completion of a batch of work. They will be expected to produce a basic minimum number of items over a given length of time, but the employer will really

hope that they will exceed this basic amount as long as the quality standards are good enough.

Hourly rate

From an employer's point of view, paying an hourly rate is ideal for the employment of part-time or casual workers. However, as we have said, a large number of full-time employees are also paid on an hourly rate. If the hours of full-time employees are always the same each week, then apart from the fact that they are paid weekly, their circumstances are almost exactly the same as those of salaried members of staff. Part-time workers may be offered a minimum number of hours per week and then if they are asked to do more hours, their wages will be amended accordingly. Casual workers, on the other hand, who cannot rely on a set number of hours per day or week, are called in by the employer to help cope with busy periods or seasonal rushes (such as packing orders for Christmas or dealing with telephone enquiries during the holiday period).

Weekly wage

Some employers, rather than quoting an annual salary, will state how much an employee will earn per week. Again, this is based on a particular number of hours that have to be worked in order to receive that wage. It is normal practice for an employer to pay a weekly wage at the end of the week, probably at lunch time or at the end of the working day on Friday. Employees who are paid in this way can find out how much they are being paid per hour by dividing the number of hours worked into the weekly wage. In a similar way, by multiplying the weekly wage by 52, they will discover their annual wage.

Monthly salary

Monthly payment is, as we have already said, the normal way to pay a salaried employee. The employer will make the payment on a particular day of the month, such as the 28th of each month, or will state that the payment will be made on the last Friday of each month. Some employers make this a little more complicated and actually pay their employees 13 times per year. This is because they pay every four weeks rather than each month and since there are 52 weeks in the year, 13 is the number of payments if you divide 52 by 4. This means that the pay is slightly more regular but, of course, each payment is slightly less since you are being paid 13 times instead of 12.

Bonuses

Bonuses are usually paid to employees for two rather different reasons:

▼ **if the employee has personally achieved a particular target or goal set by his or her employer**
▼ **if the organisation as a whole has achieved a particular target or goal set**

by the management or owners of the organisation

Sometimes, as a variation on the personal bonus, the whole department or team receives the same amount of bonus if it has achieved a particular target or goal. This serves as a way of encouraging the whole team to work together to achieve. Company bonus schemes can be quite complicated, but usually these extra payments are made either at Christmas or as soon as the organisation has worked out whether it has made a profit in a particular year, and in this case the bonuses are paid sometime in April.

Some organisations, rather than offering cash, will offer prizes to their 'star performers'. For example, a salesperson who has achieved the highest sales target in a particular month may be given an all-expenses-paid holiday abroad. More commonly though, the gift will be something a little more modest, such as an electric kettle or toaster.

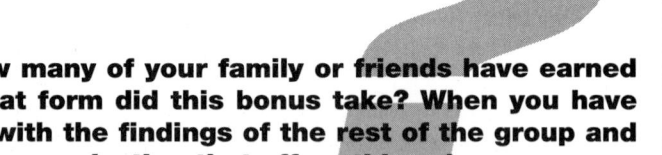

finding out

PC 9.3.1
COM 1.1, 1.2

During the next week find out how many of your family or friends have earned a bonus with their organisation. What form did this bonus take? When you have collected this information compare with the findings of the rest of the group and list the advantages of working for an organisation that offers this scheme.

Overtime

Overtime refers to any hours, or for that matter days, that have been worked in excess of the number of hours or days that the employee is normally supposed to work. For most employees this will mean that they are paid more for that hour or day than they would normally be paid for a stan-

dard hour or day. Employers do this to encourage their employees to do the overtime rather than going to the expense of having to get in new staff to cover a handful of hours or the odd day. For some workers paid by the hour, particularly those that are part time or casual, overtime just means working extra hours. They may not be paid any more money for those hours than they would normally be paid for a standard hour. However, they are often grateful for the extra work and do it all the same. You may have heard some people refer to overtime as being 'at time and a half' (which means half as much again as they are normally paid) or 'double time' (which means they are paid twice the amount they are normally paid).

As an alternative to being paid for overtime, employees may be given time off 'in lieu'. This means that they will be allowed to take the same number of hours or days off as paid leave for having done the overtime. Just as some employees are paid time and a half or double time for overtime, an extra day at Christmas, for example, may mean that they can take two or three days off in lieu for having worked that overtime. Normally if overtime is undertaken at the weekend, particularly on Sundays, or on bank holidays, the employer has to offer a good incentive for the employee to even think about doing the overtime.

FORMS OF PAYMENT

If one thing can be said about all the different forms of payment that are made to employees, then it is that the choice of payment is nearly always the one that suits the employer rather than the employee. Employers will choose the most convenient form of payment to them without necessarily thinking about whether this is best for the employee or not. As we will see, there are three main forms of payment, although credit transfer to the employee's bank is becoming the most common.

Cash

In the past, payment by cash was perhaps the most common form of receiving your wage or salary from your employer. However, many employers do not wish to take the risk of having to arrange the delivery of several thousands of pounds on, say, a Friday and then go to the trouble of splitting up that delivery into pay packets and giving those pay packets to the correct people. Not only is there a risk of robbery, but also the expense of elaborate security equipment and

accounts staff on hand to sort out the pay packets. Organising payment like this also means that pay days can be disrupted by employees having to queue for their pay packets and valuable time lost for the employer.

There are still a number of employers who insist that payment by cash is the most convenient way of paying their employees. Indeed, many employees would not like to be paid in any other way. Having cash in a wage packet means that you do not have to go to the bother of visiting the bank and you always know exactly how much money you have left. These pay packets also include a pay slip which gives details of gross pay, deductions and the net pay total. They also, normally, give a running total of how much tax and national insurance the employee has paid in that particular year.

Cash is still a very common way of being paid as a part-time or casual worker. After all, particularly with casual workers, employees do not know when they will see the employer again, if ever, and would not wish to leave work without taking their money with them.

Cheque

Cheques are probably the most inconvenient way of being paid. After all, a cheque needs to be paid into an account or cashed at a bank. Some large employers have an arrangement with their own banks which allows their employees to go into the branch (showing suitable identification) and have the cheque cashed immediately. Whether the employees then choose to take the money out in cash or have some of it or all of it transferred into their own accounts is up to them. One advantage a cheque does have for an employer, particularly if the cheque is being given on a Friday, is that the employee may not pay the cheque in until the Saturday morning or the following Monday, and then it has to clear (which could take as much as a week) before the cash is taken out of the employer's account.

As with cash, the cheque is also accompanied by a pay slip which includes all of the information we have mentioned already.

Credit transfer to bank

This form of payment is fast becoming the most common way of receiving a wage or salary. From the point of view of employers, they only need to fill in a summary sheet which details their employees' account details and the amount to be paid. For those employees who receive a regular amount at regular intervals, a standard transfer can be set up which guarantees payment on a particular day of the month. The big advantage for employees is that as soon as the money has been transferred into their account it can be drawn out again, they do not have to wait for a cheque to clear as this is an electronic transfer of funds from one account to another.

Employees will, of course, receive a statement, perhaps a day or two before the payment is due to be made, which details how much is being paid into their accounts. The statement will also include the gross pay, deductions and net pay, along with the total amount of tax and national insurance paid so far that year.

For some larger organisations who have a direct computer link with their bank, the electronic transfer of funds could not be easier. They simply type in the amount to be credited to a particular employee and, at the touch of a button, it is transferred.

9.3.2 *Identify and give examples of common fringe benefits*

COMMON FRINGE BENEFITS

Rather than offering extra pay, or higher rates of pay, some employers offer a series of fringe benefits to attract employees or keep the staff they already have. Fringe benefits are also known as 'non-financial incentives' which are aimed at providing employees with a little extra that cannot be taxed. In this way, they receive the full effect of the fringe benefit.

Subsidised meals and drinks

If you work for an organisation which is involved in the catering industry, then subsidised, or even free, meals and drinks are often commonplace. Many larger organisations, which may have no association with catering, offer their staff reduced rate (sometimes known as 'at cost') food and refreshment. Whilst the promise of a three-course lunch for under £1 may be attractive, it is rarely the only reason for someone to choose to work for that particular employer.

Some supermarket chains offer their staff extremely cheap food and drink at work, since much of the menu on offer is made up of food which is close to its sell-by date. In this way, they not only offer their employees an added bonus of cheap food, but also do not waste food which they would otherwise throw away.

As an alternative to food and drink offered on the premises of an organisation, some employers give luncheon vouchers. These can be exchanged for food and drink at a number of outlets, including supermarkets in most high streets or town centres. They have a cash value and some employees actually prefer to collect and keep their luncheon vouchers and spend them on an evening meal so they can fully enjoy the benefit of a free night out.

Travel

Another incentive to employees is free or subsidised travel. The nature of this type of incentive will differ from organisation to organisation. This incentive could take one of the following forms:

▼ *free pick-up and drop-off – for employees who live in remote areas and would otherwise find it extremely difficult to get into work. In these instances the employer provides a free* coach or bus service which makes pick-ups and drop-offs in a number of small villages and towns

▼ *free travel passes* – offered by some larger organisations, to enable their employees to travel on public transport, either in the course of work, or during their leisure time

▼ *travel loan schemes* – employers pay for the employees' season tickets in order to take advantage of discounts available. The employee pays back the employer with regular monthly payments which are interest free

▼ *company cars* – key employees or those that have to travel considerable distances in the course of their work are often provided with a company car and a credit card to pay for petrol

▼ *essential car users' allowance* – organisations who do not offer company cars give some of their key employees a credit card or a charge account at specific petrol stations to help towards the running costs of their own cars being used for company business

▼ *overseas travel* – for employees who have to make regular trips abroad, the organisation provides them with the means to purchase tickets as and when they need to. This may be done either through a recommended travel agency, or by giving these employees a credit card to buy the tickets. The organisation will be able to monitor the use of a credit card and it will be useful to the employee for other expenses as well as travel

▼ *reimbursement* – for occasional travel carried out by employees or other expenses incurred in the course of their work, organisations tend to use 'expenses claims forms' to pay back

employees for any outlay they have made in the course of their work for the organisation

Discount on purchases

Some organisations, particularly those involved in retailing, offer their employees a discount on purchases from the organisation. This not only serves as a useful incentive to employees, but also ensures that they use the company's products and, by doing so, are able to sell them more easily to other customers. In any case, it would not do for the employees of a retail organisation to be purchasing products from a competitor; this is certainly not a very good advertisement for their employer.

The procedures used when employees purchase from their employer are often very carefully monitored to avoid mis-use of the incentive. Some employers restrict the amount that employees can purchase to stop them from selling the products on to other people.

For larger purchases, the employee may also be able to obtain not only a discount, but also a reduced rate or an interest-free loan, as we shall see in the next section of this element.

Loans

Banks and building societies, in particular, offer their employees loans or mortgages at reduced rates and these are a very valuable incentive. Whilst the employee works for the organisation he or she can enjoy loans and mortgages at considerably lower rates of interest than the normal rate. Other organisations give advances on salaries and wages which are, in effect, loans, and are paid off gradually by the employee. Employees need to be aware that any loans and mortgages given to them by their current employer will have to be renegotiated or paid off if they cease to be employed by the company.

Health insurance

Key members of staff in particular may be offered health insurance as part of their overall wage or salary package. This private health insurance often covers their families too. The employer, by ensuring that key employees are covered by private health insurance, can be assured that the minimum amount of disruption occurs if the employee falls ill or needs medical attention.

From an employee's point of view, he or she can feel secure in the fact that any serious medical problem can be dealt with as quickly as possible and that valuable time will not be lost by having to wait for medical attention on the National Health Service.

Pensions

There are two different types of pension in addition to the state pension which employees receive as a result of paying national insurance. These are:

▼ **contributory pensions – where the employee and employer both pay into the pension scheme**
▼ **non-contributory pensions – where only the employer pays into the pension scheme on behalf of the employee**

Bearing in mind that anyone can pay up to around 17.5% of his or her total income to a pension scheme tax free, this can prove to be quite an incentive to both the employee and the employer.

The government is very keen for employees to be able to support themselves financially when they retire and has made it relatively easy to set up a pension scheme and monitor the payments. Some organisations offer one of the following:

▼ **company pension schemes – where a specific pension fund has been set up to pay the pension of retired employees. All employees pay into this scheme and the benefits from this joint 'saving' is passed on to the retired members of staff**
▼ **personal pension schemes – where the pension scheme is a more general one and is not company-based, but is related to the employee as an individual. One of the advantages here is that the personal pension scheme is movable from one employer to the next, as well as having the additional benefit of being part of a much larger overall pension fund**

In the past, planning for future retirement was not something that many people necessarily considered at a young age. In fact, nowadays, it is rare to find an employer who does not actively encourage staff to join a company pension scheme or set up a private one. The key aspect to consider of a company pension scheme is whether the employer makes a contribution to the employee's pension fund or not. If not, then it is not really an incentive as such, although the employer may be able to take the complication out of organising a pension for yourself by being able to offer a company scheme.

Sports and social clubs

Some organisations, particularly those who value teamwork and team building, offer their employees a range of sports and social activities to engage in at either no cost or heavily subsidised rates. Many banks and other large organisations have their own sports and social clubs, with a variety of different activities on offer. Other smaller organisations have entered into agreements with local leisure and sports clubs and have 'block membership deals' (a lump sum paid by the employer to the leisure club as payment for the membership of a large number of employees).

Some organisations take this aspect even further and positively encourage inter-departmental competitions in various sports and games. Others may organise day trips or visits for their employees, laying on the transport, food, drink and activities at the destination.

Holiday clubs are also offered by some organisations, which give employees the opportunity to travel to a holiday destination which they would not necessarily be able to afford if they were booking it themselves.

Clothing

Despite the fact that many company uniforms are not exactly to the taste of most employees, the fact that they are provided by the employer can be seen as something of an incentive. By having to wear a company uniform, employees do not have to wear their own clothes to work and can save money by not having to buy clothes for that purpose. Most organisations provide a number of sets of uniforms to each employee, but do expect employees to make sure that they are cleaned. Others merely require the employee to wear the uniform whilst at work and then leave the dirty uniform so that the employer can organise for it to be cleaned. Employees then simply pick up a clean uniform when they come into work again the next day.

As an alternative to providing uniforms, employers may give their employees a clothing allowance. With a number of restrictions, such as specifying that they choose particular colours or styles, the employer allows employees to choose their own work clothes.

FIGURE IT OUT

PC 9.3.2
COM 1.1

`00:10`

*A*s a group, discuss the advantages and disadvantages of the fringe benefits we have listed since you carried out the last activity.

9.3.3 *Identify and give examples of common deductions shown on pay slips*

COMMON DEDUCTIONS

Employees do not receive their full wage or salary. Before the money is given to them or transferred into their account, various common deductions are made. Some are required by law, such as tax, and others are voluntary, such as pension contributions.

Tax

Tax is deducted by employers on behalf of the Inland Revenue. They must do this and promptly pass the money onto the appropriate government department. Although the deduction process is complicated, it does follow a particular procedure.

The Inland Revenue works out the personal allowance of the employee based on marital status and other considerations. He or she will be taxed on all money earned above the specified personal allowance so, the more that is earned, the more tax is paid. The employee will have a clear statement on his or her pay slip stating the amount of tax that has been deducted and will receive a slip which states the total amount of tax paid in the last year annually.

The tax paid by employees and business organisations funds a great deal of government spending on schools, the civil service, the police, road building and many other expensive projects.

National insurance

National insurance is paid by all employees and a contribution is also made by the employer. Unlike tax there is no personal allowance and you pay national insurance on everything that you earn. National insurance funds all of the sick pay, maternity pay and state pensions paid out to people. Again, the employer is responsible for col-

PAY ADVICE

N.I. Number	Tax Code	Basis	Year	Period	Pay No	Pay Centre	
GROSS PAY		STANDARD DEDUCTIONS		VOLUNTARY DEDUCTIONS			NET PAY
Code				Code			
Total Gross Pay				Total Deductions			
Hours worked Normal Overtime		TOTALS TO DATE			VOL DEDUCTIONS		
					Code Balance Owed		

Figure 9.3.1 An example of a pay slip.

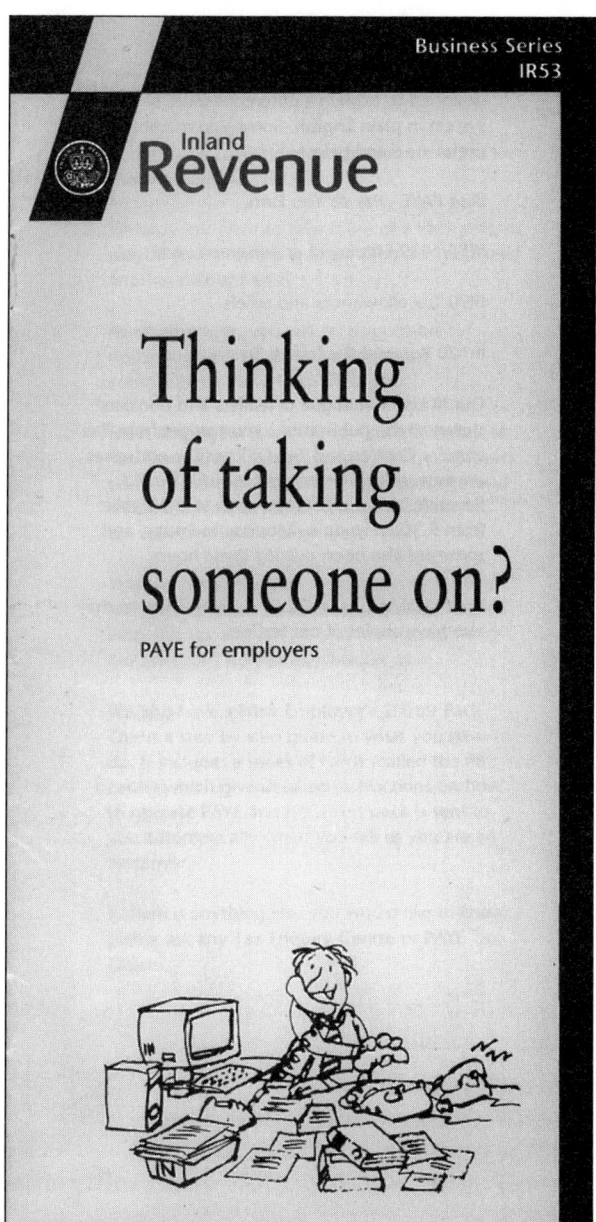

Business Series
IR53

Inland
Revenue

Thinking
of taking
someone on?

PAYE for employers

Figure 9.3.2 The front page from the Inland Revenue booklet about tax contributions for employers.

Union subscription

Members of trade unions will pay a weekly, monthly or annual subscription or membership fee. This will either be a standard amount, regardless of how much you earn, or will be on a sliding scale which increases as you earn more. Trade union subscriptions are, of course, voluntary, as you do not need to be a member of a trade union. However, many people realise the benefits of being in a trade union as it can offer additional insurance, legal advice, protection from unreasonable employers and representation in disciplinary matters and pay negotiations.

Pension

Although we all pay national insurance which goes towards our state pension when we retire, many people believe that the state pension will not give them a sufficiently high standard of living when they stop working. There are a number of different types of pension, all of which require the employee to make regular payments. These are:

▼ **state-earnings related pension scheme – which is a government-run pension**
▼ **company pension scheme – which is run and administered by the employer on behalf of the employees**
▼ **personal pension scheme – which is set up by individuals to cope with their own particular needs**
▼ **occupational pension scheme – which is run and administered nationally for all members of an occupational group and is also known as superannuation**

lecting the national insurance on behalf of the Department of Social Security and must promptly pass any money collected on to it.

Perhaps the most important user of national insurance contributions is the National Health Service.

9.3.4 *Calculate take-home pay accurately using given data*

CALCULATIONS

Where numbers are concerned it is always a good idea to get someone else to check your work. Carrying out accurate calculations is probably one of the most important duties that a business will expect of its employees. If an error is made in a calculation, it could have the following effects:

▼ **employees will be annoyed and this will not be good for the business. If their pay is wrong they will feel unhappy and will want something done about it immediately**
▼ **the overall total for the wage or salary bill will be wrong. This means that the error will be on several documents and it will not be until you have cross-checked all of the documents that you will be able to find the original error**
▼ **you will be causing work for someone else who has to trace the error back through the documents to find out where it was made**
▼ **if the mistake was serious enough then it could be brought to the attention of the senior managers and this would not be good for your career**

Even if you are using a calculator you should not assume that your figures are correct; you may have pressed the wrong key or missed out one of the figures. If you are using a spreadsheet package, then again the program will only carry out the instructions it is given. Remember to check everything thoroughly.

Percentages

Percentages will have to be calculated when working out national insurance contributions and tax deductions from wages and salaries. These totals will have to be subtracted from the gross pay of the employee.

Addition

Some employees will have a basic pay plus other forms of payment, such a bonuses and commissions, and these will have to be added together to give the total gross pay. Remember that all the deductions will have to be added together and then subtracted from the gross pay to give the net pay.

Subtraction

After you have worked out the percentage of national insurance and tax and any other deductions from the pay, such as pension contributions and a trade union subscription, you will have to subtract these from the total gross pay. You will have to make sure that you have made these calculations correctly otherwise the net pay will be wrong.

Totals

There will be several totals on a pay slip. These include the following:

▼ **total tax paid**
▼ **total national insurance paid**
▼ **total pension contribution paid**
▼ **total union subscription or membership paid**
▼ **total of other deductions, such as season ticket loans, interest free or other loans**
▼ **total of all deductions**
▼ **total of all pay, including basic pay, commission, bonus and overtime**
▼ **total gross pay**
▼ **total net pay after you have subtracted all the deductions**

Gross pay

This is the basic wage or salary before any deductions have been made. As we have seen, the typical deductions are income tax, national insurance, pension contributions (all of these are statutory deductions), trade union membership, social club membership, SAYE (Save As You Earn) and charitable contributions (all of these are voluntary deductions).

Net pay

Net pay is the amount that an employee actually receives either in cash, by cheque or directly into a bank account. Net pay is your gross pay minus any statutory or voluntary deductions. You will also be able to see the total of your net pay for that year as another item on your pay slip.

BUSINESS CONNECTION

PC 9.3

We have now looked at all the major ways of investigating payment for work. To test your memory and skill, complete the following business connection by turning payments into tax. The last letter of each word or phrase is the first letter of the next word or phrase. To help you we have put in the first and last letter on each line, but you will have to do the rest.

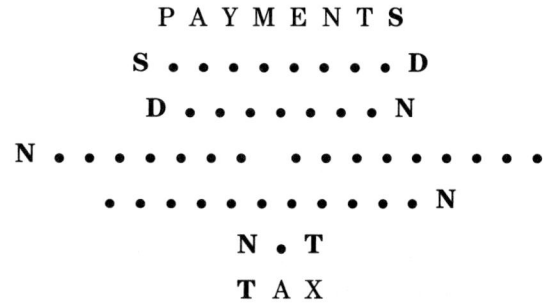

```
          P A Y M E N T S
       S . . . . . . . . D
        D . . . . . . . N
   N . . . . . . .   . . . . . . . .
       . . . . . . . . . . . N
          N . T
          T A X
```

assignment

ELEMENT 9.3

PC 9.3.1–4
AON 1.1, 1.2, 1.3, 1.4

In order to fulfil the performance criteria of this element we have created three different people and you will have to work out the take-home pay of each. You should remember to explain what you are doing when working out their net pay and describe the pay benefits and deductions that are being made.

- *Brian Appleyard (factory worker) – Brian is paid hourly and works 38 hours per week. His hourly rate is £3.62. He is married and has no other deductions apart from tax and national insurance.*

- *Georgina Bruce (personnel assistant) – Georgina is paid monthly and works 35 hours per week. Her annual salary is £8,500. She is unmarried, pays 5% of her salary into a company pension scheme and pays back £45 per month for a season ticket.*

- *Betty Davis (piece-rate worker) – Betty is paid weekly in cash. She manages to complete around 800 items per week and is paid 38p per item. She is married and pays £1.32 per week for union membership.*

243

| tasks | PC 9.3.1–4 | | notes | |

Using the three characters above, calculate their net pay showing all calculations and put this information onto a pay slip. To support your calculations and pay slip you should describe what you have done and what decisions you have made regarding the additions, percentages, subtractions and totals given.

You will have to refer to Inland Revenue statements of tax codes and personal allowances in working out the income tax that each of the people has to pay. You will also have to discover how much national insurance these people will be expected to contribute. You will find this information in your centre's library or given copies of the statements by your tutor.

WORDSEARCH

How many of the words listed below can you find? They run forwards and backwards up and down and across the grid.

```
A  S  D  F  R  E  T  L  I  U  G  W  E  O  A  P  U  Y
D  I  S  C  I  P  L  I  N  A  R  Y  A  C  T  I  O  N
Q  W  E  R  U  I  P  S  D  A  O  B  N  X  T  D  R  A
C  O  N  F  I  D  E  N  C  E  S  Q  W  E  I  E  E  U
A  B  C  P  W  E  F  G  I  E  S  O  P  L  T  S  L  A
A  D  V  E  R  T  I  S  E  M  E  N  T  S  U  I  I  P
T  M  N  N  O  S  L  O  C  X  V  B  N  P  D  D  A  L
T  A  X  S  I  Q  R  C  Q  W  E  R  T  Y  E  I  B  L
E  X  M  I  O  P  S  I  M  N  O  B  L  J  S  S  I  A
N  I  O  O  Q  R  S  A  I  O  P  M  N  S  D  B  L  U
D  M  P  N  A  S  C  L  O  T  H  I  N  G  Q  U  I  T
A  D  D  R  E  S  S  S  A  L  A  R  Y  I  O  S  T  C
N  M  N  O  P  R  V  K  P  Q  N  M  O  Z  Y  U  Y  N
C  C  V  B  X  Z  A  I  N  T  E  R  V  I  E  W  N  U
E  P  C  N  O  Z  U  L  M  O  N  Q  R  S  Y  E  O  P
I  J  K  S  O  G  O  L  N  M  A  Q  E  T  U  M  J  L
E  C  M  O  A  N  J  S  P  R  O  Z  S  I  M  I  P  O
W  E  C  N  A  R  U  S  N  I  L  A  N  O  I  T  A  N
```

ADDRESS	GROSS	RELIABILITY
ADVERTISEMENTS	INTERVIEW	SALARY
ATTENDANCE	LOAN	SOCIAL SKILLS
ATTITUDE	LOGOS	SUBSIDISED
CLOTHING	NATIONAL INSURANCE	TAX
CONFIDENCE	PENSION	TIME
DISCIPLINARY ACTION	PUNCTUAL	

*G*lossary of business terms

Academic qualifications   This usually means GCSEs and A levels. See also **vocational qualifications**.

Administration   This is a part of an organisation that tends to support the rest of the departments by providing services such as photocopying and other office duties and tasks.

After-sales service   Most organisations have now realised that good customer relations do not end with selling a product or service. After-sales service aims to provide help and advice to customers, not just for occasions when the product is faulty or when they have a complaint.

Application form   This is the document you are asked to fill in if you apply for a job. There will be various sections of the form, aimed at giving the employer the chance to find out about your qualifications, skills and other qualities.

Appointment   This is the final part of the recruitment process. The successful candidate will be 'appointed', or offered the job after the interviews have taken place.

Bonuses   These are usually extra cash payments given to employees who have performed particularly well for the employer. Perhaps they have made a large sale, or managed to reach the sales figures (targets) set by their employer.

Booking   A booking is an arrangement, or a series of arrangements, for a visit or journey for an individual or a group of people. You would have to arrange the travel and confirm with the traveller as well as the organisations involved that the arrangements are correct.

Cash book   A cash book is used to note down all the transactions (cash or cheques) that have come into the business (incomings) and been paid out by the business (outgoings).

Cash flow   This is all of the incomings and outgoings of money in a particular business. The cash flow shows that the business is either making more money than it is spending or spending more than it is making.

Charity   A charity is registered with the government and is usually involved in raising money for a particular cause. Charities are not interested in making a profit for owners, since they do not have any, but they try to make a profit or collect large sums of money so that they can fund schemes and support their causes.

Competition   In business terms, competition refers to businesses trying to make sure that the public buy from them rather than from any other organisation. They do this by advertising and promoting their products and services as well as trying to offer the best deal to customers.

Consumer   This is another word used for customer in business.

Core skills   These are the basic skills of communication and numeracy that are needed for almost any type of job.

Credit card   This is a way of paying for products and services. When customers use one of these, they sign to prove that they are the true card holder and the credit card company pays the shop or supplier. Customers must then pay the credit card company back, but are charged interest for as long as they have a balance on the card.

Credit note   This is given by a business to a customer to whom it owes money. Rather than refunding the money for faulty or returned products and services, the customer can use this as 'cash' against an **invoice** in the future.

Curriculum vitae (CV)   This is a summary of your personal details (such as name, address and telephone number) and your achievements (qualifications) which is shown to an employer when you apply for a job.

Customer services   Some larger businesses will have a separate customer services department, but for most organisations this describes the ways in which they provide advice, information and support to their customers before, during and after the sale has been made.

Distribution   In general, this is how the business transports its products to its customers. This is also a department in larger organisations and covers all those involved with transporting the products (including drivers and warehouse staff).

Electronic information   A way of describing electronic mail, faxes, notes, messages and letters.

Electronic mail   A way of sending information to another computer terminal via a telephone line and modem.

Electronic transfer of funds   A new method of moving money from one account to another. This is carried out using computer terminals and allows immediate transfer. The money transferred can be used by the account holder straightaway.

Employee contribution   This is what employees put into the business that they work for, including their skills, experience and ideas. Good employers realise that this contribution is very valuable.

Enclosures   These are items or documents put into an envelope or package in addition to the covering letter.

Fax   This is short for facsimile, sent via a telephone line from one fax machine to another.

Feedback   After some activities you will have to take part in a review of your performance in order to get feedback from your tutors. Feedback will take the form of comments, opinions and suggestions as to how you could have improved your performance during the activity.

Franchise   A franchise is a business which uses the name of another organisation, selling its range of products and services. The business offering the name is known as a franchisor and the business buying the name is called a franchisee.

Guarantee   Most products and services come with a guarantee. This states that the product or service will be of a certain quality and can be returned if there is a fault or problem with it.

Health and safety   Health and safety laws require businesses to carry out checks to ensure that there are no dangers to employees or customers as a result of the products or services the organisation produces or from the way the goods are produced.

Health and safety equipment   These are items of equipment that can be found in the workplace. Good examples of these are personal protective equipment (such as gloves), fire extinguishers, safety warning signs and first-aid equipment.

Health and safety hazards   These include an untidy and cluttered work area that could cause a health and safety problem.

Health and safety risks   These include smoking near inflammable liquids and unprotected machine wires and cords. If these are not looked out for then an accident could occur.

Human resources   In larger organisations, this is the department which deals with all of the matters relating to employees, such as recruitment and pay.

Incentives   Some organisations offer their employees rewards additional to their wages or salaries. Incentives include season ticket loans, company cars and cheap loans.

Interview   This is one of the most important parts of the recruitment process. After application forms or CVs have been received by an employer, the candidates are short listed and the best are called in for interview. After the interview one of the candidates will be offered the job.

Invoice   This is a document which is sent out to the customer and details the products and services bought and their cost. The customer is then expected to pay the total shown on the invoice.

Itemised account   This is a statement which shows the individual transactions carried out between a business and a customer. This is useful since it breaks down every order and gives the date of purchase.

Job responsibilities   These are the main duties of the employee that relate to his or her job. The job responsibilities of a wages clerk are to make sure that the wages and salaries are paid correctly and on time.

Job tasks   These are the individual duties and responsibilities of an employee. They are usually broken down into separate tasks so that they are clear.

Letter of application   This is a simple letter which can be sent with an application form or a CV when you apply for a job. A letter of application says which job you are applying for and your reasons for applying. You may also include a summary of your main qualifications, skills and experience.

Limited company   There are two main types of limited company: private and public. Although they have some differences, the word limited means that the owners only stand to lose the money that they have invested in the business should it fail.

Local authority   This is another term to describe a local council, borough council, district council or county council. They are large employers and offer a wide range of services to the public and local businesses.

Management accountant   This is the person in an organisation responsible for making sure that the accounts are correct and complete.

Managing director   This is the person that is responsible for the overall running of a business. The managing director will tell the managers what is required and take a wider view of the organisation so that all of the parts of the business are working towards the same goal.

Marketing   This is the department in an organisation that deals with the advertising and promotion of its products and services. It will carry out research to find out about its customers and the best way of getting the information about the products and services to them.

Memo   Short for memorandum. This is an internal written instruction that includes the sender, the date, the subject and the person who is to receive the message.

Oral information   A way of describing telephone and face-to-face conversations.

Oral processing   A way of describing the giving and receiving of messages and instructions.

Partnership   This is a type of business organisation that needs at least two people. They work together and share all the profits and losses that the business may make.

Paying-in slip   This is a document that is used to prove you have paid money into an account. The cashier will sign and stamp the paying-in slip and hand you back the signed and stamped counterfoil for you to use as proof of paying the money into the account.

Payment received sheet   This is a document which records incoming money. A business would make sure that all incoming payments are put onto this document.

Petty cash voucher   This is a document that is filled in by an employee who has spent some of the organisation's money on basic items such as coffee, fax paper or stamps. A receipt should always be stapled to the petty cash voucher.

Premises   This is another word for the buildings used by a business.

Production   This is the department in a business that actually makes the products.

Productivity   This is a way of measuring how hard or well the organisation is working. The business has an idea of how much it would like to produce and it will measure the actual amount produced against this total.

Profit sharing   This is when employees are given a share of the profits of the business. Employees usually get a share related to the number of years that they have been working for the organisation.

Purchasing   This is the department in an organisation that deals with buying things for the business. It buys raw materials, components and other items that the organisation needs.

Raw materials   These are basic items used by some organisations; they include coal, iron, steel, cotton and wool.

Receipt   This is handwritten or printed proof that you have bought something for a particular amount on a particular day.

Record of achievement   This is a folder or binder that includes all your certificates, personal details and career plans. Most students will have one of these by the time they leave school or be encouraged to complete one.

Refund   These are usually given if the customer returns something to the business as a result of it being faulty or not suitable. Refunds must be given by the supplier, but there are some cases when suppliers are not required to do so.

Sales   This is the department in an organisation that handles selling to customers. It usually works very closely with the marketing department so that it can be ready to sell products and services after the marketing department has advertised them.

Schedule   This includes the details and timings of

trips and events undertaken on a visit. It will include where the visit is to take place, who will be visited, arrival time, departure time and other information.

Share ownership   This is when a business gives shares to its employees. Instead of giving them cash bonuses, the shares have more value and mean that the employee is a part-owner of the business. In this way, the employer hopes that employees will put even more effort into their work.

Sole trader   This is the most basic type of business organisation. The business person may set him or herself up in business without having to go through any complicated paperwork.

Spreadsheet   This is a computerised way of dealing with lots of numbers and figures. The spreadsheet will automatically total across and down for you so that you do not have to add the figures together yourself.

Statement of account   This is a document that is sent out to customers (sometimes monthly) so that they can see all the transactions they have carried out with the supplier. The orders and payments are detailed, with the outstanding balance at the bottom of the document.

Student log   This is an outline of your activities and contribution during an assignment or, perhaps, during work experience. You should keep a detailed account of what you do, where it is done, what materials you used and what equipment was needed.

Team plan   In many group activities you will be required to organise the way in which you intend to carry out the work before you actually start the activity itself. It is wise to include all the steps that you need to follow. Your centre will have a particular form that you will need to fill in.

Telecommunication processing   A way of describing the handling of telephone, fax and modem communications and messages.

Till record   When a cash register, or till, prints a receipt, it also prints a copy onto a till roll. This is the business's record of the transaction carried out by the cashier.

Trade discount   This is a percentage off the price of products and services offered either to other businesses or to regular customers.

Travel itinerary   This includes the details of travel arrangements that will have to be organised to meet the traveller's needs and should contain the route selected, dates and calculated travel timings and all of the necessary stops.

Unique selling points   These are the features of a product or service that are different from all other products on the market. If a pencil has a rubber on the end of it, then this is a USP compared to other pencils that do not have a rubber.

Vacancy   This is when a business has a job available.

Value added tax (VAT)   This is a government tax that is added to the normal price of most products and services. This is currently at 17.5%.

Visual information   This includes charts, tables, graphs and signs.

Vocational qualifications   These are non-academic achievements based on your ability to use skills and experience.

Word-processed documents   These are documents, such as memos and letters, produced on a word processor.

Written documents   These can include letters, memos, notices and orders.

Written information   See **written documents**.

Index